MISSIONSHIFT

In memory of

Paul G. Hiebert
(1932–2007)

and

Ralph D. Winter
(1924–2009)

Thank you for your immeasurable contributions to missions.

MISSIONSHIFT

GLOBAL MISSION ISSUES IN THE THIRD MILLENNIUM

EDITED BY

David J. Hesselgrave
Ed Stetzer

B&H
ACADEMIC
www.BHacademic.com

MissionShift: Global Mission Issues in the Third Millennium
Copyright © 2010
by David J. Hesselgrave and Ed Stetzer

All rights reserved.

ISBN: 978-0-8054-4537-4

Published by B&H Publishing Group
Nashville, Tennessee

Dewey Decimal Classification: 266
Subject Heading: CHRISTIAN MINISTRY\HOME MISSIONS\
INTERNATIONAL MISSIONS

Journal, periodical, major reference work, and series abbreviations follow *The SBL Handbook of Style* (Peabody, MA: Hendrickson, 1999).

Printed in the United States of America
1 2 3 4 5 6 7 8 9 10 11 12 • 18 17 16 15 14 13 12 11 10
BP

Contents

CHAPTER 1

Introduction

ED STETZER

If you go to a shopping mall this weekend, you'll notice that the mall has anchor stores at each end. Typically malls are developed around large anchor stores like Macy's or JCPenney that are well known and advertise widely. These anchor stores attract shoppers to the mall; and while they are there, they also browse the boutiques and enjoy a double mocha latte at Starbucks. This book is like a missions mall. It is anchored by three significant essays, written by three of the foremost missiologists of our time: Charles Van Engen, Paul Hiebert, and Ralph Winter. Charles Van Engen discusses mission's past in his essay. Paul Hiebert analyzes mission's present in his articles, and Ralph Winter predicts mission's future in his. In a sense the three essayists are explaining where we have been, where we are, and where we're going in missions. We (the editors) also have enlisted outstanding writers in the field of missiology to interact with our essayists. You'll discover some lively, stimulating debate in their responses. So order your favorite coffee and sit down for an enlightening read.

CHARLES VAN ENGEN'S ESSAY: MISSION IN THE PAST

In his essay Charles Van Engen explains how the church has understood and defined its mission through the centuries. Van Engen uses this historical survey as a springboard to defining mission today. This is appropriate because how we *define* mission today determines to a great degree how we'll *do* missions today and tomorrow. He quotes Bishop Stephen Neill who wrote, "If everything is mission, then nothing is mission." Van Engen finds hope in the missional church movement. He believes this redefinition of the church in terms of its obligation to fulfill God's purpose in the world (missional purpose) will lead to great progress in mission. He concludes his essay by offering his personal and lengthy definition of *mission*. Because I've interacted with each of the essays and the responders, I won't share my responses now, but you'll find those in each section of the book.

Keith Eitel and Andreas Köstenberger express concern with Van Engen's essay, especially his enthusiasm for the missional church movement. They both fear that the missional church movement and the emergent churches have deemphasized biblical authority in order to interact with postmodern North American culture. Eitel is concerned that missiological creativity, while desirable in some respects, may lead Evangelicals away from a biblically defined mission. Of course, this was the crux of the debate between Evangelicals and the World Council of Churches in the 1960s. Who or what defines the church's mission in the world and in a particular locality? The World Council insisted that the context (the culture) must define the church's mission, while Evangelicals held that the Bible must define the church's mission. Andreas Köstenberger is a Bible scholar of note, so it is not surprising that his "12 theses" emphasize the inspiration and authority of the Scriptures. He also reminds his readers that good hermeneutics are not just necessary but a divine mandate.

Enoch Wan finds much to like in Van Engen's essay. He appreciates Van Engen's historical survey, and he likes the concept of missional churches. Wan criticizes Van Engen's theology of mission as insufficiently trinitarian. For his part Wan espouses a theology of mission that is thoroughly trinitarian.

Darryl Guder perhaps is the most affirming and appreciative responder to Van Engen. As a key figure in the missional church movement, Guder is grateful for Van Engen's endorsement, and like Van Engen he sees the missional church movement as *the* way forward for Protestant missions. Guder finds his theological inspiration in the missiology of Karl Barth, and he commends Barth's Christocentrism to a new generation of seminary students.

PAUL HIEBERT'S ESSAY: MISSION IN THE PRESENT

This essay is one of the last that Paul Hiebert wrote before he died. In the essay he addresses mission's present in terms of contextualization. Of course, contextualization is not the only thing going on in Evangelical missions today, but it is surely the most controversial. It is hard to imagine a writer more qualified than Paul Hiebert to address this topic. His writings on contextualization have shaped the thought of a whole generation of missionaries, and missions professors too.

In his essay Hiebert explains the development of contextualization in the history of missions. The early missionaries practiced minimal contextualization. That is, they did little to contextualize the gospel. This was due to ignorance of cultural anthropology and a firm belief in the absolute truth of the Bible and their theology. Later missionaries felt embarrassed by the lack of contextualization by the pioneer missionaries of the nineteenth century, and they practiced uncritical contextualization. This uncritical approach allowed the culture to dominate. The result was often syncretism (the combination of two or more religions). Hiebert rejects these two extremes and argues for critical contextualization, a contextualization that is true to biblical teaching and also sensitive to the culture.

Michael Pocock responds to his former professor at Trinity Evangelical Divinity School with great respect and affirmation. Pocock views Hiebert's critical contextualization as the solution to the problem of appropriate contextualization. In recent years much of the debate about contextualization has swirled around the radical contextualization advocated by missionaries to Muslims, such as John Travis. Pocock discusses the C1-C6 Model as an example of this debate. For himself Pocock views the C5 approach as too extreme, but he does approve the C4 approach advocated by Phil Parshall.

Darrell Whiteman expresses great appreciation for Paul Hiebert. In his response Whiteman explains that the gospel affirms most of culture, confronts some aspects of culture, and transforms all of culture. He agrees with Hiebert that critical contextualization is an appropriate response of missionaries to cultural issues. However, he applies critical contextualization to the radical contextualization employed by some missionaries to Muslims and affirms the C5 approach. Thus, both Pocock and Whiteman affirm critical contextualization, but they come to different conclusions.

Norman Geisler is a theologian, not a missiologist, much less a professor of missionary anthropology like Hiebert and Whiteman. Geisler applies a theological template to Hiebert's essay and finds it lacking. He believes Hiebert's view of propositional truth is weak, and that weakness leads to a concern about Hiebert's belief in the inerrancy and authority of the Scriptures. Geisler holds that the way to improved evangelism on the part of field missionaries is not to be found in critical contextualization but rather in worldview research and apologetics.

Avery Willis also affirms Paul Hiebert and critical contextualization. Having affirmed Hiebert's approach, he devotes much of his response to an application of contextualization—orality. In recent years Willis has been an ardent advocate of contextualized communication with people in oral cultures. As oral learners comprise approximately 60 percent of the world's population, Willis sees orality as an absolute necessity for contextualization.

RALPH WINTER'S ESSAY: MISSION IN THE FUTURE

Ralph Winter was given the assignment of writing about the future of missions. Before he addresses missions in the future, Winter recounts the history of evangelicalism. As part of that discussion, he discusses evangelical awakenings, which he calls First-Inheritance Evangelicalism and Second-Inheritance Evangelicalism. Winter combines the First Great Awakening and Second Great Awakenings into First-Inheritance Evangelicalism. This period lasted from the beginning of the First Great Awakening, about 1726, until the popularity of Dwight L. Moody (1880). In Winter's view Evangelicals during the First Inheritance engaged in intellectualism and civic leadership. They sought both to preach the gospel and to minister to the needy. Second-Inheritance Evangelicalism was dominated by the Bible college movement and the

4

Fundamentalist movement. Both movements were anti-intellectual, and their premillennial eschatology led them to reject social ministry. In his essay Winter affirms missionaries that engage in micro-projects to alleviate suffering in the world, but he challenges Evangelicals to develop and implement macro-projects on a continental scale. Though Winter does briefly mention some future trends in missions, his essay primarily is an exhortation to Evangelicals to engage in large-scale human needs ministries. He sees these ministries as a preevangelism strategy that will open doors for the gospel.

Scott Moreau agrees that evangelical missions should be holistic, but he is not sure that Evangelicals have the financial resources to operate on the scale Winter desires. Moreau undertakes to write the essay that Winter did not. He forecasts the future of missions, emphasizing the role of technology, especially the Internet, in the future of missions.

Mark Terry takes a similar track to that of Scott Moreau. Terry laments that Winter did not share his views on the future of missions. Terry agrees that the New Testament and church history support a holistic approach to missions. He then shares his vision of the future of Evangelical missions, listing a number of trends in Evangelical missions, especially missions to youth.

Chris Little's response to Winter is worth the cost of the book. He provides a thorough biblical and theological critique of Winter's call for massive human needs projects. While Little affirms the need to respond to human suffering, his biblical and theological findings lead him to reject Winter's challenge. Little sees Evangelism as the priority for evangelical missions.

Mike Barnett, who holds a Ph.D. in church history, sees Winter's historical survey of Evangelicalism as overly broad and simplistic. Barnett is not convinced that Second-Inheritance Evangelicalism was as socially deficient as Winter claims. Barnett agrees that Evangelicals need to engage in social ministry; however, he disagrees with Winter that the social ministry should come first. In Barnett's view we must see situations as different and deal with them on a case-by-case basis. Regardless of whether missionaries begin with the gospel or with social ministry, both Word and deed are necessary for a balanced approach. Ultimately, the church is the key. Churches must be mobilized to fulfill the Great Commission and the Great Commandment.

The editors wish to thank the writers, both the essayists and the responders. All wrote for their love of the Lord and a concern for missions, not for money. Mark Terry, Bob Hughes, Keith Whitfield, and Philip Nation also gave additional help to make this book what it is today.

CHAPTER 2

ESSAY 1: "Mission" Defined and Described

CHARLES VAN ENGEN

Thesis: The purpose of this essay is to offer a brief historical overview of some ways in which the Christian church has defined "mission" down through the centuries and to demonstrate how the various definitions have influenced the thought and practice of the Christian Church's ministries in the world. In this sense this essay addresses the PAST of what has traditionally been termed "missions."

INTRODUCTION

It was a Sunday noon, and I was invited to eat lunch with the members of the Global Outreach Task Force of a local church. Earlier that morning we had all been inspired by the wonderfully uplifting and celebrative worship at the church's three Sunday morning worship events at which I had been asked to preach. It was their Global Outreach Weekend. Toward the end of our lunch I turned to Gloria (not her real name), the task force's chairperson, and remarked:

> I am very impressed with the task force's organization and creative approach to this mission's weekend. The Friday evening dinner was so well done, including the interviews of members

of your church involved in ministries locally and globally. The mission fair had such a large number of display booths that highlighted all the mission activities and missionaries your church supports locally and globally. The international and local multicultural aspects of the music, the reports, and the visual presentations were so well done! Thank you for inviting me to be a part of this celebration!

Gloria grinned and replied:

Thank you for your feedback. Your observations are important to us. But please notice that we did not call this our "missions weekend." If we had called it Missions Emphasis Weekend, no one would have come. We know; we tried it before. The word *mission* turns everyone off. The members of our church do not want to be associated with anything called "mission." When we changed the name to Global Outreach, everything changed. You see, Chuck, no one seems to know what "mission" is. But a majority of our members want to be involved in some kind of local and global ministries that will benefit those in need. They are especially interested in short-term projects and visits to different parts of the world. Now you see why, when I invited you to preach, I asked you not to use the word *mission* in your sermon.

I nodded thoughtfully as I listened to Gloria. During the last several years, I have often heard comments like hers. It would appear that *mission* and *missionaries* are two of the most misunderstood words in the vocabulary of North American churches today.

THE WORD *MISSION* AS IT IS USED TODAY

Part of the confusion over the word *mission* may be the result of the way it is being overused today in numerous arenas. Out of curiosity I did a Google search for the word *mission* and received 247 million hits! Some states have towns with the name "Mission." So far there have been three *Mission Impossible* movies, and (closer to our theme here) a religious movie called *The Mission* came out in 1986. When NASA sends a shuttle to dock with the international space station, that trip is called a "mission." The word is especially prominent in the business world because a corporation often draws up a "mission statement" as a way of articulating the most fundamental purpose for which the corporation exists. Although most of these uses of the word seem to have little to do with the Christian church, each in fact describes a small portion of what the word can mean for Christian mission. The *Merriam-Webster's Collegiate Dictionary* offers a range of definitions, including its meaning with reference to Christian missionary activity.[1]

It is especially important that the Christian church wrestle with its mission in the sense of articulating the reason and purpose for which it exists. Local congregations have been encouraged to write their mission statement to focus their various ministries. Denominations have developed vision and mission statements, a process I was involved in with my denomination, the Reformed Church in America, whose mission and vision statement has guided the denominational priorities for the last seven years.

During the past decade we have also become familiar with a modified form of the word as in "missional church." In the early 1990s G. Hunsberger, D. Guder, I. Dietterich, L. Barrett, A. Roxburgh, C. Van Gelder, and others founded The Gospel and Our Culture Network to develop the implications for North America of L. Newbigin's challenge regarding the reevangelization of the West, following the lead of The Gospel and Culture movement in England of the 1980s, spearheaded by W. Shenk. The early conversations, reflection, and publications of The Gospel and Our Culture Network contributed to the creation of the concept of the "missional church." The term has now been used in so many ways as to become almost meaningless. A Google search for the term offered 933,000 hits. A quick overview demonstrates that the term now stands for any kind of new life, vision, vitality, and direction

---

[1] *Merriam-Webster's Collegiate Dictionary*, 11th ed. (Springfield, MA Merriam-Webster, 2003) 1 mis•sion \'mi-shen\ *noun* [New Latin, Medieval Latin, & Latin; New Latin *mission-, missio* religious mission, from Medieval Latin, task assigned, from Latin, act of sending, from *mittere* to send] 1 *obsolete* : the act or an instance of sending 2 a : a ministry commissioned by a religious organization to propagate its faith or carry on humanitarian work b : assignment to or work in a field of missionary enterprise c (1) : a mission establishment (2) : a local church or parish dependent on a larger religious organization for direction or financial support d *plural* : organized missionary work e : a course of sermons and services given to convert the unchurched or quicken Christian faith 3 : a body of persons sent to perform a service or carry on an activity: as a : a group sent to a foreign country to conduct diplomatic or political negotiations b : a permanent embassy or legation c : a team of specialists or cultural leaders sent to a foreign country 4 a : a specific task with which a person or a group is charged 4 b (1) : a definite military, naval, or aerospace task <a bombing *mission*> <a space *mission*> (2) : a flight operation of an aircraft or spacecraft in the performance of a mission <a *mission* to mars>

of the church—often with little or no theological or missiological reflection.[2]

For several centuries the Christian church has defined its mission in a wide variety of ways. Sidney Rooy has highlighted the differences:

> There does not exist, nor has there ever existed, only one definition of the mission of the Church; nor [one interpretation] as to what are the biblical foundations of that mission. If, like David Bosch, we define mission as *missio Dei* ["the mission of God"], we can say that this signifies the revelation of God as the One who loves the world God has created, who is concerned for this world, and who has formed the church to be a subject called to participate in the historical project of establishing the kingdom of God. . . . Our understanding of this *missio Dei* has been subjected to many interpretations down through history. . . . Each definition and all understandings of the biblical bases of that mission are tentative and are subject to new evaluation and change. Truly, each generation must define mission anew.[3]

THE ORIGINAL BIBLICAL MEANING OF THE WORD *MISSION*

Because the Bible is our foundation, we begin to build our definition of "mission" by considering the biblical perspectives. The word *mission* is rare in both the Hebrew Old Testament and the Greek New Testament. What is emphasized regularly is the concept of being sent, with an emphasis on the authority and purpose of the sender. The New Testament uses *apostellō* and *pempō*

---

[2] Foundational literature for this movement includes the following: G. R. Hunsberger and C. Van Gelder, eds., *The Church Between Gospel and Culture: The Emerging Mission in North America* (Grand Rapids: Eerdmans, 1996); D. L. Guder et al., eds., *Missional Church: A Vision for the Sending of the Church in North America* (Grand Rapids: Eerdmans, 1998); and L. Barrett et al., eds., *Treasure in Clay Jars: Patterns in Missional Faithfulness* (Grand Rapids: Eerdmans, 2003).

Some recent works that may be of interest to the reader are E. Creps and D. Kimball, *Off-Road Disciplines: Spiritual Adventures of Missional Leaders* (San Francisco: Jossey-Bass, 2006); A. Roxburgh and F. Romanuk, *The Missional Leader: Equipping Your Church to Reach a Changing World* (San Francisco: Jossey-Bass, 2006); E. Gibbs, *ChurchNext: Quantum Changes in How We Do Ministry* (Downers Grove, IL: IVP, 2000); M. Frost and A. Hirsch, *The Shaping of Things to Come: Innovation and Mission for the 21st-Century Church* (Peabody, MA: Hendrickson, 2003); N. Cole, *Organic Church: Growing Faith Where Life Happens* (San Francisco: Jossey-Bass, 2005); and E. Stetzer and D. Putnam, *Breaking the Missional Code: Your Church Can Become a Missionary in Your Community* (Nashville: B&H Academic, 2006).

[3] S. Rooy, "La búsqueda histórica de las bases b'blicas de la misión," in *Bases B'blicas de la Misión: Perspectivas Latinoamericanas*, trans. C. Van Engen (Buenos Aires: Kairos, Nueva Creación, 1998), 3–33.

somewhat interchangeably. The *Theological Dictionary of the New Testament* tells us that

> *apostellō* occurs some 135 times in the NT, mostly in the Gospels and Acts. *Pempō* occurs some 80 times, 33 in John, five in Revelation, 22 in Luke/Acts, only four in Matthew, and one in Mark. Apart from the special use of *pempō* in John, the Lucan material predominates; . . . the religious character of the NT material explains the general predominance of *apostellō*, and in the NT as a whole *pempō* seems to be used when the stress is on the sending, *apostellō* when it is on the commission, and especially (in the Synoptics) when it is God who sends.
>
> In John, Jesus uses *apostellō* to denote his full authority, i.e., to ground his mission in God as the One who is responsible for his words and works. But he uses *pempō*, e.g., in the phrase "the Father sent me," so as to state God's participation in his work by the act of sending. . . . The mission of Jesus acquires its significance and force from the fact that he is the Son, not from its description in terms of *apostellō*.
>
> In the NT *apostellein* certainly begins to be a theological word for "sending forth to serve God with God's own authority," but only in context and not with any radical departure from its normal sense. . . .[4]
>
> In relation to the general use of apostellein in the NT we must say finally that the word does begin to become a theological term meaning "to send forth to service in the kingdom of God with full authority (grounded in God)."[5]

In Luke 9 Jesus sends the 12, and in Luke 10 the 70, on their mission to the Jews and to the world. After the resurrection Jesus commissions His followers as those being sent. Jesus says, "Peace be to you! As the Father has sent *[apostellō]* Me, I also send *[pempō]* you" (John 20:21). Paul uses the term in its noun form *(apostolos)* to refer to himself, his calling, his commission, and his authority derived from his being sent by Jesus the Messiah, at the beginning of Romans, 1 and 2 Corinthians, Galatians, Ephesians, Colossians, 1 and 2 Timothy, and Titus. The author of 1 and 2 Peter does the same.

---

[4] G. Kittel, G. Friedrich, and G. W. Bromiley, *Theological Dictionary of the New Testament* (Grand Rapids: Eerdmans, 1995, c1985), 68 [Greek original has been transliterated].
[5] Ibid., 406.

So the first element of a definition of *mission* should be based on the concept of "sending." The church is sent by her Lord. Throughout the Bible the covenant people of God are clearly sent by God to the nations who are not yet part of the people of God.[6] Jesus refers to Himself as one who is sent: "I must proclaim the good news about the kingdom of God to the other towns also, because I was sent *[apostellō]* for this purpose" (Luke 4:43). Like Jesus, His followers are also sent to proclaim the coming of the kingdom of God, to invite all peoples to become Jesus' disciples and responsible members of Christ's church (Matt 28:18–20). This understanding of the word *mission* is most basic and should never be lost or eclipsed by subsequent discussions and refinements.

The church in the twenty-first century needs to keep the "sending" element of Christian mission in the foreground. Biblical mission is God's mission. Mission is participation in the mission of Jesus Christ, the Lord of the Church, in the power of the Holy Spirit. Mission is not merely church extension, nor is it merely doing good works of compassion. Mission is not to be determined by a mission agency's particular bias or agenda. Today, as many cross-cultural missionaries are sent from and supported by churches and mission agencies in Asia, Africa, and Latin America as the total sent from Europe and North America. Yet in the final analysis the "senders" are not the denomination, not the mission agency, not the megachurch or its senior pastor, not a nongovernmental relief agency. The authority of the mission enterprise is not the denomination, mission agency, self-proclaimed apostle, large relief agency, or a more advanced culture. The Sender is Jesus Christ, whose authority defines, circumscribes, limits, and propels Christian mission.

THE CONSTANTINIAN REDEFINITION OF *MISSION*

For almost three centuries after the coming of the Holy Spirit at Pentecost, the Christian church understood "mission" as outlined above. But with the changes effected by the emperor Constantine (306–337), the definition of *mission* changed dramatically. Sidney Rooy has given us an excellent summary of the impact that the

---

[6] E.g., A. F. Glasser et al., *Announcing the Kingdom: The Story of God's Mission in the Bible* (Grand Rapids: Baker, 2003).

Constantinian era had on the church's understanding of mission. Rooy explains:

> With the recognition of Christianity as an officially permitted religion based on the Decree of Milan in 313 AD, the context in which Christians exercised their mission changed dramatically. After that first large step, the next came in rapid succession: in 325 [Christianity] became the favored religion, in 380 it became the official religion, and by 392 it was the only tolerated religion [in the Holy Roman Empire]. That is, in the brief span of eighty years, Christianity went from being a persecuted religion to the persecuting religion. . . . During the Middle Ages, in the West, the king was considered the vicar of Christ and of God. . . .
>
> Thus, in addition to the church, the [nation-state] became an agent of mission represented by the persons designated by the emperor. The method by which the church was extended included the imposition of the faith by [forcibly] destroying the pagan religions and the institution of the new religion. It is true that at times the Gospel was extended through the work of missionaries, . . . but most of Europe was Christianized by conquest, the mass baptism of the pagans, and the construction of churches, monasteries and schools with the direct support of the political powers [of the day].
>
> In the Constantinian [model of mission], the dominant motivation was the temporal and spiritual extension of [what was then considered to be] the "kingdom of God" [embodied in the emperor]. Without a doubt, there was confusion regarding the two kingdoms: the state and the church. Together with the huge masses that entered the church, many [popular] beliefs and customs were also accepted. Popular [or folk] religion, which has always existed, took on new directions that affected not only the doctrines and ceremonies of the church, but also influenced the way mission was understood.[7]

Forms of this model continued into the colonial era of the eighteenth and nineteenth centuries. Christian missions at times looked quite similar to the medieval model sketched above. S. Neill says:

---

[7] Rooy, 10–12, in C. R. Padilla, ed., *Bases b'blicas de la misión: perspectivas latinoamericanas* (Buenos Aires: Nueva Creación/Eerdmans, 1998, inserts author's); cf. S. B. Bevans and R. P. Schroeder, *Constants in Context: A Theology of Mission for Today* (Maryknoll: Orbis, 2004), 173–74.

Whether we like it or not, it is the historic fact that the great expansion of Christianity has coincided in time with the world-wide and explosive expansion of Europe that followed the Renaissance; that the colonizing powers have been the Christian powers; that a whole variety of compromising relationships have existed between missionaries and governments; and that in the main Christianity has been carried forward on the wave of western prestige and power.[8]

We who live in the twenty-first century should not be too hard in our judgment of the medieval and colonial models of mission. During the past 150 years, Protestant mission endeavors from the north and west of the globe to the south and east at times implanted a cultural Protestantism that was too often more interested in propagating a particular form of civilization than in helping women and men come to faith in Jesus Christ. Culture, civilization, education, and technology too often replaced the emperor in eclipsing the gospel of faith in Jesus Christ. In today's mission activities, when denominations, mission organizations, or mega-churches set out to "plant" new churches that are essentially identical branch offices of the sending organization, the parallels to the medieval view of mission are quite troubling.[9]

WILLIAM CAREY'S GREAT-COMMISSION DEFINITION OF *MISSION*

In the late 1700s W. Carey (1761–1834) suggested a different way of understanding mission. Carey "preached that the church's primary responsibility was foreign missions."[10] In his ground-breaking work, "An Enquiry into the Obligation of Christians to Use Means for the Conversion of the Heathens," Carey based his view of mission on Matt 28:18–20, a passage that eventually would be known throughout the Christian church, particularly among Protestants, as the Great Commission.[11] During the nineteenth and early twentieth centuries, the Great Commission (together with

---

[8] S. Neill quoted in D. J. Bosch, *Witness to the World: The Christian Mission in Theological Perspective* (London: Marshall, Morgan, & Scott, 1980), 116.

[9] For discussion of this from a Latin American perspective, see C. E. Van Engen, "¿Por Qué Sembrar Iglesias Saludables? Bases B'blicas y Misionológicas," in *Sembremos Iglesias Saludables*, ed. J. Wagenveld (Miami: FLET, 2004), 43–96.

[10] J. Reapsome, "William Carey," *Evangelical Dictionary of World Missions (EDWM)*, ed. H. N. A. Scott Moreau, H. Netland, and C. Van Engen (Grand Rapids: Baker, 2000), 162–63.

[11] D. Hesselgrave, "Great Commission," in *EDWM*, 412–14.

Mark 16:15–16; Luke 24:46–49; John 20:21; Acts 1:8) "came to play an extremely important role in missions and Missiology."[12]

The Matthean version of the Great Commission drew from and contributed to a particular view of mission. Matthew's Great Commission was a primary component of the biblical foundation for the "Watchword" of the Student Volunteer Movement of the late 1800s that was later popularized by J. R. Mott (1865–1955) as a motto for the great missionary conference held at Edinburgh in 1910: "the evangelization of the world in this generation."[13] We have space here to mention only a few of the related assumptions.

For about 150 years prior to the 1960s, Protestants who used the Great Commission as their foundation for mission assumed the following:

- that salvation was individualistic;
- that salvation had to do primarily with a spiritual and personal relationship with Jesus Christ;
- that the primary calling of the church's mission was geographic: Christians were called to "go";
- that the "going" was primarily from the west and north of the globe to the east and south;
- that the "make disciples" portion of the Great Commission was more important than the "baptizing" and "teaching" portions;
- that new converts should be gathered into churches resembling—and often belonging to—the sending churches and missions;
- and (especially during the last half of the nineteenth century) that new individual converts should be extracted from their non-Christian contexts, gathered into Christian mission stations, and taught the culture and civilization of the missionaries.

In 1955 D. McGavran (1897–1991) published *The Bridges of God: A Study in the Strategy of Missions*, in which he affirmed but radically reinterpreted the Great Commission missiology of Matt

---

[12] Ibid., 414.
[13] For a brief biographical sketch of this great missionary statesman, see J. D. Douglas, "Mott, John Raleigh," in *EDWM*, 664.

28:18–20. McGavran questioned the "mission station" approach; suggested that the word "nations" *(ethnē)* meant people groups rather than individuals; affirmed that the imperative, the mandate, was to "disciple" people and not the geographically defined "going" as emphasized by earlier mission thought; and suggested that the result of such activity should be measured in terms of the numbers of persons—in ethnically cohesive groups—who become members of Christ's church.[14] Founded by McGavran in 1955, the church growth movement built upon the basic tenets of the missiology of his book. By the 1970s and 1980s, in some Protestant evangelical circles, the *ethnē* had come to be understood as being "unreached people groups," a view that combined some geographic and individualistic assumptions with certain cultural and group-oriented emphases. But there was never a clear or precise theological or missiological comprehension of what "unreached" or "resistant" meant.[15]

MISSION AND THE INDIGENOUS CHURCH MODEL

The Great Commission understanding of mission emphasized the evangelization of those who were not yet followers of Jesus. Parallel to this view was a more institutionalized perspective advocated by H. Venn (1796–1873) in England and R. Anderson (1796–1880) in the United States. These two mission administrators stressed that the goal of mission was the birth, nurture, and development of "self-supporting, self-governing, and self-propagating churches." J. Scherer describes this view as follows:

> The new church-centered view [of mission], prominent around the middle of the nineteenth century through the work of Henry Venn and Rufus Anderson, . . . set forth the view that "church planting"—especially the planting of local "three-self" churches with their own autonomy and indigeneity—should be considered alongside personal conversion an important goal of missions. The acknowledged "father" of mission science, Gustav Warneck, could declare that mission activity was "the road from [existing] church to church [in the mission field]."[16]

---

[14] D. McGavran, *The Bridges of God* (New York: Friendship/World Dominion, 1955), 605.

[15] C. Van Engen, "Reflecting Theologically About the Resistant," *Reaching the Resistant: Barriers and Bridges for Mission*, ed. J. D. Woodberry (Pasadena: William Carey Library, 1998), 22–78.

[16] J. A. Scherer, "Church, Kingdom, and *Missio Dei*: Lutheran and Orthodox Correctives to Recent Ecumenical Mission Theology," in *The Good News of the Kingdom: Mission Theology for the Third Millennium*, ed. C. Van Engen, D. S. Gilliland, and P. Pierson (Maryknoll:

Though they may not have intended it so, the goal of mission advocated by Venn and Anderson as a principle of mission administration became a virtual definition of mission that dominated mission theology and practice among almost all older denominations and mission agencies for a hundred years, beginning in the mid-nineteenth century.[17] Many of those who followed Venn and Anderson tried to soften the institutional aspects of their view of mission. J. Nevius (1829–1893), R. Allen (1868–1947), M. Hodges (1909–1986) and A. Tippett (1911–1988) offered refinements to the "three-self" formula that sought to stress the development of the spiritual, organic, theological, relational, social, cultural, and contextual aspects of missionary congregations. Yet the original "three-self" concept has continued to dominate in Africa, Asia, and Latin America to such an extent that one can find "three-self" churches originally established by Western European and North American mission endeavors which today exhibit another kind of "self": they tend to be self-centered and selfish.

During the 1970s and 1980s, many denominations in the USA adopted a form of the "three-self" formula as the administrative philosophy for planting new churches in the suburbs of North American cities, with very mixed results. Vestiges of this movement remain in some denominational church-planting endeavors in the USA.

More recently the "emerging church" movement appears to be searching for ways to birth, nurture, and develop congregations that are indigenous to the center cities of the USA. This new movement shows striking parallels to the search by the baby-boomer generation to form kingdom-oriented, transformational faith communities in the cities of the USA during the 1960s. Those who

---

Orbis, 1993), 82; Scherer cites Duerr (1947). R. Bassham writes (*Mission Theology: 1948–1975, Years of Worldwide Creative Tension, Ecumenical, Evangelical and Roman Catholic* [Pasadena, CA: William Carey Library Publishers, 1979]): "Evangelical mission thought [in the 1930s and 1940s] revolved essentially around evangelism, often understood in terms of individual conversions, with the implied aim of gathering believers into self-supporting, self-governing, and self-propagating churches on the basis of a closely defined basis of faith."

[17] For an excellent summary about indigenous churches and mission, see J. M. Terry, "Indigenous Churches," in *EDWM*, 483–85. I grew up in the National Presbyterian Church of Mexico in which the "three-self formula" was the dominant mission perspective advocated by missionaries and national leaders alike. With over one million members, that denomination is one of the largest single denominations in Latin America. Yet it is in its infancy in both local and global mission-sending. I believe the "three-self formula" is one of the major reasons for that denomination's lack of missionary vision and practice.

are leading these contemporary efforts could learn much from what their predecessors experienced in local and global mission in terms of birthing, nurturing, and developing indigenous churches around the world.

MISSION IN THE 1960s

Following the Second World War, many Western European missiologists and theologians, along with some of their counterparts in the older mainline denominations in North America, began to formulate a new view of mission. Having seen the disastrous consequences of the church's silence and irrelevance in the crisis of Western Europe during the 1930s and early 1940s, and following the inspiration of D. Bonhoeffer among others, the churches associated with the fledgling World Council of Churches (founded in 1948) began to search for what they considered to be a more relevant missiology. They wanted to mobilize the churches to become involved with what God was doing in the world. This new view of mission crystallized around the phrase *missio Dei*, "the mission of God," and represented a radical secularization of mission. Missiologists like J. C. Hoekendijk demonstrated a deep pessimism about the church as a viable agent of God's mission. In fact Hoekendijk suggested that the best thing the church could do was to turn itself "inside out" and essentially cease to exist.[18] This led to an emphasis on God's mission oriented toward, and centered in, the kingdom of God and the world rather than the church. J. Scherer summarizes this development as follows:

> The latter half of the nineteenth century and the first half of the twentieth were largely dominated by the church-centered concept as the practical goal for what were then called "foreign missions." Church-centrism replaced earlier individualistic mission theories derived from pietism and evangelical revivalism that focused on personal conversion *[conversio gentium]* and "soul-saving" . . . .
>
> From 1860 to 1960 the church-centered goal of mission served a useful purpose in replacing the earlier missionary pattern of individual conversions, in that it clearly defined the necessary steps toward planting churches among all nations. But as

---

[18] J. C. Hoekendijk, *The Church Inside Out* (Philadelphia: Westminster, 1966).

the task of church-planting advanced in all six continents, it was rapidly becoming obsolete as a missionary goal. . . .

After [the meeting of the International Missionary Council at] Willingen [in 1952], the church-centered mission framework . . . was no longer adequate for dealing with the problems facing churches engaged in mission *in, from* and *to* all six continents in the post-colonial era. Those problems required a *missio Dei* ["mission of God"] response, with a clearer understanding of the Trinitarian basis and nature of the church's mission, and an openness and sensitivity to the eschatological character of the kingdom, and the church's subordinate relationship to it.

[But] in the decade of the 1960s, *missio Dei*[19] was to become the plaything of armchair theologians with little more than an academic interest in the practical mission of the church but with a considerable penchant for theological speculation and mischief making. . . .

God was seen to be working out the divine purpose in the midst of the world through immanent, intra-mundane historical forces, above all secularization. The Trinitarian *missio Dei* view was replaced by a theory about the transformation of the world and of history not through evangelization and church-planting but by means of a divinely guided immanent historical process, somewhat analogous to deistic views of the Enlightenment. This secular view of God's mission made the empirical church virtually dispensable as an agent of divine mission, and in some cases even a hindrance. . . . The world set the agenda for the church, and the real locus of God's mission was no longer the church but the world. Accordingly, the church must now receive its marching orders from the world. . . . Humanization was the new keyword.[20]

This radical redefinition of mission, with its strong impetus toward secularizing Christian mission, became a reason for concern among many of the most loyal participants in the World Council of Churches. S. Neill, for example, warns, "When everything is mission, nothing is mission."[21] Neill felt it necessary to

---

[19] H. H. Rosin states that G. F. Vicedom's book (*Missio Dei, Einfurung in eine Theologie der Mission*), which was published in German in 1958, played a decisive part in the spreading of the term *missio Dei*, appearing in 1965 in the USA in an English translation entitled *The Mission of God: An Introduction to a Theology of Mission*; cf. H. H. Rosin, "*Missio Dei:* An Examination of the Origin, Contents and Function of the Term in Protestant Missiological Discussion" (Leiden: Interuniversity Institute for Missiological and Ecumenical Research, 1972), 24.

[20] Scherer, "Church, Kingdom, and *Missio Dei*," 82–88.

[21] S. Neill, *Creative Tension* (London: Edinburgh House, 1959), 81; J. Blauw, *The Missionary Nature of the Church* (Grand Rapids: Eerdmans, 1962), 109, 121–22.

emphasize that "the one central purpose for which the Church has been called into existence is that . . . it should preach the Gospel to every creature. Everything else—ministry, sacraments, doctrine, worship—is ancillary to this."[22] Bevans and Schroeder comment, "It is important to heed Stephen Neill's warning that if everything is mission, then nothing is mission. Nevertheless, we need also to pay attention to David Bosch's warning to 'beware of any attempt at delineating mission too sharply.'"[23] In the twenty-first century Evangelical mission agencies are becoming increasingly committed and involved in humanitarian and compassion ministries through agriculture, education, medicine, AIDS-related ministries, children-at-risk movements, and so on. Given these new emphases in Evangelical mission activism, it behooves us to consider carefully how Evangelical views of mission today may be tempted to repeat the same errors made when mission was redefined and eventually lost in the World Council of Churches between the 1960s and the 1990s.

EVANGELICAL REACTION, REDEFINITION, AND RECONSTRUCTION OF MISSION: 1980s TO 2000

The 1960s were a time of great ferment around the globe. "In 1960 alone, seventeen new African nations were born."[24] In Latin America, dictatorships were rising and falling. Western Europe was regaining its strength. The cold war was still going strong, as was the war in Vietnam. The Roman Catholic world was in an uproar after the Second Vatican Council. The baby boomers were changing the face of North America. Older churches and mission agencies were in a deep crisis as to their identity, purpose, direction, and priorities for mission action, while a host of new mission agencies begun after the war were beginning to dominate the missions scene.

In its April 1969 issue, *The International Review of Missions* (the oldest missiological journal in the world) dropped the "s" to

---

[22] Neill, *Creative Tension,* 112.

[23] Bevans and Schroeder, *Constants in Context,* 9; Bevans and Schroeder cite D. J. Bosch, *Witness to the World: The Christian Mission in Theological Perspective* (London: Marshall, Morgan, & Scott, 1980), 512.

[24] C. Van Engen, "A Broadening Vision: Forty Years of Evangelical Theology of Mission, 1946–1986." Pages 203–32 in *Earthen Vessels: American Evangelicals and Foreign Missions, 1880–1980,* ed. J. A. S. Carpenter and W. Shenk (Grand Rapids: Eerdmans, 1990), 212, citing C. Forman, *The Nation and the Kingdom: Christian Mission in the New Nations* (New York: Friendship, 1964), 17.

become *The International Review of Mission.*[25] Many older denominations in the USA abandoned the words *mission* and *missionary* and adopted the vocabulary of "fraternal workers" and "ecumenical sharing of resources."

The departure from a church-centric view that included the idea of individual conversion to faith in Jesus Christ was so drastic that McGavran accused the World Council of Churches of "betraying the two billion."[26] And in *Crucial Issues in Missions Tomorrow*, published in 1972, McGavran says:

> The [air]plane of missions has been hijacked. . . . Helping older churches as well as helping younger churches is to be considered mission. From this new angle, mission ceases being gospel proclamation to non-Christians and becomes inter-church aid or good work done anywhere.[27]

The integration of the International Missionary Council (IMC) into the World Council of Churches greatly impacted the Evangelical mission theology of the 1960s.[28] Reacting against the mission thinking of the World Council outlined in the section above, a significant number of important Evangelical leaders came together in two major mission conferences in 1966, inspired by the Billy Graham Association: the Congress on the Church's World Mission at Wheaton and the World Congress on Evangelism in Berlin.[29] These

---

[25] W. H. Crane, "Editorial," *International Review of Mission* 58 (1969): 141–44. In the editorial for that issue, Crane writes: "Missions in the plural have a certain justification in the diplomatic, political, and economic spheres of international relations where their nature, scope, and authority are defined by the interests of both those who initiate and those who receive them, but the mission of the Church is singular in that it issues from the One Triune God and His intention for the salvation of all men. His commission to the Church is one, even though the ministries given to the Church for this mission, and the given responses of particular churches in particular situations to the commission, are manifold. . . . The various studies and programmes initiated by the Division of World Mission and Evangelism in the past few years since integration into the life of the World Council of Churches also reflect this concern for the one mission of the Church in six continents rather than the traditional concern for missions from three continents to the other three."

[26] D. McGavran, "Yes, Uppsala Has Betrayed the Two Billion, Now What?" *Christianity Today* 16 (1972): 16–18.

[27] D. McGavran, *Crucial Issues in Missions Tomorrow* (Chicago: Moody, 1972), 190; cf. C. Van Engen, *The Growth of the True Church: An Analysis of the Ecclesiology of Church Growth Theory* (Amsterdam: Rodopi, 1981), 20; and Van Engen, "A Broadening Vision," 212–13.

[28] H. Lindsell, *The Church's Worldwide Mission* (Waco: Word, 1966), 2; cf. Van Engen, "A Broadening Vision," 203–32. In 1966 the Congress on the Church's Worldwide Mission convened, representing a large cross-section of Evangelical mission leaders. The delegates stated, "The birth of the World Council of Churches and the pressures to integrate the [IMC] into the framework of that organization brought to the forefront the problem of conservative theological missionary cooperation."

[29] Lindsell, *Church's Worldwide Mission*, 3.

gatherings later flowed into the large world mission congresses at Lausanne (1974), Pattaya (1980), and Manila (1989), among others.[30]

Out of this great ferment in Evangelical mission thinking came a new Evangelical synthesis and new definitions of *mission* for the twenty-first century. During the 1980s and 1990s Evangelicals called for mission among "unreached people groups" in locations where they saw no "viable" church present. This motivated Evangelicals to send a multitude of missionaries to the former Soviet-bloc countries after the dismantling of the USSR. This view of mission also led to an emphasis on mission in the "10–40 Window," the area between 10 and 40 degrees north of the equator, spanning from the eastern edge of Western Europe to the north Pacific, the least-evangelized area of the world where the greatest number of poor people lived.[31]

R. Winter sparked a movement for "frontier missions," mission among those who have no natural contacts with Christians. After the Lausanne II Congress in Manila, the AD 2000 and Beyond movement was born to mobilize Christians around the globe for world evangelization, following a vision similar to that of Edinburgh in 1910.

Along with these new initiatives, one can observe Evangelicals struggling to bring together evangelism and social action once again. In their extreme reaction to the WCC emphases of the 1960s, Evangelicals ended up splitting word and deed, speaking and doing, verbal proclamation and social transformation. Through a series of consultations, they sought to bring the two closer without necessarily giving one priority over the other.

Today, at the beginning of a new century, Evangelical mission is searching for new, appropriate, creative, and motivating definitions of mission. Increasingly, Evangelical missiologists have adopted the biblical notion of God's mission *(missio Dei)* as pointing toward a more holistic view of mission. O. Costas, S. Escobar, R. Padilla, and others called for a much stronger emphasis on the

---

[30] Van Engen, "A Broadening Vision," 203–32.
[31] R. Love, "10/40 Window," *Evangelical Dictionary of World Missions*, ed. S. Moreau and C. Van Engen (Grand Rapids: Baker, 2000), 983.

kingdom of God as a helpful paradigm of holistic and transformational mission action.[32] Evangelicals today would probably agree with this observation by Scherer:

> Abandoning the church-centered framework in no way implies forsaking the church's mission, but rather a re-visioning of that mission from a fresh biblical, missiological, and above all, eschatological point of view. This remains a priority task for the theology of Christian mission today.[33]

Evangelical missiology has been searching for a new cohesive synthesis. In 1999 V. Samuel and C. Sugden compiled a collection of essays entitled *Mission as Transformation*. The kingdom-of-God framework for mission is strong in this volume. In 2000 evangelical theologians of mission gathered in Iguassu, Brazil, to dialogue regarding the church's mission. A rapid scan of the topics shows an inclusive view of mission that sought to address many different missional agendas.[34] At a large Evangelical mission congress in Thailand in 2004, the concept of "transformation" was suggested. In their desire to develop a holistic understanding of mission, Evangelicals probably need to heed Neill's warning that "when everything is mission, nothing is mission."[35] A cohesive, consistent, focused, theologically deep, missiologically broad,

---

[32] O. Costas, *The Church and Its Mission: A Shattering Critique from the Third World* (Wheaton: Tyndale House, 1974); Costas, *Theology of the Crossroads in Contemporary Latin America* (Amsterdam: Rodopi, 1976); Costas, "The Whole World for the Whole Gospel," *Missiology* 8 (Oct 1980): 395–405; Costas, *Christ Outside the Gate: Mission Beyond Christendom* (Eugene, OR: Wipf & Stock, 2005); S. Escobar, "Beyond Liberation Theology: Evangelical Missiology in Latin America," *IBMR* 6 (July 1982): 108–44; C. R. Padilla, *Mission Between the Times: Essays on the Kingdom* (Grand Rapids: Eerdmans, 1985); Padilla, *Misión Integral: Ensayos sobre el Reino y la Iglesia* (Grand Rapids/Buenos Aires: Nueva Creación, 1986); Costas, *Liberating News: A Theology of Contextual Evangelization* (Eugene, OR: Wipf & Stock, 2002); Escobar, *De la Misión a la Teolog'a* (Buenos Aires: Kairos, 1998); Escobar, *Tiempo de Misión: América Latina y la Misión Cristiana Hoy* (Guatemala: Semilla, 1999); Escobar, *The New Global Mission: The Gospel from Everywhere to Everyone* (Downers Grove, IL: IVP, 2003).

[33] Scherer, "Church, Kingdom, and *Missio Dei*," 85.

[34] W. D. Taylor, ed., *Global Missiology for the 21st Century: The Iguassu Dialogue* (Grand Rapids: Baker, 2000). This work was published in Portuguese as *Missiologia Global para o Século XXI: A Consulta de Foz de Iguaçu*, ed. W. D. Taylor (Londrina: Descoberta ed., 2001).

[35] Neill, *Creative Tension*, 81. The present trend for Evangelical schools of world mission to change their name to "school of intercultural studies" is missiologically disturbing. "Intercultural studies" is not mission. When Evangelical mission thought and actions are reduced to "intercultural studies," the heart and soul of a biblical perspective of mission has been lost. J. Verkuyl (*Contemporary Missiology: An Introduction* [Grand Rapids: Eerdmans, 1978], 6) correctly affirms, "Missiology may never become a substitute for action and participation. God calls for participants and volunteers in his mission. . . . If study does not lead to participation, whether at home or abroad, Missiology has lost her humble calling."

and contextually appropriate Evangelical missiology has not yet emerged for this new century.[36]

DEFINING *MISSIONAL* AND *MISSION*: A SUGGESTION

A possible way forward in defining *mission* for the twenty-first century might involve an attempt to describe what a missional church would look like. I can suggest one way to go about that.

With the term *missional,* I emphasize the essential nature and vocation of the church as God's called and sent people. A missional ecclesiology is biblical, historical, contextual, praxeological (it can be translated into practice), and eschatological. With reference to the church, the term sees the church as the instrument of God's mission in God's world. Following L. Newbigin and others, a church that is missional understands that God's mission calls and sends the church of Jesus Christ, locally and globally, in the power of the Holy Spirit, to be a missionary church in its own society, in the cultures in which it finds itself, and globally among all peoples who do not yet confess Jesus as Lord. Mission is the result of God's initiative, rooted in God's purposes to restore and heal creation and to call people into a reconciled covenantal relationship with God. *Mission* means "sending," and it is the central biblical theme describing the purpose of God's action in human history, with God's people (now the church) being the primary agents of God's missionary action.[37]

Thus, if a church is missional, it will be:

- *Contextual:* A missional church understands itself as part of a larger context of a lost and broken world so loved by God.
- *Intentional:* A missional church understands itself as existing for the purpose of "following Christ in mission."

---

[36] Bosch, *Transforming Mission*, 390–91. Bosch offers the following definition of mission: "Mission [is] understood as being derived from the very nature of God. It [is] thus put in the context of the doctrine of the Trinity, not of ecclesiology or soteriology. The classical doctrine of the *missio Dei* as God the Father sending the Son, and God the Father and the Son sending the Spirit [is] expanded to include yet another 'movement': Father, Son and Holy Spirit sending the church into the world. . . . Our mission has no life of its own: only in the hands of the sending God can it truly be called mission, not least since the missionary initiative comes from God alone. . . . To participate in mission is to participate in the movement of God's love toward people, since God is [the] fountain of sending love. . . . In its mission, the church witnesses to the fullness of the promise of God's reign and participates in the ongoing struggle between that reign and the powers of darkness and evil."

[37] This definition is based on D. Guder, ed., *Missional Church: A Vision for the Sending of the Church in North America* (Grand Rapids: Eerdmans, 1998), 4–5, 11–12; cf. Bosch, *Transforming Mission*, 390.

- *Proclaiming:* A missional church understands itself as intentionally sent by God in mission to announce in word and deed the coming of the kingdom of God in Christ.
- *Reconciling:* A missional church understands itself to be a reconciling and healing presence in its contexts, locally and globally.
- *Sanctifying:* A missional church understands itself as a faith community gathered around the Word preached, thus personally living out its truth and serving as a purifying influence to society.
- *Unifying:* A missional church understands itself as an embracing, enfolding, gathering community of faith, anxious to receive persons into its fellowship.
- *Transforming:* A missional church is "the salt of the earth" (Matt 5:13), a transforming presence as the body of Christ in mission, called to be, embody, and live out in the world the following biblical concepts of mission, among others: *koinōnia, kērygma, diakonia, martyria*, prophet, priest, king, liberator, healer, sage.[38]

Such a conception of a missional church would need to take into consideration the interrelationship of what Bosch calls the church's "mission intention" and the church's "mission dimension."[39]

CONCLUSION

So, what do I tell Gloria and her Global Outreach Task Force? She is also aware that the ways in which we define *mission* influences our motivations, the agents, the means, the goals, and the way we measure the results of our lives, ministries, and actions as Christians in the world.

Maybe I could help Gloria and the members of her church begin to gain a biblical view of mission centered in Jesus Christ and shaped by the gospel of the kingdom of God. Scherer says:

> One of the crucial missiological problems of the second half of the twentieth century has been how to accomplish a successful transition from an earlier *church-centered* theology of mission

---

[38] The description offered above is drawn from C. Van Engen, *God's Missionary People* (Grand Rapids: Baker, 1991), 65–70; and Guder, *Missional Church*, 254–64.

[39] Bosch, *Transforming Mission*, 199–201.

to a *kingdom-oriented* one without loss of missionary vision or betrayal of biblical content. It can scarcely be denied that we are in the midst of such a transition. It is equally clear that we have not yet fully grasped the meaning of a move toward the *kingdom* orientation, which closely correlates with the Trinitarian *missio Dei*. . . . The fuller implications of this changeover for our missionary practice still lie in the future.[40]

In 1986 I wrote, "A Broadening Vision: Forty Years of Evangelical Theology of Mission, 1946–1986." Although evangelical missiology has undergone some development in relation to the observations I made then, I leave it to the reader to examine the extent to which evangelical definitions of *mission* have changed during these intervening years.[41]

Toward the end of my Sunday lunch with Gloria and her task force, I suggested they consider thinking, sharing insights, and working together to write their own definition of *mission*. Once they had crafted their definition as a task force, they could use the word again, teaching and promoting it in their church in order to further mobilize their congregation to participate in God's mission in God's world. They found the idea intriguing and challenging. Then, as I was getting ready to leave for the airport, with a twinkle in her eye, Gloria asked me, "So, how do you define *mission*?" This is what I told her:

---

[40] Scherer, "Church, Kingdom, and *Missio Dei*," 82. Bevans and Schroeder (*Constants in Context*, 9) suggest a definition of *mission* for this new century: "Mission happens wherever the church is; it is how the church exists. Mission is the church preaching Christ for the first time; it is the act of Christians struggling against injustice and oppression; it is the binding of wounds in reconciliation; it is the church learning from other religious ways and being challenged by the world's cultures. . . . Mission is the local church focusing not on its own, internal problems, but on other human beings, focusing elsewhere, in a world that calls and challenges it."

[41] Twenty years ago, I wrote, "Where to from here? Evangelicals have the possibility of exciting new developments ahead. They will probably find one of these to involve the theology of the Kingdom of God. . . . This motif could provide a vehicle for greater breadth of vision, including wiser and more careful use of technology, more sensitive understanding of other Christians, and increased cooperation between churches. Second, Evangelicals have yet to understand thoroughly and incorporate the pneumatological developments of the 'Third Force in Missions' of the Pentecostal and charismatic movements. . . . [P. Pomerville, *The Third Force in Missions* (Peabody, MA: Hendrickson, 1985). G. B. McGee, "Assemblies of God Mission Theology: A Historical Perspective," *IBMR* X (1986): 166–70.] Third, the relationship of evangelism and social action as goals of holistic mission has not yet been resolved. Evangelicals have the possibility of developing a new concept of evangelism for the whole person that combines a deep spirituality with a concern for each individual's total welfare. . . . The motif that keeps emerging through all forty years as the principal driving force behind evangelical theology of mission is the 'spirit of Edinburgh 1910.' The 'Watchword' still captures the imagination of the Evangelicals. They still consider themselves compelled to proclaim the gospel to the billions of people who have not yet believed in Jesus Christ. So, while some things about Evangelicals' mission theology have changed a great deal, this theme endures. Without it, Evangelicals would not be evangelical." Van Engen, "A Broadening Vision," 203–32.

I've been working on that for about 40 years now. Thus far in my own search for a definition, I have arrived at the following tentative attempt: "God's mission works primarily through Jesus Christ's sending the people of God to intentionally cross barriers from church to nonchurch, faith to nonfaith, to proclaim by word and deed the coming of the kingdom of God in Jesus Christ through the Church's participation in God's mission of reconciling people to God, to themselves, to one another, and to the world and gathering them into the church, through repentance and faith in Jesus Christ, by the work of the Holy Spirit, with a view to the transformation of the world, as a sign of the coming of the kingdom in Jesus Christ."

May the Holy Spirit teach us how to be and to become more authentically "God's missionary people"[42] in this new century, sent to a lost and hurting world so loved by God.

BIBLIOGRAPHY

Barrett, L. et al. *Treasure in Clay Jars: Patterns in Missional Faithfulness.* Grand Rapids: Eerdmans, 2004.

Bassham, R. *Mission Theology: 1948–1975, Years of Worldwide Creative Tension, Ecumenical, Evangelical, and Roman Catholic.* Pasadena: WCL, 1979.

Bevans, S. B., and R. P. Schroeder. *Constants in Context: A Theology of Mission for Today.* Maryknoll: Orbis, 2004.

Blauw, J. *The Missionary Nature of the Church.* Grand Rapids: Eerdmans, 1962.

Bosch, D. J. *Transforming Mission: Paradigm Shifts in Theology of Mission.* Maryknoll: Orbis, 1991.

———. *Witness to the World: The Christian Mission in Theological Perspective.* London: Marshall, Morgan, & Scott, 1980.

Cole, N. *Organic Church: Growing Faith Where Life Happens.* San Francisco: Jossey-Bass, 2005.

Costas, O. *Christ Outside the Gate: Mission Beyond Christendom.* Maryknoll: Orbis, 1982.

———. *The Church and Its Mission: A Shattering Critique from the Third World.* Wheaton: Tyndale, 1974.

---

[42] See Van Engen, *God's Missionary People*, 78.

————. *Liberating News: A Theology of Contextual Evangelization*. Grand Rapids: Eerdmans, 1989.

————. *Theology of the Crossroads in Contemporary Latin America*. Amsterdam: Rodopi, 1976.

————. "The Whole World for the Whole Gospel." *Missiology* 8 (October 1980): 395–504.

Crane, W. H. "Editorial." *International Review of Mission* 58 (1969): 141–44.

Duerr, J. *Sendende und Werdende Kirche in der Missions-theologie Gustav Warneck*. Basel: Basler Missionbuchhandlung, 1947.

Hesselgrave, D. "Great Commission." Pages 412–14 in *Evangelical Dictionary of World Missions*. Edited by S. Moreau and C. Van Engen. Grand Rapids: Baker, 2000.

Hoekendijk, J. C. *The Church Inside Out*. Philadelphia: Westminster, 1966.

Kittel, G., G. Friedrich, and G. W. Bromiley. *Theological Dictionary of the New Testament*. Grand Rapids: Eerdmans, 1995, c1985.

Love, R. "10/40 Window." Page 938 in *Evangelical Dictionary of World Missions*. Edited by S. Moreau and C. Van Engen. Grand Rapids: Baker, 2000.

McGavran, D. *The Bridges of God*. New York: Friendship/ World Dominion, 1955.

————, ed. *Crucial Issues in Missions Tomorrow*. Chicago: Moody, 1972.

————. "Yes, Uppsala Has Betrayed the Two Billion, Now What?" *Christianity Today* (1972): 16–18.

Neill, S. *Creative Tension*. London: Edinburgh House, 1959.

————. *A History of Christian Missions*. Baltimore: Penguin Books, 1964.

Padilla, C. R., ed. *Bases B'blicas de la Misi—n: Perspectivas Latinoamericanas*. Buenos Aires/Grand Rapids: Nueva Creacion/Eerdmans, 1998.

Reapsome, J. "Carey, William." *Evangelical Dictionary of World Missions*. Edited by S. Moreau and C. Van Engen. Grand Rapids: Baker, 2000.

Rooy, S. "La Búsqueda Histórica de las Bases B'blicas de la Misión." Pages 3–33 in *Bases B'blicas de la Misión: Perspectivas Latinoamericanas*. Translated by C. R. Padilla. Buenos Aires/Grand Rapids: Kairos, Nueva Creación, 1998.

Rosin, H. H. *"Missio Dei:* An Examination of the Origin, Contents and Function of the Term in Protestant Missiological Discussion." Leiden: Interuniversity Institute for Missiological and Ecumenical Research, 1972.

Samuel, V., and C. Sudgen. *Mission as Transformation: A Theology of the Whole Gospel*. Oxford: Regnum Books International, 1999.

Scherer, J. A. "Church, Kingdom, and *Missio Dei*: Lutheran and Orthodox Correctives to Recent Ecumenical Mission Theology." Pages 82–88 in *The Good News of the Kingdom: Mission Theology for the Third Millenniu*. Edited by C. Van Engen, D. S. Gilliland, and P. Pierson. Maryknoll: Orbis, 1993.

Stetzer, E., and D. Putman. *Breaking the Missional Code: Your Church Can Become a Missionary in Your Community*. Nashville: B&H, 2006.

Taylor, W. D., ed. *Global Missiology for the 21st Century: The Iguassu Dialogue*. Grand Rapids: Baker, 2000.

Van Engen, C. "A Broadening Vision: Forty Years of Evangelical Theology of Mission, 1946–1986." Pages 203–32 in *Earthen Vessels: American Evangelicals and Foreign Missions, 1880–1980*. Edited by J. A. S. Carpenter and W. Shenk. Grand Rapids: Eerdmans, 1990.

———. *God's Missionary People*. Grand Rapids: Baker, 1991.

———. *The Growth of the True Church: An Analysis of the Ecclesiology of Church Growth Theory*. Amsterdam: Rodopi, 1981.

———. "Reflecting Theologically About the Resistant." Pages 22–78 in *Reaching the Resistant: Barriers and Bridges for Mission*. Edited by J. D. Woodberry. Pasadena: William Carey Library, 1998.

Verkuyl, J. *Contemporary Missiology: An Introduction*. Grand Rapids: Eerdmans, 1978.

CHAPTER 3

On Becoming Missional: Interacting with Charles Van Engen

KEITH E. EITEL

A STORY

A former student was tasked to take photographs of a missionary's work in a predominantly Hindu area. The missionary he was to photograph did a startling thing near the end of a day of filming. The missionary lined up behind the Hindu worshippers in a temple, then went up and bowed before an image of Shiva, followed the same ritual prayer formula before the image as the Hindus were doing, then placed the red dot on his forehead and bowed one more time as he backed away from the image, never turning his back so as not to offend Shiva.

When asked by my former student what on earth he had just done, the missionary said, "If these people don't view me as a spiritual and relevant person, they'll not listen to me when I try to evangelize them."

So here we have the oddity of a Christian missionary contextualizing the gospel message while using a method that presumes the validity and truth of spirituality exhibited by Hindu worshippers of Shiva! Here, and in other instances, similar things are done on the pretense of being contextual, relevant, or even missional toward the host culture.

This story illustrates what happens when there is too little care regarding biblical boundaries or safeguards as we create methods for contextualizing the gospel and being missional in a host culture. If the outcome undermines, destroys, threatens, or contradicts the message we wish to communicate, then we have surpassed biblical boundaries and lost touch with Christ's mission entrusted to His Church.

Missional methods or models used to engage a given culture with the gospel reflect an underlying set of assumptions about what missionaries are commissioned to do. Something seems awry with the Shiva sham described above. Are there limits to what Christians can say or do when being relevant? How does being relevant translate into being *missional* or even just doing missions? If so, what do all these things mean? Where are we headed on the front end of this century as Christians called to be prophetic voices discharge their duties to a lost world?

Charles Van Engen of Fuller Theological Seminary has keen insight and proven qualifications for addressing these contemporary challenges Christians face. He graphically illustrated the level of embarrassment about the term *missions* today in his opening and ending story. Missions—in the parlance of some cutting-edge, globalistic believers today—is discounted as a relic of the modernistic past because we now reside in a postmodern future. Hence, there is a search for new ways to do missions that reflect the futures now crashing in on us with Internet speed.

The term *missional* is commonly written about and spoken of as the viable alternative. Van Engen suggests contouring or defining that term in light of our *missions* history. Along the way he exposes numerous caveats we need to hear and raises new ones for the journey ahead. The present piece is an interaction with his chapter and aims to note a resounding support where possible and to take alternative positions when needed. This writer's desired outcome is to affirm the term *missional* but to do so with some distinct and emphatic qualifications.

CONTENT

Van Engen returns to biblical soil to determine what the term *missions* has meant and what parallels there may be for the emerging meaning of *missional*. The English term carries purposeful or goal-oriented connotation. While there is no New Testament usage of the term *missions*, the parallel concept is rooted in the translated Greek word meaning "to send out." This presupposes a sender and one that complies with being sent. His conclusion is that Jesus alone is the Sender and the Church is sent out into the world. This comprises the *missio Dei*. Van Engen indicates that things eventually went off course because the church began to view itself as being sent by some intervening agency, administrative entity, board, or human structure and lost sight of its divine purpose. "The Sender is Jesus Christ, whose authority defines, circumscribes, limits, and propels Christian mission." In one sense this is a warranted reminder of the foundation of all missions. In another it is an overstatement of the obvious and neglects dealing with the practical and logistical problems of humanly organizing, facilitating, and implementing the missions of the sent out ones. Some level of organization is necessary. The contrary notion is aimless scattering of people and resources to achieve undefined goals. While those obeying the Great Commission must always keep the Sender clearly in view, the ways and means of accomplishing missions necessarily entail structure.

Between the biblical eras and modern times, Van Engen describes what he calls the "Constantinian" era. The premise is that with Constantine a state-controlled purpose or set of purposes emerged that have driven the engine of missions. He sweeps broadly the backdrop of nearly two thousand years of Church history and contends that intermingling Church interests with those of temporal powers down through the centuries taints missions. This is, according to Van Engen, still evident as sending agencies or megachurches mirror the motives and models used in the medieval and colonial periods. He sounds an alarm. Yet his survey is editorial and ends up creating a caricature of reality. Not all missionaries, their models, or their methods were necessarily given over to serve the ends of earthly rulers. While all were human, not all were agents with ulterior and pretentious motivations.[1]

---

[1] One thinks of the ministries of William Carey or Hudson Taylor in this regard. Each of them opposed colonial authorities and their edicts to practice missions biblically in their respective settings.

A HISTORICAL SURVEY

The essential focus of the essay is to dissect the historical pieces of postmodernity's preference for the term *missional* and look at what is inside. There is more to this change in terminology than simple semantics; it is philosophical and reflective; and it makes new applications of old theological assumptions while adding some new ones. In four sections Van Engen tours the reader through the modern missions era from William Carey to the turn of this century. A conversionist theology gave impetus to Carey as well as most of those who rose to the missions challenge throughout the nineteenth century and into the early twentieth. Van Engen notes that the simple belief in the Great Commission's mandate to go and make disciples by teaching and baptizing was what launched the movement. However, he adds value judgments regarding the application of principles that are not necessarily indicative of a whole era of missions. For example, disciple making, he says in reference to these earlier missionaries, "was more important than the 'baptizing and teaching' portions"; convert churches resembled sending churches and agencies; and extraction from the social network was normative. While there are certainly historic incidents of each, Van Engen seems overgeneralized in his depiction of the era.

During these same years an administrative emphasis emerged regarding the development of indigenous churches.[2] Church-centered missions was status quo until the dawning of the 1960s when a stress on the kingdom of God and engagement of the world surfaced to help coordinate human efforts more closely with God's ultimate purposes. Van Engen rightly spells out that there was an inherent secularization process in missions during this time because the world, and its overwhelming social needs, set the premise for engaging missions rather than the need to proclaim or evangelize lost souls.

Evangelicals reacted by prioritizing evangelism over social engagement from approximately 1980 to 2000. Separation of word and deed, speaking and doing, or verbal proclamation and

---

[2] K. E. Eitel, "'To Be or Not to Be?': The Indigenous Church Question," in *Missiology: An Introduction to the Foundations, History, and Strategies of World Missions*, ed. J. M. Terry, E. Smith, and J. Anderson (Nashville: B&H, 1998): 301–17.

social ministries resulted as per Van Engen's historical scenario. He concludes that David J. Bosch and others then shifted the mission world's focus from being Church- or kingdom-centered to a trinitarian theology that would demonstrate the functional plurality of the Godhead mirrored in true missions.

Each plank in the platform has parallel or embedded practical assumptions that mirror developments in both the realms of philosophy (regarding the character and content of truth) and theology (the nature and substance of religious truth) and thereby sets the stage for the current identity crisis among those who are engaging in missions or claiming to be missional.

ENGAGING THE IDEAS

We live in a time of dangerous creativity in missionary circles. Creative tensions without biblically firm boundaries will result in compromises that undermine the message we have to offer to the world. Unless believers set hermeneutical measures in place that will safeguard the integrity of the gospel message itself, missions will falter.

A distinct attitudinal similarity is roving through some churches in North America today that is reminiscent of the counterculture movements of the late 1960s and early 1970s; namely there was a loss of confidence in the "establishment" (known in the literature today as "modernity" or "Christendom"). Hippies that came to Christ in yesteryear reacted so strongly against established authority and the corresponding structures that they declared social war and scheduled institutions to be burned down figuratively and sometimes literally. Their radically secular ideas spilled over into religious circles and emerged as the Jesus People movement that actually took on various splintered forms.[3] Today there are those choosing to call themselves "emergent" claiming they are something new under the sun. They are caught between paradigms. I suspect they are related to the movement of the 1960s but are not yet fully chiseled to be what they are becoming.

Numerous terms are used and redefined with emergent or missional meanings.[4] These terms provide traceable evidence of

---

[3] A. Reid, "The Impact of the Jesus Movement on Evangelism Among Southern Baptists" (Ph.D. diss., Southwestern Baptist Theological Seminary, 1991): 45–47.

[4] Literature delineating the concept of missional or missional theologies predates the

what is actually emerging. *Missional* is one of those distinctly emergent terms. These two concepts are not necessarily interchangeable. Yet much is made of the term *missional* by those who identify with various branches of the emerging church movement. The scope of meaning ranges from simply being intentional and outwardly focused in living a Christlike life while engaging in an evangelistic conversation with the secular world to incorporating elements of postmodern philosophy, especially regarding views of truth, relativism, and contextualization.[5] Embedded in these trends are spirits of cultural ancestors from the 1960s because they tend to disdain denominationalism, traditionalism, and modernity. Some even claim their desire is to skip over nearly 2,000 years of Christian history to rediscover true biblical Christianity.[6] They are not the first to desire to do so. Christian history is replete with radical or root cause movements. Denominations, agencies, boards of trustees, and the like all smack of traditionalism or establishments that many emergents deem outmoded or inconsequential for the new century. Hence, missional proponents wish to reconfigure the Christian Church to be much more localized, even to a level of intimacy experienced only in small cells or house churches. Times, places, and logistics for their congregating are fluid, sometimes changing rapidly to avoid institutionalization or bureaucracy. Leadership is suspect if they claim to know truth especially if it is deemed biblical since truth is personally derived. Highly individualized theological opinions are each considered

---

appearance of emergent or emerging churches. L. Newbigin's concerns regarding Western culture, as articulated in the 1980s, gave rise to a network of concerned thinkers entitled "Gospel and Our Culture Network." See www.gocn.org. Some traditional, denominational churches embrace evangelistic and culture-engaging aspects of missional theology while others break with denominational pasts and freelance in cultural engagement without the theological constraints of a church tradition or, as others may argue, without biblical safeguards against theological syncretism. For backgrounds of these developments see E. Gibbs and R. K. Bolger, *Emerging Churches: Creating Christian Community in Postmodern Culture* (Grand Rapids: Baker, 2005) and D. L. Guder, *Missional Church: A Vision for the Sending of the Church in North America* (Grand Rapids: Eerdmans, 1998).

[5] For an example of the more conservative use of the term *missional,* see E. Stetzer, "Toward a Missional Convention," in *Southern Baptist Identity: An Evangelical Denomination Faces the Future*, ed. D. S. Dockery (Wheaton: Crossway, 2009), 175–202. For various theological elements within the emerging church movement, and accompanying uses of the terms in view, see R. Webber, ed., *Listening to the Beliefs of Emerging Churches: Five Perspectives* (Grand Rapids: Zondervan, 2007). Finally, for the impact of these influences on rethinking denominationalism, see C. Van Gelder, "An Ecclesiastical Geno-Project: Unpacking the DNA of Denominations and Denominationalism," in *The Missional Church & Denominations: Helping Congregations Develop a Missional Identity*, ed. C. Van Gelder (Grand Rapids: Eerdmans, 2008), 12–45.

[6] See J. D. Hall, *The End of Christendom and the Future of Christianity* (Valley Forge: Trinity Press, 1997).

valid and real even if they may conflict with the Bible. Saving the world is the purpose that drives the Church. Salvation is holistic; it includes faith but not in a common set of doctrines that smack of traditionalism. Instead it is a journey, a walk, or an existential sojourn. "They [emergent advocates] view the emerging church as a missional effort to engage in post-modern culture through a rediscovery of the kingdom of God that Jesus proclaimed."[7]

Underlying this matrix of ideas expressed in an atmosphere of multiple changes that are coming at broadband velocity is a set of theological adjustments that allow for a journey less fettered by biblical restraints. Missiologists of a different generation are sounding an alarm. *"Although changes there must and will be, the future of Christian missions will depend more on changes that are not made than it will on changes that are made."*[8] Hesslegrave's warning is echoed by one living and working in an Asian context.

> Theology is not only to be *thought*; it is also to be *lived*. Whereas philosophy has traditionally been the dialogue partner with theology, today it is sociology. . . . While it is certainly true that theology must be enculturated, it is also true that theology must stand in judgment over culture. Theology, at least as we understand it in the Christian sense, does have its parameter.[9]

---

[7] P. Hertig, "Fool's Gold: Paul's Inverted Approach to Church Hierarchy (1 Corinthians 4), with Emerging Church Implications," *Missiology: An International Review*, vol. 35, no. 3 (July 2007): 299.

[8] D. J. Hesselgrave, *Paradigms in Conflict: 10 Key Questions in Christian Missions Today* (Grand Rapids: Kregel), 20. Emphasis is his.

[9] D. J. Adams, "Toward a Theological Understanding of Postmodernism," www.crosscurrents.org/adams (accessed August 19, 2007), 6. Also, in an earlier publication, Van Engen erected a model of "covenantal" contextualization that deals with the challenge of universal truth expressed and lived out in local settings. If God's Word is indeed absolute truth, then how do local people in their own contexts interpret and apply said truth? Van Engen concludes that "if by 'theology' we mean the knowledge of God in context, we must also allow the revelation of God's self-disclosure in each new context to influence all other understandings, all other 'theology' arising in other times and cultures." See C. Van Engen, "The New Covenant: Knowing God in Context" in *The Word Among Us: Contextualizing Theology for Mission Today*, ed. D. S. Gilliland (Dallas: Word, 1989), 91. Hiebert cautions contextualizers not to repeat the error of "postmodern anthropology" and end up with no means by which one may engage in "accurate communication . . . because there are no external reference points against which two subjective perceptions can be compared." He continues and illustrates the tension herein when he says a "requisite in a metatheology [absolute biblical truth or external reference point of truth] is to differentiate between God's revelation in Scripture and human understandings expressed in theologies." See P. G. Hiebert, "The Missionary as Mediator of Global Theologizing," in *Globalizing Theology: Belief and Practice in an Era of World Christianity*, ed. C. Ott and H. A. Netland (Grand Rapids: Baker, 2006), 303, 306. The oddity is that by affirming absolute truth of the Bible yet overemphasizing the relativized, conditioned, and humanly determined nature of interpretation of the text handicaps the flow of God's truth and divorces His meanings from human experiences undermining biblical authority. In other words, what use is it to affirm the

Why is there such a fuss? Partly it stems from Bosch's seminal work in the early 1990s in which he wove together a tapestry of what seems like a new academic discipline. He surveyed the panoramic development of missions since biblical times to the end of the twentieth century with multiple scholarly perspectives conjoined from the disciplines of biblical studies, theology, history, and missiology. The net effect is something akin to the way historical theology relates to sister disciplines of church history and systematic theology. In chapter 12, he describes the "Elements of an Emerging Ecumenical Missionary Paradigm."[10] Bosch did not live to see the effects of his treatise, but many of those advocating emergent and missional changes benchmark off of his ideas.[11]

Theological methodologies are of utmost importance. Presuppositions regarding the integrity and reliability of the biblical text set in motion interpretative mechanisms that build one's theology into a set of strategic initiatives and practices. Inherent in some emergent or missional schools is a bipolar attitude. On one hand there is an affirmation of the truth and reliability of the Bible. On the other hand there is a methodological disconnect that encourages relativistic flirtation with cultural modes of thought and actions. Alan Hirsch rightly points out that the Church must turn outward and assume a "sent" posture. Yet he adopts a theological method that bypasses discussion of biblical authority and then prioritizes Christology that then determines missiology and consequently shapes ecclesiology.[12] Without the foundational assumption of biblical authority, accessibility, and applicability, the net effect is some degree of relativism. When intentionally flirting with the world's systems, this can be dangerous. Hirsch even notes

---

Bible as truth yet have no reliable way to access, interpret, or apply it? This phenomenon ends up affirming the very thing Hiebert cautions us against that is evident in postmodern anthropology. What makes theologians or missiologists immune from this dilemma is to recognize the literal and practical meaning of the Bible's teachings. Adams's contention is magnified in practice then. The "dialogue partner" for theology now is not philosophy (questions of existence, meaning, purpose, and truth) but the social sciences, especially sociology and anthropology that begin with human experiences as determinate of truth.

[10] D. J. Bosch, *Transforming Mission: Paradigm Shifts in Theology of Mission* (Maryknoll, NY: Orbis, 1991), 368. See the whole chapter for detailed development of this paradigm.

[11] See the critique rendered by D. A. Carson, *Becoming Conversant with Emergent: Understanding a Movement and Its Implications* (Grand Rapids: Zondervan, 2005).

[12] A. Hirsch, *The Forgotten Ways: Reactivating the Missional Church* (Grand Rapids: Brazos), 143.

that this is a concern. He comments that a "Designer Christianity" model or make-your-own-theology approach,

> poses one of the most potent threats to the EMC [Emergent Missional Church]. . . . As a late-twentieth-century, early-twenty-first-century phenomenon, the EMC *is very susceptible to the postmodern blend of religious pluralism and philosophical relativism. This makes it very hard to stand for issues of truth in the public sphere.* Claims of truth are thus pushed into the sphere of private opinions. This creates massive pressure to deny the uniqueness of Christ and his work in our behalf. I have seen many emerging churches succumb to theological liberalism a la Spong [Bishop John Shelby Spong] and then die off. The adaptive challenge must drive us closer to our original message, not further away from it. This, I believe, is critical.[13]

Oddly, while the sentiment is right, the DNA will breed theological error. Scripture must always critique cultural experiences and never the reverse.

CONCLUSION

Perhaps the globalized Church today is suffering from a deep-seated sense of insecurity that results from embarrassment about what the Bible clearly says, "Thus says the Lord" and "I am the way." These are exclusive definitions of truth. In order to fit in or relate to the trends, we are jeopardizing the foundations upon which God's truth is built. If Shiva now determines the characteristics of the Christian missionary witness and spirituality, then our rush to be relevant is too costly. If being missional means relationships that entail little or no intentional and verbal proclamation of the gospel, service without concern for the eternal destiny of human souls, or finally relevance without responsibility for truth, then let us simply reaffirm the Great Commission and be willing to keep on telling the old, old story to everyone that *wills to listen.* The results may merely be godly disciples and New Testament churches, but we could spend our lifetimes accomplishing far less if we are not careful and at the same time being quite trendy in the process.

---

[13] Ibid., 156–57. Emphasis added by this writer.

BIBLIOGRAPHY

Adams, Daniel J. "Toward a Theological Understanding of Postmodernism." Available at www.crosscurrents.org/adams (accessed August 19, 2007), 6.

Bosch, David J. *Transforming Mission: Paradigm Shifts in Theology of Mission.* Maryknoll, NY: Orbis, 1991.

Carson, D. A. *Becoming Conversant with Emergent: Understanding a Movement and Its Implications.* Grand Rapids: Zondervan, 2005.

Eitel, Keith E. " 'To Be or Not to Be?': The Indigenous Church Question." In *Missiology: An Introduction to the Foundations, History, and Strategies of World Missions.* Edited by John Mark Terry, Ebbie Smith, and Justice Anderson. Nashville: B&H, 1998.

Gibbs, Eddie, and Ryan K. Bolger. *Emerging Churches: Creating Christian Community in Postmodern Culture.* Grand Rapids: Baker, 2005.

Guder, Darrell S. *Missional Church: A Vision for the Sending of the Church in North America.* Grand Rapids: Eerdmans, 1998.

Hall, John Douglas. *The End of Christendom and the Future of Christianity.* Valley Forge: Trinity Press, 1997.

Hertig, Paul. "Fool's Gold: Paul's Inverted Approach to Church Hierarchy (1 Corinthians 4), with Emerging Church Implications." *Missiology: An International Review*, vol. 35, no. 3 (July 2007): 299.

Hesselgrave, David J. *Paradigms in Conflict: 10 Key Questions in Christian Missions Today.* Grand Rapids: Kregel, 2005.

Hiebert, Paul G. "The Missionary as Mediator of Global Theologizing." In *Globalizing Theology: Belief and Practice in an Era of World Christianity.* Edited by Craig Ott and Harold A. Netland. Grand Rapids: Baker, 2006.

Hirsch, Alan. *The Forgotten Ways: Reactivating the Missional Church.* Grand Rapids: Brazos, 2006.

Reid, Alvin. "The Impact of the Jesus Movement on Evangelism Among Southern Baptists." Ph.D. Diss., Southwestern Baptist Theological Seminary, 1991.

Stetzer, Ed. "Toward a Missional Convention," in *Southern Baptist Identity: An Evangelical Denomination Faces the Future*. Edited by David S. Dockery. Wheaton: Crossway, 2009: 175–202.

Van Engen, Charles. "The New Covenant: Knowing God in Context." In *The Word Among Us: Contextualizing Theology for Mission Today*. Edited by Dean S. Gilliland. Dallas: Word, 1989.

Van Gelder, Craig. "An Ecclesiastical Geno-Project: Unpacking the DNA of Denominations and Denominationalism," in *The Missional Church & Denominations: Helping Congregations Develop a Missional Identity*. Edited by Craig Van Gelder. Grand Rapids: Eerdmans, 2008: 12–45.

Webber, Robert, ed. *Listening to the Beliefs of Emerging Churches: Five Perspectives*. Grand Rapids: Zondervan, 2007.

CHAPTER 4

"Mission" and *Missio Dei*

Response to Charles Van Engen's "'Mission' Defined and Described"

ENOCH WAN

My response to Charles Van Engen's "'Mission' Defined and Described" is organized in the following order: observation, evaluation, and suggestion. Observation and evaluation are conducted on the basis of the stated purpose and proposed definition in Van Engen's piece. A shorter and more holistic definition of *mission* is then proposed with explanation as to why it is a better alternative.

OBSERVATION

Purpose and Presentation

The stated purpose of the article is quoted below for the sake of easy reference and review:

> The purpose of this essay is to offer a brief historical overview of some ways in which the Christian church has defined "mission" down through the centuries, and to demonstrate how the various definitions have influenced the thought and practice of the Christian church's ministries in the world. In this sense this essay addresses the PAST of what has traditionally been termed "missions" (p. 7).

Van Engen is to be credited for having achieved the stated purpose by providing "a historical overview" of how the term *mission* has been defined, and he has successfully demonstrated how variations in this definition have impacted the thought and practice of the Christian Church.

The format of the presentation is creative and realistic. It begins with his meeting with the Global Outreach Task Force of a local congregation on a Sunday afternoon and closes with his attempt to answer Gloria's question: "So, how do you define mission?" By using this device, the author avoids the typical dry and boring historical narration and provides a sense of realism in dealing with the questions, including details of place, personnel, and process.

Definition and Description

The entire study chronicles the changes in the understanding and practice of "mission," drawing from the author's 40 years of experience in teaching, research, and publication. It describes the shift of emphasis in the conception and implementation of "mission" throughout the centuries. The author's review of varying definitions of the term *mission* by mission statesmen, scholars, and mission leaders is clear and to the point. The diachronic description of the practice of "mission" by various groups of different periods is both interesting and helpful.

Emphasis on the Institutional Dimension of Mission

In this study, however, there is a tendency to focus more on the institutional dimension of "mission" at the expense of the individual dimension. The author is conscious of the difference in these two dimensions, as indicated by the illustrative samples below:

- the reference to H. Venn's "more institutionalized perspective" (pp. 16–17);
- the extensive quote of J. Scherer's comments on "church-centrism" (pp. 19–20);
- the reference to D. McGavran versus the World Council of Churches in terms of "the departure from a church-centric view" (p. 21).

The evaluation below is provided in light of the author's awareness of two dimensions of Christian mission, that is, "individual" and "institutional."

EVALUATION

Overcorrection of Evangelical Emphasis on Individual/Spiritual Salvation

In the review on W. Carey and the Student Volunteer Movement of section 4, the author observes that "for about a 150 years prior to the 1960's, . . . Protestants who used the 'Great Commission' . . . assumed the following: that salvation is individualistic . . . personal relationship with Jesus Christ . . . new individual converts" (pp. 15–16). This is the only portion in the entire study that deals with the individualistic aspect of mission. The rest of the paper deals with the institutional aspect of mission. This institutional focus of mission is clearly shown in the last section ("Defining 'Missional' and 'Mission': A Suggestion") where the definition of *mission* is being narrowed down to become "missional church" (pp. 24–26).

Theological Understanding of "Mission"

It is good and proper that the author begins with word studies (Greek and English) and continues with exegetical work on key texts (e.g., Matt 28:18–20; Luke 4:43; John 20:21). But the author does not unpack the theological significance of these passages for his readers. Instead of being true to the texts that are trinitarian—and despite the fact that the author does cite some key trinitarian texts (Matt 28:18–20; Luke 4:43; John 20:21)—the author limits the theological understanding of *mission* to "the Sender is Jesus Christ, whose authority defines . . . Christian mission" (p. 12). Thus the richness of the theological foundation of *mission* being trinitarian has been reduced merely to being Christocentric. This runs counter to the contemporary trend in missiological and theological literature that is richly trinitarian in orientation. Significantly, trinitarian missiological studies have entered into the recent discourse between contemporary theologians such as C. LaCugna, D. Coffey, E. Jüngel, E. Johnson, J. Bracken, J. Moltmann, L. Boff, L. Newbigin, R. Jensen, and Y. J. Lee. This trend has also impacted the theology of Christian missions, stimulating it toward a new trinitarian orientation. I have provided a brief bibliography of these recent publications at the end of this chapter. Hopefully, the works I have selected are sufficient to show a trend toward trinitarian orientation in missiological and theological studies. Yet Van Engen, though citing many Scripture references to the Trinity, unnecessarily limits the theological understanding of *mission* to "the Sender [who] is Jesus Christ, whose authority defines . . . Christian mission."

SUGGESTION

Missio Dei of the Trinity and Christian Missions at Two Levels

One of the most outstanding features of this study is the author's repeated references to *missio Dei* (pp. 10, 18–20, 23, 26) in key places. In light of these multiple references, this reviewer would like to use figure 1 to explain "The Interactive Relationship Within the Trinity and Beyond" at two levels:

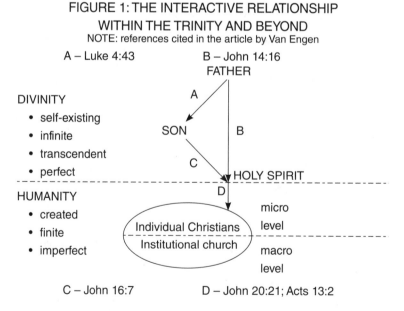

FIGURE 1: THE INTERACTIVE RELATIONSHIP
WITHIN THE TRINITY AND BEYOND
NOTE: references cited in the article by Van Engen

A – Luke 4:43   B – John 14:16
FATHER

DIVINITY
- self-existing
- infinite
- transcendent
- perfect

SON   B

C

HOLY SPIRIT

HUMANITY
- created
- finite
- imperfect

Individual Christians
Institutional church

micro level

macro level

C – John 16:7   D – John 20:21; Acts 13:2

Figure 1 shows the two realms (i.e., divinity and humanity) with a dotted line in between to denote the converging of the two. Using the references from Van Engen's piece, there are internal interactions within the Triune God (i.e., "A" Father–Son, "B" Father–H.S., and "C" Son–H.S.).

Figure 1 also shows interaction of the Triune God with humanity ("D" in fig. 1) at two levels (i.e., micro-individual Christians and macro–institutional church).

Van Engen cites trinitarian texts but unnecessarily reduces *missio Dei* to being Christocentric only, and mission is reduced to becoming the missional church at the institutional level. In addition to the needed emphasis on the individual career missionary, there is also a personal dimension of Christian mission for all believers. For example, while the apostle Paul was a key figure in the spread of the gospel (obeying the Great Commission) in the book of Acts, his conversion, calling, and commission had much to do with the "little mission" that God had entrusted to a relatively unknown figure of the Bible, Ananias (Acts 9). Yes, the missional church in Antioch (Acts 13) was prominent in carrying the Great Commission, but it had much to do with individual leaders (e.g., Simeon, Lucius of Cyrene, Manaan, Barnabas, Saul) and with the sending of Barnabas and Saul by the church. There is no dichotomy between the individual and institutional dimensions of the Christian mission (see the dotted line in fig. 1). It is therefore not correct to leave out the individual aspect and focus exclusively on the institutional missional church as Van Engen does.

Figure 1 can help correct the unbalanced treatment in Van Engen's piece and rectify its reductionistic tendency. Figure 1 clearly portrays the complexity of divine and human realms converging, plus the dynamic interaction of the triune God with personal human beings and the institutional Christian church. Figure 1 also shows the more holistic understanding of Christian mission to be inclusive of individual Christians (at the micro level) and the institutional church (at the macro level as marked by the dotted line). From the point of this reviewer, Van Engen's institutional focus is an overcorrection of the individualistic character of Christianity and mission in the Western tradition. In this case it is not a matter of either-or but both-and at two levels.

Definition of "Mission"

The title of the article is "'Mission' Defined and Described," yet the entire piece has the missional church as the only focus. Mission is broader in scope than the missional church. The Christian mission cannot be accomplished apart from individuals obedient to the Great Commission. The personal dimension of mission somehow escaped Van Engen's attention. He does a good job describing mission historically but fails to define mission holistically and realistically.

Toward the end of the article, after providing a diachronic review of the description and definition of *mission*, Van Engen makes the following observation: "A cohesive, consistent, focused, theologically deep, missiologically broad, and contextually appropriate evangelical missiology has not yet emerged for this new century." Then at the conclusion, in his response to Gloria's quest for a definition of *mission*, Van Engen proposes one that is eight lines long but which does not measure up to the criteria he himself provides. This reviewer proposes the following definition as an alternative, believing it to be closer to the above criteria and more true to the title of "'Mission' Defined":

> "Mission" is the endeavor of both individual Christians and the institutional church to continue on and carry out the *missio Dei* of the Triune God at both micro and macro levels, spiritually (saving souls) and socially (ushering in *shalom*[1]), for redemption, reconciliation and transformation.

This definition is a better alternative for several reasons. First, it is shorter in length but more comprehensive in scope. Second, it is holistic (i.e., spiritual and social) and balanced (i.e., not anti-individualistic) instead of being reductionistic. Third, it is enriched by the trinitarian orientation rather than impoverished by being merely Christocentric in emphasis. Fourth, it truly reflects the essence of the key texts Van Engen cites (see notes in fig. 1). Fifth, it includes spiritual and social aspects of Christian mission in general and particularly in the missions of redemption, reconciliation, and

---

[1] *"Shalom."* The opposite of "shalom" is described in John 12:31; 1 John 3:8; 5:19 and Jesus had overcome the world and the evil one who is its ruler (1 John 2:13–14; 5:4). *Shalom* is a Hebrew word with connotations of peace, wholeness, and wellness in the context of right relationships with God, people, and nature (Jer 33:8–9; Job 5:24; Ps 30:11; Isa 11:6,9; 53:5).

transformation. Sixth, the key elements of "redemption, reconciliation, and transformation" in the proposed definition are relational in nature[2] thus more relevant to the postmodernist of the twenty-first century who are starving for relationship. This proposed alternative definition is hopefully measured up to the criteria[3] Van Engen had imposed on himself. It is hoped that this definition can lead to the emergence of an "evangelical missiology . . . for this new century."

BIBLIOGRAPHY ON THE RELATIONSHIP
BETWEEN MISSIOLOGY AND TRINITARIAN STUDIES

Boff, L. *Holy Trinity, Perfect Community.* Translated by
	P. Berryman. Maryknoll, NY: Orbis, 2000. Originally
	published in Portuguese, *Santisima Trindade e a Melhor
	Communidade,* 1988.

Chester, T. *Mission and the Coming of God: Eschatology, the
	Trinity and Mission in the Theology of Jurgen Moltmann.*
	Paternoster Theological Monographs Series. Cambridge:
	Paternoster, 2007.

Cunningham, D. *These Three Are One: The Practice of
	Trinitarian Theology.* Holden: Blackwell, 1998.

Feenestra, R. J., and C. Plantinga Jr., eds. *Trinity, Incarnation,
	and Atonement.* Notre Dame: University Press, 1989.

Foust, T. F., G. R. Hunsberger, J. A. Kirk, and W. Ustorf,
	eds. "Trinitarian Missiology: Mission as Face-to-Face
	Encounter." Pages 76–83 in *A Scandalous Prophet:
	The Way of Mission After Newbigin.* Grand Rapids:
	Eerdmans, 2001.

Greene, C. J. D. "Trinitarian Tradition and the Cultural
	Collapse of Late Modernity." Pages 65–72 in *A
	Scandalous Prophet: The Way of Mission After Newbigin.*
	Edited by T. F. Foust, G. Hunsberger, J. A. Kirk, and
	W. Ustorf. Grand Rapids: Eerdmans, 2001.

Gunton, C. E. *The One, the Three and the Many: God, Creation
	and the Culture of Modernity.* New York: Cambridge
	University Press, 1993.

---

[2] For extensive explanation and discussion on "relationalism," see Wan 2006, 2007, 2010.
[3] The criteria are "cohesive, consistent, focused, theologically deep, missiologically broad, and contextually appropriate."

———. *The Promise of Trinitarian Theology,* 2nd ed. New York: T&T Press, 1997.

Hoffmeyer, J. F. "Should Christianity Be Missionary? The Missional Trinity." *Dialog: A Journal of Theology* 40 (published online December 17, 2002): 108–11.

Holmes, S. R. "Trinitarian Missiology: Towards a Theology of God as Missionary." *International Journal of Systematic Theology* 8 (2005) 1:72–90.

Horrell, J. S. "In the Name of the Father, Son and Holy Spirit: Constructing a Trinitarian Worldview," http://www.bible.org (accessed November 26, 2005).

———. "Toward Clarifying a Biblical Model of the Social Trinity: Avoiding Equivocation of Nature and Order." *Global Missiology* (January 2004). http://www.globalmissiology.net (accessed February 16, 2005).

Kimel, A. F., ed. *Speaking the Christian God: The Holy Trinity and the Challenge of Feminism.* Grand Rapids: Eerdmans, 1992.

LaCugna, C. M. "God in Communion with Us—the Trinity." Edited by C. M. LaCugna. *Freeing Theology: The Essentials of Theology in Feminist Perspective.* New York: HarperCollins, 1993.

Lim, D. S., and S. Spaulding. *Sharing Jesus in the Buddhist World.* Pasadena: William Carey Library, 2003.

Moltmann, J. *The Trinity and the Kingdom.* Minneapolis: Fortress, 1993.

Newbigin, L. *The Open Secret: An Introduction to the Theology of Mission.* Eerdmans, 1994.

Peters, T. *God as Trinity: Relationality and Temporality in Divine Life.* Louisville: Westminister Knox Press, 1993.

Philip, T. V. *Edinburgh to Salvador: Twentieth Century Ecumenical Missiology.* New York: Community Service Society of New York, 1999.

Piper, J. *Let the Nations Be Glad! The Supremacy of God in Missions.* Grand Rapids: Baker, 1993.

Rahner, K. *The Trinity.* Translated by J. Donceel. New York: Herder, 1970.

———. *The Trinity.* Translated by J. Donceel. With introduction, index, and glossary by C. M. LaCugna. In *Milestones in Catholic Theology.* New York: Crossroad, 1997.

Ross, L. *The Word Made Flesh: Towards an Incarnational Missiology.* Lanham, MD: University Press of America, 2004.

Schmidt-Leukel, P. "Mission and *Trinitarian* Theology." Pages 57–64 in *A Scandalous Prophet: The Way of Mission After Newbigin.* Edited by T. F. Foust, G. Hunsberger, J. A. Kirk, and W. Ustorf. Grand Rapids: Eerdmans, 2001.

Smith, R. A. "The Trinitarian Covenant in John 17." *Global Missiology* (Trinitarian Study), January 2005. http://www.globalmissiology.org (accessed Feburary 16, 2005).

———. "Tritheism and Christian Faith." *Global Missiology* (Trinitarian Study), October 2006, http://www.globalmissiology.org (accessed February 16, 2005).

Taylor, W. D., ed. *Global Missiology for the Twenty-first Century: The Iguassu Dialogue.* Grand Rapids: Baker. 2000.

Van Engen, C., D. S. Gilliland, and Paul Pierson, eds. *The Good News and the Kingdom: Mission Theology for the Third Millennium.* Maryknoll, NY: Orbis, 1993.

Wan, E., and M. Hedinger. "Understanding 'Relationality' from a Trinitarian Perspective." *Global Missiology* (Trinitarian Study), January 2006, http://www.globalmissiology.org (accessed Feburary 16, 2005).

Wan, E. "Missionary Pneumatology: Towards an Understanding of Spiritual Dynamics in Missions from a Trinitarian Perspective." Paper presented at the Evangelical Theological Society meeting, Jackson, MS (November 21–23, 1996).

———. "Missio-relational Reading of the Epistle to Romans: A Complementary Study to Various Approaches," *Occasional Bulletin* (Spring 2010).

———. "The Paradigm of 'Relational Realism.'" Pages 1–4 in *Occasional Bulletin* vol 19, no. 2 (Spring 2006). Evangelical Missiological Society.

———. "Relational Theology and Relational Missiology."
Pages 1–7 in *Occasional Bulletin,* 21, no. 1 (Winter
2007). Wheaton: Evangelical Missiological Society.

CHAPTER 5

Defining and Describing "Mission"

A Response to Charles Van Engen, Keith Eitel, and Enoch Wan

DARRELL L. GUDER

APPRECIATION AND CRITIQUE

Charles Van Engen's survey of the ways, in the history of Western Christianity, *mission* has been defined and described fulfills its intention admirably. I have always appreciated the way Van Engen's publications reflect his commitment to and giftedness for teaching. He organizes his material clearly and understandably. He lays out complex contents in ways that aid the learner's comprehension. He cites authorities respectfully, relates their insights to one another, and articulates a reliable consensus of the missiological conversation. And he does all this while avoiding jargon. He describes the contemporary discussion of mission judiciously and fairly. Yet he does not hesitate to make the judgment that "a cohesive, consistent, focused, theologically deep, missiologically broad, and contextually appropriate evangelical missiology has not yet emerged for this new century."

In terms of the missiological initiatives he so ably summarizes, his judgment must be confirmed—although his citation of D. Bosch's admirable definition of *mission* in footnote 36 is puzzling.

Does this citation imply that Bosch's formulation illustrates the deficiency he has just posited? Or does he see Bosch's wording as a twentieth-century formulation that needs further development for the twenty-first century? While agreeing with Van Engen's critique in general, I suggest there are encouraging and productive evidences of the emergence of the kind of missiology he is seeking, and Bosch was certainly one of the major examples of such evidence.

In their engagement with Van Engen's survey, our colleagues K. Eitel and E. Wan contribute important insights. Some of their arguments, however, appear to contribute little to the envisioned articulation of an "evangelical missiology . . . for this new century." Of the two I have found Eitel's essay to be the more problematic. It appears to be driven by a polemic that is hinted at but not fully developed. Perhaps the telling clue is his anxiety about the dangers of too little regard for "biblical boundaries or safeguards" in the ongoing task of Gospel translation or contextualization. But there is also an uncritical emphasis on the importance of structure, strategy, and organization, which links with a defensive posture with regard to "denominationalism, traditionalism, and modernity[?]." The answer to all the threatening problems he appears to find in the contemporary missiological process appears to be a particular doctrine of biblical authority, ensuring that the "biblically firm boundaries" will be respected. Beyond that, there appears to be little actual concern for a "theologically deep" missiology. Nor does there seem to be any engagement of the missiological challenge presented by the decline of Western Christendom and the dynamic development of a truly global Christian movement in the course of the twentieth century. A great deal of the discussion analyzed by Van Engen is dealing with the massive paradigm shift in world Christianity and mission theology since 1910. Many participants in that discussion share with Eitel a deep concern that the task of Gospel translation within the multicultural reality of the global church should not dilute the gospel. I am thinking here of Newbigin, Sanneh, and Walls in addition to Bosch. Certainly that concern is itself substantively addressed in Van Engen's work.[1]

---

[1] E.g., C. Van Engen, "Mission Theology and the Bible," in *Mission on the Way: Issues in Mission Theology* (Grand Rapids: Baker, 1996), 35–68.

THE PROMISE OF MISSIONAL HERMENEUTICS

The concern for the role of the Bible in mission highlights a theme in contemporary missiology that is not expressly developed in Van Engen's essay, although it is implied. Parallel to the increasingly vibrant and controversial missiological debates of the twentieth century have been developments in biblical studies that relate in important ways to how biblical authority works in the mission encounter. This has recently coalesced around an emphasis on "missional hermeneutics."[2] The developing consensus in this discussion is that the scriptural witness is the Holy Spirit's instrument for the formation of faithful witnessing communities in every culture—and thus Bible translation is a necessary part of all cross-cultural mission. A missional approach to the interpretation of Scripture is shaped by the insight that the apostolic strategy was the formation of witnessing communities and that their formation of these communities emphasized how their corporate life both together and scattered in the world could faithfully witness to the good news of God's redeeming love and inbreaking reign in Jesus Christ. The New Testament Scriptures continued that apostolic formation. The authority of these Scriptures is not, therefore, merely a static characteristic of them but their Spirit-empowered capacity to form Easter communities for their continuing vocation as witnesses for Christ. This understanding of the purpose of the Scriptures renders them authoritative in the church because the Holy Spirit works through them to enable us to "be [Christ's] witnesses in Jerusalem, in all Judea and Samaria, and to the ends of the earth" (Acts 1:8). The authority of Scripture is not then defined so much by our anxiety about boundaries and guidelines but by the powerful way in which God's written Word written continues our conversion to our vocation (more about that below). The Scriptures are, in fact, constantly addressing the issues of cultural encounter and the dangers of overassimilation and culturally defined distortion of the gospel. These issues are what is really at

---

[2] See J. Brownson, *Speaking the Truth in Love: New Testament Resources for a Missional Hermeneutic* (Harrisburg: Trinity Press, 1998); D. Guder, "Missional Hermeneutics: The Missional Authority of Scripture" and "Missional Hermeneutics: The Missional Vocation of the Congregation and How Scripture Shapes that Calling," *Mission Focus: Annual Review* (2007) 15: 106–42; R. Bauckham, *Bible and Mission: Christian Witness in a Post-Modern World* (Grand Rapids: Baker, 2003); cf. the "Missional Hermeneutical Conversation" on the Web site of the Gospel and Our Culture Network, www.gocn.org.

stake in the discussions of meat offered to idols, observing dietary rules, and even the debates about circumcision.

THE CHALLENGE OF THE "MISSIONAL" CHURCH

Then there is the term *missional*, which Van Engen receives and understands to denote "the essential nature and vocation of the church as God's called and sent people." As one of the team that proposed the term *missional church* as a way to focus theologically the questions that challenge Western Christianity as Christendom fades, I can gratefully confirm Van Engen's definition of the term's intended meaning.[3] I say "intended" because it is abundantly clear that the term has become a cliché today that means everything and nothing. Its original purpose was to stimulate a conversation about the church's missional vocation in our North American context. That has happened, for which we are thankful, but the term in itself must always be defined to enable a cogent conversation to continue. The intended emphasis of the term is reflected wherever it stimulates a theologically rigorous engagement of the fundamental issues of the church, the gospel, and their interaction within culture.[4]

E. Wan criticizes Van Engen's alleged distinction between the "institutional dimension" and the "individual dimension" of mission. This surely is an important discussion, although it might be more constructively pursued if we used the concepts "personal" and "corporate" for the matter being addressed. It is a problem of the Christendom legacy that the corporate character of the people of God has been almost exclusively defined in institutional categories. That has invariably been a reductionistic move when viewed from the biblical perspective of the Christian calling. The biblical emphasis on God's calling, forming, and sending of a people has been diluted and distorted by church institutions. But the answer to that is not to resort to (Western!) individualism as shaped by enlightened modernity. Rather, the scriptural emphasis

---

[3] See D. Guder et al., eds., *Missional Church: A Vision for the Sending of the Church in North America* (Grand Rapids: Eerdmans, 1998).

[4] I am at a loss to understand Eitel's argument that the term can be taken to refer to a "preference of postmodernity." Similarly, one must question whether the "development of indigenous churches" is properly explained as an "administrative emphasis," against deeply biblical and theological struggles with the question of faithful community formation as the continuation of the apostolic mission.

on the essentially intertwined significance of the personal and corporate must be reclaimed. The personal encounter with Christ is always and immediately linked with incorporation into his body, the Church. The purpose of personal calling is the formation of the witnessing community. We need constantly to be reminded that the New Testament Scriptures are largely addressed to the community, to the plural "you," and they are appropriately and faithfully read, heard, and interpreted in that corporate context. The apostolic strategy was not only to "save souls" but to form witnessing communities whose members' testimony to God's salvation formed the center of their gospel proclamation.

The tendency to individualize God's gift of salvation and to separate it from God's healing purposes for the world must be rejected as unbiblical. D. Bosch's excellent exposition of the "ecumenical paradigm of evangelism" stresses that

> if the offer of [individual salvation] gets center-stage attention in our evangelism, the gospel is degraded to a consumer product. It has to be emphasized, therefore, that the personal enjoyment of salvation never becomes the central theme in biblical conversion stories (cf. Barth 1962:561–614). Where Christians perceive themselves as those enjoying an indescribably magnificent private good fortune (:567f), Christ is easily reduced to little more than the "Disposer and Distributor" of special blessings (:595f) and evangelism to an enterprise that fosters the pursuit of pious self-centredness (:572). Not that the enjoyment of salvation is wrong, unimportant, or unbiblical; even so, it is almost incidental and secondary (:572, 593). It is not simple to *receive* life that people are called to become Christians, but rather to *give* life.[5]

I have elsewhere used the term *reductionism* in reference to this focus on the individual benefits of salvation to the exclusion of the missionary duty that accompanies the calling to follow Christ, and I regard it as the pervasive problem of Western Christianity.[6] Thus, I cannot agree with Wan that Van Engen has an

---

[5] D. Bosch, *Transforming Mission: Paradigm Shift in Theology of Mission* (Maryknoll: Orbis Books, 1991), 414. The citations are references to K. Barth, *Church Dogmatics*, IV.3,2 (Edinburgh: T&T Clark, 1962).
[6] See D. Guder, *Be My Witnesses: The Church's Mission, Message, and Messengers* (Grand Rapids: Eerdmans, 1985); Guder, *The Continuing Conversion of the Church* (Grand Rapids: Eerdmans, 2000), esp. 97ff.

"overcorrection of Evangelical emphasis on individual/spiritual salvation." In full concurrence with Wan's well-documented emphasis on the resurgence of trinitarian thought and its reflection in emerging trinitarian missiology, I would emphasize that the thrust of a trinitarian exposition of the *missio Dei* is God's sending of the Son, the sending of the Spirit by the Father and the Son, resulting in the sending of the Church by the triune God. Each Christian's personal calling is an integral part of that corporate dimension, with each one's distinctive and complementary giftedness. But it is as the "body of Christ" that the church carries out its mission, not as distinct toes, fingers, and elbows. The corporate witness of the community is the central thrust of Jesus' teachings and of the apostolic formation. Paul called on the community to lead its life worthy of its calling (see Eph 4:1; Phil 1:27).

To be sure, "'mission' is broader in scope than the 'missional church,'" as Wan emphasizes. The church, as Newbigin constantly emphasizes, is the sign, foretaste, and instrument of God's reconciling mission to the world. The focus of mission is the world, not the church. That is perhaps the simplest way to describe the turning from ecclesiocentric to trinitarian mission, which is the paradigm shift in the twentieth century that Van Engen ably describes. But it does not help to make the overcorrection of emphasizing the individual at the expense of corporate calling, corporate discipleship, and corporate apostolate. Beginning with the basic liturgical fact that one cannot baptize oneself, the personal and the corporate are inseparable. Paul challenged the entire Corinthian community to live its vocation as "Christ's letter to the world." That is an eminently personal image of the Christian life, but in 2 Cor 3:2–3, the letter is spoken of in the singular, and its writing is a work of the Spirit in the community.

THE RESOURCE FOR MISSIONAL CONVERSION: KARL BARTH'S THEOLOGY OF CHRISTIAN WITNESS

This discussion points, for me, to another major theological resource of the twentieth century that certainly contributes to a "cohesive, consistent, focused, theologically deep, missiologically broad, and contextually appropriate evangelical missiology." This resource is absent from Van Engen's survey, which validly reflects the state of affairs in the guild generally. I am speaking of K. Barth, whom Johannes Aagard described as "the most decisive Protestant missiologist in this generation."[7] Bosch concurs with that assessment:

> In light of Barth's magnificent and consistent missionary ecclesiology there may indeed be some justification for such a claim. Under the overarching rubric of soteriology, Barth develops his ecclesiology in three phases. His reflections on soteriology as justification (1956:514–642) are followed by a section on "The Holy Spirit and the *Gathering of* the Christian Community" (:643–749). His exposition on soteriology as *sanctification* (1958:499–613) leads to a discourse on "The Holy Spirit and the *Upbuilding* of the Christian community" (:614–726). And his discussion of soteriology as *vocation* (1962:481–680) is followed by a treatise on "The Holy Spirit and the *Sending of* the Christian Community" (:681–901). From three perspectives, then, the entire field of ecclesiology is surveyed; each of these perspectives evokes, presupposes, and illuminates the other two.[8]

The context of Barth's theological project is the end of Western Christendom as it unfolded in the twentieth century. His conversion to the gospel of grace during World War I was shaped by his shock at the fact that his great (liberal) theological professors all endorsed the Kaiser's war. His perplexity drove him to Scripture and especially to Romans. He discovered sin, grace, promise, and mission in his reclamation of the biblical message. From then on, his theological work is pervasively shaped by the basic biblical conviction that God's purpose for the world is its healing, its reconciliation; and therefore the purpose of God's calling of a people to faith is to render a witness to that good news. Although there are few so-called Barthians who recognize the fundamental mission focus of Barth's *Church Dogmatics*, it is the shaping force of his vast theological enterprise.

In the exposition of the gospel of reconciliation, outlined by Bosch in the citation above, Barth proposes a correction of the

---

[7] J. Aargard, "Some Main Trends in Modern Protestant Missiology, *Studia. Theologica* 19 (1965): 238, quoted in D. Bosch, *Transforming Mission*, 373.

[8] Bosch, *Transforming Mission*, 373. The references in the text are to the corresponding volumes in Barth's *Church Dogmatics*, IV.1; IV.2; IV.3.

Reformation's understanding of the gospel, which is of great missiological significance. He expounds the doctrines of justification and sanctification with incisive discussions of Christ's office, human sin, and the doctrine of the church. His argument builds to a climax when he comes to the assertion that the vocation of the Christian is the necessary outworking of justification and sanctification. Justification and sanctification remain inward, individualistic, and nonmissional, if they do not issue into the Christian calling to be the witness of God's healing grace and loving reign in Jesus Christ. He questions the classic definition of the identity of the Christian, which is to enjoy the benefits of the gospel. (I refer to this evangelistic reductionism above.) Rather, Barth says, the Christian experiences the incomparable grace of God precisely in order to be called, equipped, and sent as a witness to Christ. This vocation defines all Christians, not just the ministers, or the full-time servants. And it defines everything about the person. It is remarkable that this discussion does indeed focus on the personal dimension of the Christian faith, but it is integrated into the larger discussion of the "sending" of the Christian community. The personal and corporate are exemplarily interactive here.

This exposition of missional vocation comes in the last full volume of *Church Dogmatics* (IV.3.2). Barth's missiological ecclesiology is basically the climax of the entire multivolume project. But it is constantly anticipated as Barth moves from one doctrinal discussion to the next. Back in volume III.4, in which he addresses "The Doctrine of Creation," Barth expounds "the active life" of the Christian in community. Here, in four propositions, he defines the purpose of Christian action in the world:

> What the community owes to the world, and each individual within it, is basically that in its life, and in the lives of all its members, there should be attempted an imitation and representation of the love with which God loved the world. But this means that the Christian community cannot be against the world; it can only be for it. . . .[9]
>
> The second thing to be considered is the task of mission committed to the community. We understand the concept primarily in the narrower and external sense as the task of self-renewal by

---

[9] Barth, *Church Dogmatics,* III.4, 502.

the winning of new human members from the world around, of summoning non-Christians to an understanding of their call and therefore to faith, to obedience and to cooperation in the service of the community. The community cannot make a Christian. This is God's own act. But the community cannot exist in the world without calling men out of it, without inviting them to participate in its work. . . .[10]

The third point to be mentioned is what we might call the *opus proprium* of the community, namely, its commission to preach the Gospel to the world. It is in this wider, deeper and more material sense that it is a missionary community. It is for this purpose that it must expand in the world, that it wills to renew itself by admission of men from the world. . . .[11]

We cannot conclude this survey without finally and emphatically pointing to the prophetic service of the community. It always serves, i.e., it always loves and reaches out and evangelises, at a specific time, in a particular phase of universal occurrence, among men who in accordance with this phase take a specific active or passive part in world events, acting and suffering, impelling and being impelled, in this or that specific way. Always, at all times and to all men, it has to attest with its service the same eternal Word of God.[12]

When Van Engen proposes his own definition of *missional* and *mission*, he quite properly suggests that such a definition "might involve an attempt to describe what a 'missional church' would look like." Missiology, properly understood, must focus on the church called by God to be his witness in the world. It must be about the equipping of such a community so that both corporately and in the lives of each of its members, the church can lead its life worthy of the calling with which it has been called (Eph. 4:1). There is, I suggest, a remarkable convergence between the missiological vision of Van Engen, the Reformed American theologian, and Barth, the Reformed Swiss theologian. Like Van Engen, Barth's doctrinal project intends the equipping of the church for its missional vocation. That is why he renamed the project *Church Dogmatics* when he restarted it in the 1930s. In neither approach is there an ultimate separation between the personal experience

---

[10] Ibid., 504.
[11] Ibid., 506; *opus proprium* means "proper work."
[12] Ibid., 510.

of salvation and the corporate vocation to witness. Van Engen's exposition of such a missional church proposes characteristics which, as I review them, seem to relate clearly to central emphases of Barth's theological vision of the church faithful to its calling.

In fact, there is a twentieth-century resource that is truly "theologically deep, missiologically broad, and contextually appropriate." It is certainly a daunting task to read and grapple with Barth's massive *Church Dogmatics*. But perhaps that difficulty is appropriate to the task we face as Christendom disintegrates, which is to rediscover that mission is truly the mother of theology (M. Kähler).[13] It has taken centuries of reductionism, cultural captivity, and compromise to bring us to our current place as "post-Christendom Christians." It will take much prayerful, thoughtful, and not seldom painful work to discover how we are to walk worthy of our calling today. Barth may well be the mentor we need for this missiological challenge.

BIBLIOGRAPHY

Aargard, Johannes. "Some Main Trends in Modern Protestant Missiology." *Studia Theologica* 19 (1965): 238–59.

Barth, Karl. *Church Dogmatics*, IV.3, 2. Edinburgh: T&T Clark, 1962.

Bauckham, Richard. *Bible and Mission: Christian Witness in a Post-Modern World*. Grand Rapids: Baker, 2003.

Bosch, David. *Transforming Mission: Paradigm Shift in Theology of Mission*. Maryknoll: Orbis Books, 1991.

Brownson, James. *Speaking the Truth in Love: New Testament Resources for a Missional Hermeneutic*. Harrisburg: Trinity Press, 1998.

Guder, Darrell. *Be My Witnesses: The Church's Mission, Message, and Messengers*. Grand Rapids: Eerdmans, 1985.

_____. *The Continuing Conversion of the Church*. Grand Rapids: Eerdmans, 2000.

---

[13] M. Kähler, *Schriften zur Christologie und Mission* (Munich: Chr. Kaiser Verlag, 1971), 190.

_____. "Missional Hermeneutics: The Missional Authority of Scripture." *Mission Focus: Annual Review* 15 (2007): 106–24.

_____. "Missional Hermeneutics: The Missional Vocation of the Congregation and How Scripture Shapes that Calling," *Mission Focus: Annual Review* 15 (2007): 125–42.

Guder, Darrell, et al. *Missional Church: A Vision for the Sending of the Church in North America* Grand Rapids: Eerdmans, 1998.

Kähler, M. *Schriften zur Christologie und Mission*. Munich: Chr. Kaiser Verlag, 1971.

Van Engen, Charles. *Mission on the Way: Issues in Mission Theology*. Grand Rapids: Baker, 1996.

CHAPTER 6

Twelve Theses on the Church's Mission in the Twenty-first Century

In Interaction with Charles Van Engen, Keith Eitel, and Enoch Wan

ANDREAS J. KÖSTENBERGER

INTRODUCTION

It is hard to imagine a more important task than to reflect on the church's mission in the world today. I count it a privilege to be part of this conversation and of the collaborative effort of reflecting biblically, critically, and constructively on the church's missionary task. It is not necessary to agree with everything Charles Van Engen says to appreciate his useful and competent essay, which is eminently suitable to serve as the basis for further discussion. I am writing this response as a New Testament scholar, born and raised in Vienna, Austria, theologically trained at Columbia International University and Trinity Evangelical Divinity School, and now teaching at Southeastern Baptist Theological Seminary. I am not attempting to provide my own definition of mission, but (with apologies to Luther) I am setting forth 12 theses that I hope will be useful guideposts for further discussion on this vital topic. These theses flow from my reading of Van Engen's essay, with which I will interact along the way. At times I will also touch on the responses by K. Eitel and E. Wan.

THE TWELVE THESES

1. *The church's mission—in both belief and practice—should be grounded in the biblical theology of mission.* This requires sustained reflection on the biblical teaching on mission in both Testaments, an awareness of the complexities involved in apprehending such a biblical theology of mission, and the adoption of a humble stance toward Scripture as the church's sole legitimate source of divine revelation and thus of the church's understanding of its mission.[1]

By "biblical theology" I mean, in essence, the theology of the Bible and of the biblical writers themselves, in contrast to our contemporary efforts to lay out what we believe the church's mission ought to be. A. Schlatter wrote:

> We turn away decisively from ourselves and our time to what was found in the men through whom the church came into being. Our main interest should be the thought as it was conceived *by them* and the truth that was valid *for them*. . . . This is the internal disposition upon which the success of the work depends.[2]

Once the biblical teachings have been apprehended in their respective historical contexts and in the terms used by the biblical authors, it is possible to systematize the theology of the various biblical writers.[3] In this way the teaching of God's Word is allowed to set the proper parameters for the church's reflection on

---

[1] Van Engen's discussion of the Old Testament material is only one sentence (see the massive recent volume by C. J. H. Wright, *The Mission of God: Unlocking the Bible's Grand Narrative* [Downers Grove: InterVarsity, 2006]), and his treatment of the New Testament teaching is sketchy at best. The lengthy quote of the *Theological Dictionary of the New Testament* is insufficient not only because of its nature as a secondary source but also because its methodology is questionable. See the critique of the *TDNT* entry on *apostellō* by K. H. Rengstorf in A. J. Köstenberger, *The Missions of Jesus and of the Disciples According to the Fourth Gospel* (Grand Rapids: Eerdmans, 1998), 99–102; and, more generally, J. Barr, *The Semantics of Biblical Language* (London: SCM, 1961), chap. 8. On a biblical theology of mission, see A. J. Köstenberger and P. T. O'Brien, *Salvation to the Ends of the Earth: A Biblical Theology of Mission* (NSBT 11; Leicester, UK: InterVarsity, 2001); cf. E. J. Schnabel, *Early Christian Mission*, 2 vols. (Downers Grove: InterVarsity, 2004). Van Engen also insufficiently distinguishes between the concept of "sending," the sender and sent one(s), and the task with which those sent are charged (e.g., preaching the gospel).

[2] A. Schlatter, *The History of the Christ: The Foundation of New Testament Theology*, trans. A. J. Köstenberger (Grand Rapids: Baker, 1997), 18.

[3] See A. J. Köstenberger, "The Challenge of a Systematized Biblical Theology: Missiological Insights from the Gospel of John," *Missiology* 23 (1995): 445–64.

the nature of its mission. Rather than anthropology, psychology, sociology, or any of the other social sciences setting the parameters, it is the divine revelation in Scripture that forms the starting point of the church's reflection.

2. *Reflection on the church's mission should be predicated on the affirmation of the full and sole authority of Scripture.*[4] Unless the church's convictions regarding its mission and strategies are committed to the authority of Scripture, the purity of its missionary thought and practice will be compromised. Thinking derived from the social sciences will inevitably leaven the dough of its missiology.

3. *The church's mission should be conceived primarily in terms of the church's faithfulness and responsiveness to the missionary mandate given by the Lord Jesus Christ as recorded in Scripture.* If the church is to engage in mission as prompted by God's initiative in Christ (as is surely the case), then the church's mission is to be conceived as essentially responsive and representational in nature.[5]

The gospel is conceived in the New Testament in terms of stewardship and responsibility. Timothy, for example, is enjoined by Paul to "guard the good deposit" of the gospel (2 Tim 1:14) and to eschew "youthful lusts" (2 Tim 2:22 NASB), which may refer not merely to sexual temptation but also dangers of embracing the latest theological trends. The gospel is certainly not new, for Paul says it is "the gospel of God—the gospel he promised beforehand through his prophets in the Holy Scriptures" (Rom 1:1–2 NIV). The message of God's salvation in Christ is timeless and true.

4. *The church's understanding of its mission should be hermeneutically sound.*[6] This requires the consideration of facts; for example, the Synoptic Gospels focus on Jesus' teaching about the "kingdom of God," but John's Gospel speaks instead of "eternal

---

[4] In this I echo K. Eitel's call for "the foundational assumption of biblical authority, accessibility, and applicability" in "On Becoming Missional: Interacting with Charles Van Engen."

[5] On the term "representational," see A. J. Köstenberger, *Missions of Jesus and the Disciples*, chap. 5; and D. J. Hesselgrave, *Paradigms in Conflict* (Grand Rapids: Kregel, 2006), chap. 5.

[6] I agree with Eitel's warning against "dangerous creativity" and against "creative tensions without biblically firm boundaries" and his call for "hermeneutical measures" to be put in place "that will safeguard the integrity of the gospel message." At the same time, when Eitel says, "let us simply reaffirm the Great Commission and be willing to keep on telling the old, old story," this may unduly recognize the fact that the Great Commission still needs to be interpreted and has been interpreted in different ways over the centuries as Van Engen's essay has demonstrated.

life."[7] This seems to caution against elevating the "kingdom of God" as the only paradigm by which the church's mission is to be understood. Also, Paul emphasizes the centrality of the gospel (e.g., Rom 1:1–2,16–17) and provides teaching on the church as the body of Christ, on spiritual gifts, and on the proper organization of the church, including qualifications for its leaders (see Rom 12:3–8; 1 Corinthians 12–14; and 1 Tim 3:1–13).[8]

Sound hermeneutics also requires that one Great Commission passage (Matt 28:18–20) not be treated as if it were the only commissioning passage in the New Testament.[9] Nor should these commissioning passages be understood in isolation from the book of which they are a part. For example, Matt 28:16–20 shows the commission to be an extension of God's command to Abraham that he would be a blessing to all the nations, and John 20:21–22 climaxes the Gospel's portrait of Jesus as the Son sent from the Father and construes the relationship between Jesus and the church on the basis of this paradigm.[10]

5. *The church's mission is to be conceived ultimately in theocentric rather than anthropocentric terms.* Mission is part of the church's obedience to God, just as dying on the cross for the sins of the world was part of the sent Son's obedience to the one who sent Him, God the Father (cf. John 17:4; 19:30). Thus the gospel and its abiding truth and relevance for lost sinners should be the primary point of reference as the church engages in its mission rather than human need and the contemporary cultural, political, economic, and social contexts.

6. *The church's mission, properly and biblically conceived, is to be trinitarian in its orientation but not at the expense of neglecting the distinct roles of the three Persons within the Godhead.*[11] The church's mission is to be prompted by God the Father's initiative, to proceed on the basis of Christ's redemptive mission

---

[7] The term "kingdom" *(basileia)* is found in John's Gospel only in John 3:3,5; 18:36.

[8] The term "kingdom" *(basileia)* is found in Paul's letters only 14 times, and at least eight of them have a future reference (1 Cor 6:9–10; 15:24,50; Gal 5:21; Eph 5:5; Col 1:13; 2 Tim 4:18; note that five of these passages feature the term "inherit" or "inheritance").

[9] See Luke 24:46–49; John 20:21–22; Acts 1:7–8. Although Wan elsewhere acknowledges several commissioning passages, at one point in his essay he does speak of individuals being obedient to the Great Commission.

[10] See Köstenberger and O'Brien, *Salvation to the Ends of the Earth*, chaps. 5, 8; and Köstenberger, *Missions of Jesus and the Disciples*, passim.

[11] See A. J. Köstenberger and S. R. Swain, *Father, Son and Spirit: The Trinity and John's Gospel* (NSBT 24; Leicester, UK: InterVarsity, 2008), especially chap. 9.

and commission, and to be empowered by the Holy Spirit. In this sense, there is no dichotomy between the church's mission being trinitarian *and* Christocentric—it is to be both.[12]

Scripture does indeed teach that Jesus is the sender (John 20:21) and the one who commissioned the church on the basis of His authority (Matt 28:18). Jesus is "the way, the truth, and the life, and no one comes to the Father except through" Him (John 14:6). In Jesus, God will bring all things to their end-time consummation (Eph 1:10). It is therefore vital to affirm both the trinitarian nature of the church's mission (Matt 28:19; John 20:21–22) and the preeminence given to Christ in that same mission.

In terms of both revelation and redemption, the New Testament writings state unequivocally that Jesus is preeminent (John 1:1–2,14,16–18; Col 1:15–20; Heb 1:1–4). A church that opts to be broadly trinitarian yet holds that focusing on Christ is being unduly narrow may open the door to the notion that there are ways of salvation other than faith in Christ. Yet the exclusivity of Jesus Christ in salvation is an indispensable part of faithful gospel proclamation (e.g., Acts 4:12).

7. *The contemporary context of the church's mission, while important, ought not to override the church's commitment to the authority of Scripture, its need to be grounded in the biblical theology of mission, and the understanding of its task in terms of faithfulness to the gospel.*[13] Once contemporary context and experience are put on a par with Scripture, the former two take precedence and Scripture's authority is undermined, with the inevitable result that the gospel's integrity is compromised.[14] At the same time, of course, it is vital for the church to find ever-new ways to present the truth of the gospel in ways that are relevant to the culture.

8. *The church is the God-ordained agent of His mission in this world today.* Just as it is *in Christ* that God has chosen to center

---

[12] Compare the way of putting things by Wan, who speaks of "the trinitarian orientation rather than [the church being] impoverished by being merely Christocentric in emphasis."

[13] This is why Van Engen's definition of "theology" as "the knowledge of God in context" is potentially slippery (see Van Engen, "The New Covenant: Knowing God in Context," in *The Word Among Use: Contextualizing Theology for Mission Today*, ed. D. S. Gilliland (Dallas: Word, 1989), 91 (cited by Eitel, "On Becoming Missional," n. 9).

[14] For a demonstration of this with regard to the feminist portrayal of Jesus, see M. E. Köstenberger, *Jesus and the Feminists: Who Do They Say That He Is?* (Wheaton: Crossway, 2008).

His salvation-historical program, Christ is the head of His body, *the church*. Paul stated, "In *Him* you also, when you heard the word of truth, the gospel of your salvation—in *Him* when you believed—were sealed with the promised Holy Spirit" (Eph 1:13, emphasis added). Paul's desire was that "to Him [God] be glory *in the church* and in Christ Jesus to all generations, forever and ever. Amen" (Eph 3:21, emphasis added).

This recognition of the agency of the church in God's plan also requires that the kingdom of God and the church be properly related to each other. While related, the two concepts are nonetheless distinct. The kingdom, while having been inaugurated through Jesus Christ at His first coming, is to a significant extent still future. At the present time the life of the kingdom is to be displayed in an anticipatory fashion in the life of the church. Nevertheless, there are also differences, such as that marriage is part of the present way of life in the church while there will be no marriage in the kingdom (Matt 22:30).

9. *The way the kingdom of God is extended in this world today is through regenerate believers acting out their Christian faith in their God-assigned spheres of life: the church, their families, their workplaces, the societies in which they live* (see Eph 5:18–6:9; 1 Pet 2:13–3:7). This realization precludes both an overrealized eschatology and an otherworldly escapism or heroism that has the effect of bypassing the primary God-ordained familial and social structures in this life. Instead, believers are to live out the gospel in their natural social and political environment by being good spouses, parents, citizens, and so on.

10. *There is no true lasting social transformation apart from personal conversion through repentance and faith in the Lord Jesus Christ*. Wan is right to stress the indispensable personal and individual nature of faith in Christ and to caution against an overreaction against an unduly individualistic understanding of the biblical teaching on mission. At the same time it should be acknowledged that mission is the Church's task, not the task of individuals apart from their membership in a given local church.

11. *Human organization is perfectly compatible with an acknowledgment of God and his initiative in mission*. While at times in the history of the church and its mission human organization

became a substitute for faith in God, it is also true that the opposite of organization is chaos. The New Testament writings (especially the book of Acts) indicate that the early church took concerted steps to organize itself to carry out its mission successfully. It appointed and commissioned missionaries, planted networks of churches, and set up leaders, and so on.

While not addressing every conceivable challenge with which the church would be confronted in its missionary task, the book of Acts therefore constitutes an abiding, divinely inspired casebook to guide its missionary practice. But the study of the book of Acts reveals that the church must remain open to God's direction and redirection and must be aware that God's purposes, not human strategizing, are to be primary. This includes Paul, who is depicted in Acts not so much as a master strategist but as one who remained open to God's leading.

12. *The church's task today is to nurture, renew, and plant churches composed of a spiritually regenerate membership and constituted in keeping with the biblical teaching regarding church leadership.*

In this the apostle Paul's example is unsurpassed. We would do well to immerse ourselves in Scripture—particularly the book of Acts and Paul's letters—and to emulate Paul's priorities, values, strategies, and missionary practice.[15]

In my local church, Richland Creek Community Church, I teach a class called Kingdom Families. In this class, which is made up of families and singles from over a dozen countries, I am blessed to experience a foretaste of life in the kingdom. We worship, fellowship, study, pray, serve, go and share the gospel; and above all we love. May the work of God continue to flourish until the gospel has been preached to all the nations (Mark 13:10). And may we, both individually and corporately, be prepared to follow where God leads us, wherever that may be.

CONCLUSION

Van Engen has provided a helpful thumbnail sketch of the various definitions of *mission* over the history of the church. In fact,

---

[15] See E. J. Schnabel, *Paul the Missionary: Realities, Strategies and Methods* (Downers Grove: InterVarsity, 2008).

he has been part of this history himself for several decades. While I was reading his essay, it occurred to me that while the church should certainly be prepared to learn all it can from the past as it reflects on the nature of its mission, in the final analysis it should take its cue not from the history of missions but from the biblical teaching regarding the mission of the church. Toward the end of his essay, Van Engen suggests today's church should be missional and proposes a rather lengthy definition of mission.

Yet I wonder if the way forward in the church's quest for a proper understanding of its mission is to be found in adopting a new terminology or in crafting an elaborate definition of *mission* that commands widespread support. Instead, I offer these 12 theses as a small contribution to the conversation of how the church should conceive of and go about her mission. "Now to Him who is able to do above and beyond all that we ask or think—according to the power that works in you—to Him be glory in the church and in Christ Jesus to all generations, forever and ever. Amen" (Eph 3:20–21).

BIBLIOGRAPHY

Bosch, David J. *Transforming Mission: Paradigm Shifts in Theology of Mission.* Maryknoll, NY: Orbis, 1991.

Hesselgrave, David J. *Paradigms in Conflict: 10 Key Questions in Christian Missions Today.* Grand Rapids: Kregel, 2006.

Köstenberger, Andreas J. *The Missions of Jesus and of the Disciples According to the Fourth Gospel.* Grand Rapids: Eerdmans, 1998.

_____. "The Challenge of a Systematized Biblical Theology: Missiological Insights from the Gospel of John." *Missiology* 23 (1995): 445–64.

_____, and Peter T. O'Brien. *Salvation to the Ends of the Earth: A Biblical Theology of Mission.* NSBT 11. Leicester, UK: InterVarsity, 2001.

_____, and Scott R. Swain. *Father, Son and Spirit: The Trinity and John's Gospel.* NSBT 24. Leicester, UK: InterVarsity, 2008.

_____, and Terry L. Wilder, eds. *Entrusted with the Gospel: Paul's Theology in the Pastoral Epistles.* Nashville: B&H Academic, 2010.

Köstenberger, Margaret E. *Jesus and the Feminists: Who Do They Say That He Is?* Wheaton: Crossway, 2008.

Moreau, A. Scott, ed. *Evangelical Dictionary of World Missions.* Grand Rapids: Baker, 2000.

Rommen, Edward, and Harold Netland, eds. *Christianity and the Religions: A Biblical Theology of World Religions.* EMSS 2. Pasadena, CA: William Carey Library, 1995.

Schlatter, Adolf. *The History of the Christ: The Foundation of New Testament Theology.* Translated by Andreas J. Köstenberger. Grand Rapids: Baker, 1997.

Schnabel, Eckhard J. *Early Christian Mission.* 2 vols. Downers Grove: InterVarsity, 2004.

_____. *Paul the Missionary: Realities, Strategies, and Methods.* Downers Grove: InterVarsity, 2008.

Senior, Donald, and Carroll Stuhlmueller. *Biblical Foundations for Missions.* Maryknoll, NY: Orbis, 1983.

Tidball, Derek. *Skilful Shepherds: Explorations in Pastoral Theology.* 2nd ed. Leicester, UK: Apollos, 1997.

Van Engen, Charles. "The New Covenant: Knowing God in Context." In *The Word Among Us: Contextualizing Theology for Mission Today.* Edited by Dean S. Gilliland. Dallas: Word, 1989.

Wright, Christopher. *The Mission of God: Unlocking the Bible's Grand Narrative.* Downers Grove: InterVarsity, 2006.

CHAPTER 7

Responding to "'Mission' Defined and Described" and the Four Responders

ED STETZER

INTRODUCTION

Charles Van Engen's task was to write about the PAST of "missions," or what we as Western Evangelicals often call "mission." That very distinction is among the major issues of this discussion, and Van Engen has dealt with the subject quite capably. Guder rightly acknowledges that Van Engen is a consummate teacher who is concerned with clarifying complicated information for students, which allows them to quickly engage in conversation. He has effectively provided a starting point for this conversation. Moreover, Van Engen lays out the problem of definition and challenges us to seek a "cohesive, consistent, focused, theologically deep, missiologically broad, and contextually appropriate evangelical missiology."

Some who have responded to him have sought to meet that challenge. Others seem to have taken offense at the thought that our missiological definition needs to be examined. They react with a defense of biblical authority and a fear of what it means to be "contextually appropriate"—which suggests this entire enterprise might be dangerous to the gospel. But, if the book of Acts tells us anything about the strategy of missions, it tells us that strategic changes in approach to mission often make those representing the status quo uncomfortable.

Actually, these objections, fears, and warnings lead into our next section of this book, which deals directly, and hopefully appropriately, with the problem and promise of contextualization. I am setting that aside for the moment to reflect on some of Van Engen's insights regarding the task of defining mission.

Looking at Van Engen's article from the reader's perspective, Wan notes that the definition of mission Van Engen provides for Gloria is quite . . . well, long. Van Engen subtly defends its length in advance by pointing out that he has been working on this for 40 years. Each new clause anticipates, or reflects on, a battle over definition from somewhere along the way. Still, the reader might respond that Van Engen's definition is too complicated, suggesting that we *just know* what we mean by "missions."

But who are "we"? And do "we" really know what "we" mean by missions? In fact, as I read Van Engen's piece, I was reminded of the reality that some of the things understood by the missionary community since the beginning of the last century (e.g., the indigenous principle) have still not penetrated the missionary practices of many—let alone most—evangelical churches today. The indigenous principle appears to have been caught in a time warp, slowed by various factors that deter valuable insights, from reaching this or that group of Christians. Thus, it becomes evident that we in fact don't really know what "we" mean by missions. It reveals the reason that we struggle to articulate definitions (albeit with the limited benefits of such a definition). The reality is that still many of the concepts and practices of mission/missions that are affirmed and practiced today are often locked in another time period and are out of sync with Christians elsewhere.

Furthermore, we need a well-articulated definition of missions/mission because we can't all get on the same page, which has been one of the main reasons that a "theologically deep, missiologically broad, and contextually appropriate evangelical missiology" has not yet been developed. The reason that we have not all been able to get on the same page is not because people are not trying to do so. This book is an example of such an attempt. But, the fact is, even if this book should help some of us arrive at what we think constitutes such a missiology, we should not pretend to think that every individual, congregation, or denomination would then adopt it. It would only serve as an example of the continuing process in the church to find what Guder, through Bosch and Barth before him, calls the church's "vocation." Therefore, an expanded and nuanced definition like Van Engen's helps us to think more deeply about missiology and is useful to direct our missiological conversation.

Van Engen's chapter contributes to our discussion in a number of important ways in addition to his helpful definition. I return below to what I think is the most significant aspect of Van Engen's words. But, first I would like to respond to the responders.

RESPONDING TO EITEL

Keith Eitel, it seems to me, departs from responding directly to Van Engen and takes this assignment as a window of opportunity to address what is clearly a thorn in his side (and in the sides of many other missiologists). He takes aim at the issue of contextualization and his concern over the use of the term "missional."

Eitel attempts to wrestle with the question, When do attempts to identify contextually with the culture (such as wearing the facepaint of Shiva) cease being missional and start being syncretistic— or worse, heretical? This is an important question. When dealing with specific practices (like the example Eitel offers), careful and critical thinking is required. My concern with Eitel's article is that his argument moves from a specific instance to wide-sweeping conclusions. Eitel links his Shiva example to the emergent church. Then, he applies his concerns to any "creative" missiology. This is the slippery slope argument—which the Pharisees applied to Jesus and the Judaizers to Paul. In this argument, "creative" can never be applied to the things of God. It is not my intention to defend every practice that Eitel critiques, but to suggest that his argument is flawed and ultimately leads to suspicious questioning of any mission strategy that is non-traditional.

I suggest that we return to first-century thinking. What we find in the New Testament is that to be biblical requires contextualization. Dean Flemming develops this point in *Contextualization in the New Testament*. He argues, "Scripture itself can offer us a more adequate approach to the challenge of reappropriating the gospel," because "each book of the New Testament represents an attempt by the author to present the Christian message in a way that is targeted for a particular audience within a sociocultural environment."[1]

Let's take Eitel's warning for what it is—a warning in the face of change that is coming at "broadband velocity." In addition, let's recognize that young Christians, who by generational training swim comfortably at broadband speed, need the freedom to respond to the postmodern relativism coming at them. After all, postmodern culture exists, and we are forced to interact with it, like it or not. Therefore, let's also presume that this is not a slippery slope problem but a problem in effective communication. Further, let me add that most of the emerging Christians I have met are not responding to this cultural reality by wearing Shiva's dot. Instead, they are finding new ways to state effectively, "Thus says the Lord" and "Jesus is the way." This may be where the "definition" problem surfaces at its highest level. Members of the churches living on mission in an emerging culture are less capable of explaining their definition of mission to traditionalists than they are relating the gospel to their peers, which they often do quite effectively. Perhaps, we need to think more in terms of mission described rather than mission defined.

RESPONDING TO WAN

Enoch Wan's main critique of Van Engen regards his trinitarian views. Wan considers that his trinitarian view is "reduced" by Van Engen's emphasis on the Father sending the Son. Conceivably, Wan is reacting to the propensity toward Arianism reflected in the theologies of some, who have taken the concept of *missio Dei* to such an extreme that they have cast the church aside. While Van Engen discusses that view, he does not endorse it. Rather, Van Engen is setting that view up for his own critique while seeking to help other evangelicals learn about that perspective. That was part of his assignment, and he performs it well.[2]

In addition, Wan objects to Van Engen's apparent failure to separate the "institutional" church from the "individual" Christian.

---

[1] Dean Flemming, *Contextualization in the New Testament: Patterns for Theology and Missions* (Downers Grove: InterVarsity, 2005), 15.

[2] See also Köstenberger's comments on Wan's concerns of Van Engen at this point on p. 66, footnote 12. Contra Wan, Köstenberger correctly argues that there is no conflict between the church's mission being both trinitarian and Christocentric in orientation.

I don't perceive that from Van Engen either. He is merely responding to the need for this "corporate" dimension of mission to be infused within a new evangelical missiology, if it is to be holistic and genuinely biblical. Wan gives his definition (in response to Van Engen's long one). Both definitions are similar to other definitions.

Allow me to return here to my reticence with defining mission(s). I have in fact defended above the need for a working definition to guide the missiological conversation, but I question the intimation that any definition can provide a truly defining picture of what all evangelical churches are seeking to accomplish in our day. Perhaps we are coming closer to the point of saying, "I cannot define this without getting into controversy, but I can certainly describe what I think God is doing." It could be that some agreed-upon description would provide what no definition can.

I will continue my reflection on the value of describing missions as I respond to Köstenberger's chapter in the next section.

RESPONDING TO KÖSTENBERGER

Think for a moment about what the title of Acts actually means. Can you really condense all that happened surrounding the early church into one definition? Is it the Acts of the Apostles, the Acts of the Holy Spirit, the Acts of Church Planting, or the Acts of "Movemental" Christianity? Acts is definitely more of a description than a prescribed definition because Acts is about what occurred through, in, and to the early church.

The Christians of New Testament times emphasized praxis (practice). They were about doing. Köstenberger affirms this to some extent, as he emphasizes that the church's mission comes from a faithful response to the missionary mandate given by Jesus Christ (thesis 3) and that the kingdom of God is extended through Christians actively living out their faith in every area of life (thesis 9).

Köstenberger's chapter, however, is a critical response to Van Engen. He responds as a New Testament scholar, whose theological concern is to apprehend the theology of the biblical writers in their historical context and in the very terms they use. Then, for him, systematic theological reflection and presumably missiological reflection must be based solely on this work. Köstenberger's twelve theses are offered as "guideposts" for this journey.

Though Köstenberger does not interact with the substance of Van Engen's chapter directly in the body of his own chapter (see footnotes 1 and 13 for the only interaction with Van Engen, albeit minor), his concerns with Van Engen are clear. Köstenberger is uncomfortable with how Van Engen uses the history of missions to help shape his definition, with his adoption of the term "missional," and with his attempt to propose a definition of mission that could be widely adopted.

So, it seems that Köstenberger clings to his method for biblical theology so tightly that he cannot appreciate how the history of missions has shaped our understanding of the task and is resistant to the possibility of a new term being useful to articulating the biblical concept of mission. It might appear from Köstenberger's chapter that the issue that distinguishes him and Van Engen concerns the doctrines of biblical authority and sufficiency (and it may be true that they may have differing views on these doctrines). However, I believe the issue that distinguishes them is how Köstenberger applies and integrates his discipline of biblical theology with another discipline, such as missiology.

I will attempt to shine some light on this point by interacting with the first five of Köstenberger's twelve theses. Below, I summarize Köstenberger's theses (in italics) with my comments immediately following (in plain text).

1. *Any definition of "mission" must be based on biblical theology.* As a simple statement, I hardly think anyone seeking to follow the biblical mission would disagree. However, this statement is loaded, and as Köstenberger demonstrates in his explanation, it assumes his particular approach to biblical theology and to interdisciplinary theological studies as necessary. On these issues, there is room for evangelicals to have a lively debate.[3]

2. *Reflections on the church's mission must be predicated upon the full and sole authority of Scripture.* While I

---

[3] For an example of such a debate, see Gary T. Meadors, ed., *Four Views on Moving Beyond the Bible to Theology* (Grand Rapids: Zondervan, 2009).

affirm *sola scriptura* and privilege the authority of biblical revelation in all theological and missiological reflection, these convictions do not preclude us from gaining favorable insights from the history of the church, philosophy, a community of believers, the social sciences, and other sources where God's truth about the world and the people who live in it maybe discerned. Furthermore, it is the case that the reflections on the church's mission from theologians and missionaries throughout the history of the church have been shaped in part by the particular cultural factors, concerns, and questions of their day.

3. *Mission should be conceived in terms of the church's faithfulness to the missionary mandate of Christ as recorded in Scripture.* Insofar as Köstenberger is referring to the gospel content of the mission, I affirm this point fully. With reference to the goal of missions, I can largely agree with this statement, with perhaps some minor qualifications. But, with respect to actually being engaged in the mission, I have a question: do the unique challenges of particular locations have no merit in the way the mission is conceived? Often, I think it can appear that for Köstenberger that they do not.

4. *It must be hermeneutically sound.* Köstenberger is helpful in reminding us here that hermeneutics is a crucial aspect of what it means to be biblical. I agree that we need to interpret and apply the Bible carefully and correctly. But, I suggest that being hermeneutically sound requires more than merely recognizing that the "kingdom of God," "eternal life," and "the gospel" are all important biblical concepts that shape the church's mission and that there is more than one passage where Jesus commissions His disciples. For us to be biblical (or, hermeneutically sound) in our reflections on the church's mission, we must have a theological interpretation of the message of Scripture, a theological interpretation of our culture, and a theological application of the gospel to our culture.

5. *It must be theocentric, not anthropocentric.* This thesis is stated in either/or terms, and the fact is, mission is by

definition both/and. It was, after all, Paul who said, "I would be cut off from Christ for the sake of my Israelite brothers" (Rom 9:3). Further, it was also Paul who said to the church at Philippi, "I desire to be in the presence of Christ, but for your sake, I will remain here" (Phil 1:23-25). There are significant anthropocentric considerations in these biblical examples.

These theses appear to be one thesis reformulated in multiple ways. The core conviction is "biblical authority over contextual thinking in every situation." In principle, I affirm this statement. (In chapter 13, I will discuss in more detail my view on Scripture, as we delve into the contextualization question.) I would be fine with the principle that biblical authority is privileged if it allows for contextual thinking to interact with the interpretation of Scripture. The inescapable challenge is to interpret and apply the message of God's Word that was written in a particular cultural context to all cultures for all time. We look to interpret Scripture faithfully and also contextually for our time and place, believing it is part of the faithful application of God's inerrant Word.

Biblical scholars study the history of interpretation because they recognize that within the history of the church, interpretations of Scripture were often shaped by contemporary context. The fact that interpretation is shaped by context is a hard pill for some people to swallow. It certainly was for the Pharisees when Jesus called into question their rabbinic interpretations of the Old Testament.

Köstenberger follows Eitel's argument down the slippery slope. I smile at his inclusion of trendy theologies in the definition of "youthful lusts." In 1 Tim 4:12, Paul also instructs Timothy not to let anyone despise his youth. Personally, I think God provides the insights of new thinkers from time to time. While I realize that an established hermeneutical context resides behind the interpretation of that passage, such a glib reference to it is exactly what raises the ire of traditionalist New Testament scholars. But again, hasn't such a glib interpretation of "youthful lusts" violated the same hermeneutical principle?

What I like best about Köstenberger's chapter is his final

analysis—really, his own contextual description—of what the church should be doing. That description comes out of his own multicultural context, which establishes for him its biblically true nature. Or, to put it another way, it is "contextually appropriate."

RESPONDING TO GUDER

Next, we come to Guder's response. I agree with much of what Guder has to say. His emphasis on "reductionism" as the bane of Western theology—meaning that "Christ is easily reduced to little more than the 'disposer and distributor' of spiritual blessings"— describes all too powerfully the theology of many supposedly evangelical churches. The "pious self-centeredness" of Western (especially American) Christians echoes in my mind as I think about the practice of "short-term missions," which is so often really Christian tourism in disguise. The focus of missions must be the world, not the church, but when the church hears that, the knee-jerk reaction is, "Hey, what about us?"

What was most impressive to me, however, was the way in which Guder went back through Bosch to Barth, relating them back to Van Engen. And yes, reading Barth is painful, especially since most modern-day evangelicals (like me) have buried Barth with a neo-orthodox good riddance. Barth's one-word title in his response to Brunner's general revelation shows that he is clearly on the side of all these writers regarding the Christocentric mission of God through the church: "Nein!" he emphatically wrote. Jesus is the only way. While he could not define for all-time the vocation of the church even with the length of *Church Dogmatics*, Barth could certainly describe the need with a single illustration: he wrote of seeing his congregation look to him for bread, and he had only a stone to give them. Hasn't every preacher had that kind of moment at some point in the ministry? The mission is dependent on God and his actions through the body of Christ.

CONCLUSION

Finally, I return to Van Engen. The bulk of his paper is Van Engen describing mission, both bad and good. If you read the article again, you'll see that his final definition was added to teach Gloria a working definition for what was already being done by this woman's church through her Global Outreach Taskforce. Isn't that a pretty good name for what the church should be—"global outreach taskforce"? Would that every church have such a Global Outreach Taskforce that is striving to reach the world! It never has been—not the entire church anyway—except perhaps in certain unusual (and supernatural) periods of missionary expansion. Why not? Why can't we all ever get on the same page and practice what we preach?

And Van Engen's description of the church is that it is "missional." That one word does not define the mission of the church, but rather, it describes its actions. He also uses the word "praxeological," which incorporates the Greek name for "Acts." This term comes from the social sciences. It means the science of the study of humanly willed behavior, which harkens back to W. Carey's idea of the "Obligation of Christians to Use Means." You may recall that Carey's observation was met by a sharp retort: "Carey, sit down. If God wants to save the heathen He can do so without your help." Isn't this the nexus of contextualization? God does want us to be involved. The question of missions is not only the "what" (as some of Van Engen's responders concentrated on), but it is also the "how."

The making of definitions is in the nature of thinking. The describing of effective actions is in the nature of doing. I'm reminded of the old saying, "When all is said and done, far more will have been said than done." That certainly has applied to the church up to and including the present age. I also think of the real positive result of short-term missions (which I have already criticized in this chapter)—namely, getting people to do missions. Doing missions helps make a person a disciple of missions. My response to Van Engen's challenge is to add one of Van Engen's ideas to the tag line of his article. What we need is a "cohesive, consistent, focused, theologically deep, missiologically broad, contextually appropriate, and praxeologically effective, evangelical missiology."

Definitions are dangerous things. They can confuse and clarify, but the discussion of such can help provide clarity in the midst of the conversation. For certain readers, agreeing with missiologists and theologians (like Barth, for example) will be difficult. It will require an acknowledgment that someone can be right on one issue but wrong on another (for that matter, this would apply to many other agreements and disagreements among the respondents). For example, theologically I would be closer to Köstenberger and Eitel (particularly on issues of biblical authority), but missiologically, I more often agree with Guder and Van Engen. Although we start with different presuppositions in some cases, we come to similar conclusions on the mission of God and his church. At the end of the book, David Hesselgrave will weigh in with his thoughts on both—and give another important perspective on this conversation.

Definitions are dangerous things. They can confuse and clarify, but the discussion of such can help provide clarity in the midst of the conversation. For certain readers, agreeing with missiologist and theologians (like Barth, for example) will be difficult—it will require an acknowledgement that someone can be right on one issue but wrong on another (for that matter, this would apply to many other agreements and disagreements among the respondents). For example, theologically I would be closer to Köstenberger and Eitel (particularly on issues of biblical authority), but missiologically, I more often agree with Guder and Van Engen. Although we start with different presuppositions in some cases, we come to similar conclusions on the mission of God and his church. At the end of the book, David Hesselgrave will weigh in with his thoughts on both—and give another thought on these very definition issues.

BIBLIOGRAPHY

Flemming, Dean. *Contextualization in the New Testament: Patterns for Theology and Missions*. Downers Grove: InterVarsity, 2005.

Meadors, Gary T., ed. *Four Views on Moving Beyond the Bible to Theology*. Grand Rapids: Zondervan, 2009.

CHAPTER 8

ESSAY 2: The Gospel in Human Contexts

Changing Perceptions of Contextualization

PAUL G. HIEBERT

Thesis: The purpose of this essay is to offer some discussion of the state of "contextualization" as a critical aspect of missions, and of the changing perceptions of contextualization among missionaries and missions scholars. Any analysis of the current status of the Christian mission in the world must take social, historical, personal, and other contexts into account, and examine the relationships between the different contexts in which the people we serve live. In this sense this essay addresses the PRESENT of what has traditionally been termed "missions."

INTRODUCTION

As humans we live in particular contexts: our family, our neighborhood, our town, our country. We seldom give specific thought to them, but these contexts affect what we see, feel, and value, and what we believe without question is true, right, and proper. These beliefs are so obvious to us that they seem to be universal. They simply *are* the way things truly are. We assume that others see things the way we do. Houses have bathrooms, bedrooms, kitchens, and living rooms. Cars drive on the right side of the road and stop at stop signs. We must put postage stamps on letters before dropping them in the mailbox. We fail to recognize that many of the assumptions and values that underlie our culture are not biblical.

Many of us, particularly in our childhood, are *monocultural.* Only when things go wrong, or change rapidly, or when our views of reality come in conflict with the assumptions from another culture, do we question them. Such experiences make us aware that we live in contexts and force us to start thinking about them— their structures and underlying assumptions.

Others of us have grown up or live in multicultural contexts— missionaries, missionary kids, immigrants, business people, and diplomats. Such people are aware of cultural differences and have learned to negotiate between two worlds in daily living, but even they often do not stop to consciously examine these contexts, how they shape their thinking, or the deep differences between them. These people are, to some extent, *bicultural*, but they would find it hard to explain to others what this means.

In a rapidly globalizing world it is important that all of us give thought to human contexts and how these shape others and ourselves. We need to learn how to live in a multicontext world, to build bridges of understanding and relationship between different contexts, and to judge between them. This is true for social, cultural, linguistic, religious, and historical contexts. How do we and how should we relate to people from other cultures?

As Christians, we are often unaware that we are shaped more by our contexts than the gospel. We take our Christianity as biblically based and normative for everyone. We do not stop to consider what aspects of our contexts come from our sociocultural and historical situations and what comes from Scripture. Missionaries are forced to deal with sociocultural differences and, therefore, with social and cultural contexts. But even they often take little time to study systematically and deeply the contexts in which they serve, even though the effectiveness of their ministries is determined in large measure on how well they do so.

Humans live in many contexts: geographical, social, cultural, political, and historical. Here we will focus only on cultural contexts and the importance of understanding them for the sake of missions. Missionaries seek to plant churches in local social contexts and to communicate the gospel in local cultural contexts. The church without the gospel ceases to be the church. The gospel dies without humans and social institutions, such as families and congregations. A full analysis of missions must take social, historical, personal, and other contexts into account and examine the relationships between the different contexts in which the people we serve live.

VIEWS OF CONTEXTUALIZATION

Our conscious awareness of cultural contexts, including our own, often goes through changing perceptions as we encounter other cultures. Everyone does not go through them in a linear fashion, and those who grow up in multicultural settings develop at least some awareness of social and cultural differences and therefore of cultures and societies themselves. The changing perceptions outlined below are a model—a way of looking at our growing awareness of other cultures and people from other cultures—in cross-cultural ministries. This model is not a descriptor of the phases all people go through in their encounters with other cultures. Rather, it is a tool to help us understand ourselves, to understand the history of the modern mission movement in which missionaries from Europe and North America went to the ends of the earth, and to learn from past experiences.

Both personal and corporate views of contextualization change as we encounter other cultures and face the questions raised by our "otherness," our "differentness." These changes are not necessarily linear and may overlap.

VIEW 1. MINIMAL CONTEXTUALIZATION

Most monocultural people are largely unaware of the contexts in which they live or the depth to which these contexts shape how and what they think and do. For them the contextualization of the gospel is not an issue.

Noncontextualization

When my boss learned I wanted to be a missionary but wanted first to complete college, seminary, and graduate studies, he said,

"Just go and preach the gospel. Why waste time going to college and seminary?" His is a widespread attitude in the church.

When people go as missionaries, we know they need to understand the gospel, but we are sure they know enough from church and Sunday school to reach the lost abroad. Even if we recognize their need for more Bible training, most of us are unaware of the profound issues raised by cultural, social, and historical differences. We know that missionaries might benefit from a class or two on the culture in which they plan to serve. We are confident that in a few years they will naturally learn the local language and customs and be able to minister as they have in our church. All they need to do is proclaim the gospel to the people, and the people will understand and believe. They need to persuade the people to leave their old gods and receive Jesus as their Savior, and then they need to move on to new areas where the gospel has never been proclaimed. The gospel is seen as acultural and ahistorical in its very nature.

In this first phase we equate the gospel with our Christianity. New converts should learn from us and our ways and join us because we are Christians and this is the way we practice it. To do Christianity differently raises difficult questions. How differently can Christians in other cultures do it? Is our Christianity normative for all? To what extent have our ways of doing Christianity been shaped by the gospel and to what extent by our culture? We come as outsiders and assume new converts will join and imitate us.

An example of this view, one that can be found around the world, is the Methodist Church in Sri Lanka. In 1841, R. S. Hardy, a Methodist missionary, wrote:

> The national religion of Ceylon is Buddhism, accompanied by the worship of demons and the propitiation of malignant infernal spirits. . . . I rest my argument for the necessity of its destruction upon the simple fact that it is opposed to the truth—denies the existence of God—is ignorant of the only way of salvation, by faith in our Lord Jesus Christ—and is utterly impotent as a teacher of morals, or as a messenger of peace to the awakened consciences of its deluded votaries.[1]

---

[1] R. S. Hardy, *The British Government and the Idolatry of Ceylon* (London: Crofts and Blenkarn, 1841), 9.

Assessing the results of this view, W. T. J. Small wrote:

There was no attempt to adapt the form of worship to a national or truly [Sinhalese] form produced and sung to Western tunes, to the accompaniment of an organ or harmonium; the few lyrics included in the hymn book were hardly used in the services inside the church, and were reserved for open air services. No one dared to play an eastern musical instrument or a drum in a Methodist church in Ceylon. In short, a visitor from the West entering one of our churches during this period would find nothing to suggest to him in the ritual music or appointments that he was in an eastern church.[2]

K. M. de Silva writes:

The Christian missions had come to Sri Lanka as the apostles of a new faith and as critics of indigenous society, and in preaching their new ideas the missionaries had been fortified usually by an unquestioning faith not merely in their own rightness but also in the intrinsic depravity of many traditional customs and beliefs. This latter had given the Christian missionary movement its characteristic feature of cultural intolerance. . . . Christianity was interpreted on western lines and in non-indigenous concepts. The missionaries imposed on their adherents in Sri Lanka the conventional forms of western Christianity almost in their entirety.[3]

This view was not restricted to Methodists or to missionaries in Sri Lanka. It was characteristic of most Protestant missions around the world. The epistemological foundation for this second phase was positivism, which holds that our scientific knowledge is an accurate, true photograph of the world and corresponds one-to-one with reality. Its theories are not models but facts. Scientists seek objective truth and must eliminate feelings and morals from the rational and empirical processes used to ascertain truth because they introduce subjectivity.

Theological positivism holds that our central concern is truth and that our theology corresponds one-to-one to Scripture. Other theologies and religions are false and must be attacked. We are

---

[2] W. J. T. Small, ed., *A History of the Methodist Church in Ceylon 1814–1964* (Colombo, Sri Lanka: The Wesley Press, 1971), 367.
[3] K. M. de Silva, ed., *Sri Lanka: A Survey* (Honolulu: The University Press of Hawaii, 1977), 395.

concerned with truth and define it in rational terms. We divorce it from feelings and values because these undermine the objectivity of the truth. Our concern is that people believe the truth of the gospel because that determines whether they are saved. We define the truth in propositional terms and seek to transmit it unchanged. We see ourselves as God's lawyers, and we put our trust in experts who have studied Scripture deeply.

Finally, we see the gospel as acultural and ahistorical. It is unchanging and universal and can be codified in abstract rational terms and communicated in all languages without loss of meaning. The sociocultural contexts of neither the listeners nor the messengers need be taken into account.

Most missionaries, when they enter another culture, move quickly to the second phase, but some remain in the first phase all their lives. They work through translators and control the converts and churches. They make certain that new Christians conform to the cultural norms introduced by the missionary. They must wear clothes, learn to read, and have only one wife. They cannot do theological reflection on their own. They must learn theology from the missionary.

Minimal Contextualization

When we enter another culture, we soon encounter deep differences. We experience culture shock: the feeling of disorientation that arises when all our familiar cultural ways no longer hold. We experience language shock: the inability to communicate even the simplest messages and the growing realization that languages shape the way we experience and see reality. We also experience religious shock: the fact that other religions make sense to their followers, even though to us these are strange and obviously wrong. We meet Muslims and Hindus who are good people, often better than some of the Christians we know. They can articulate their beliefs clearly and persuasively. How can we say they are lost? Why are we Christians? Was it a matter of conviction or of birth and upbringing? We are forced to examine our own beliefs more deeply and the bases for our convictions. Such encounters with cultural differences force us to deal with "others" and ultimately with the question of "otherness."

This encounter with "otherness" requires missionaries to decide on matters of lifestyle in a new land. What kind of food should we eat at home? What kind of clothes should we wear? What kind of homes should we live in? In this view we try to preserve our culture abroad for the psychological survival and for our children, who, we assume, will eventually return to our home culture.

"Otherness" also raises the question of the messengers' attitudes toward the local people. They are so different—so "other"! In the modern view we are "civilized," and they are "primitive" or at least "backward" and in need of help to become like us. When we learn to know them personally, they become more human to us—friends and neighbors—but we keep a psychological barrier between us and them. They are "others," not "us." We do not think seriously of migrating and becoming citizens of the country or that our children might marry locally and settle down as "natives." We think of returning "home" when we retire.

The more we live with and study the people we serve, the more we become aware of the depth and power of the people's culture and the need to contextualize both the messenger and the message for them to understand and live the gospel; but we are afraid that this can distort the gospel, so it must be done minimally. We realize that we must speak and translate the Bible into their language and that we must organize their services and churches in ways the people understand, but we equate Christianity with our beliefs and practices.

In this paradigm we link Christianity to civilization. Since we see ourselves as "modern" and others as "primitive" (i.e., in need of development), we do not need to study other cultures deeply except to find the distortions they bring to the people's understanding of the gospel. We bring schools and hospitals to teach people the truths of science and civilize them. We see other cultures as primitive or evil, with little to contribute to our understanding of reality. There is little in the old culture worth preserving. The minds of the "natives" are a *tabula rasa* on which we can write Christianity and science. In order to become Christian and civilized, the people must become like us. As the Chinese used to say, "One more Christian, one less Chinese."

The semiotic foundations for positivism are formal or literal signs. Signs, such as words and mathematical formulas, are thought to correspond directly to empirical realities. The word *tree* refers to real trees, *cow* to real cows. This view assumes that all people live in essentially the same world but simply attach different labels to realities. Their thought categories, logic, ways of ordering realities, and worldview are essentially like our own. In communication and Bible translation, missionaries needed simply to find the corresponding words in another language, adjust the grammar, and the people would understand the message accurately.

One characteristic of this view of signs is its strong affirmation of *truth*. Feelings and morals are eliminated from the rational process because they introduce subjectivity. In mission work this stresses communicating the gospel as truth, with little focus on its affective and moral dimensions. In evangelism and teaching, an emphasis is placed on accurate, rationally developed arguments and an apologetic confrontation with other religions.

A second characteristic is that communication is measured by what is said or transmitted. It is sender-oriented communication. Communication is measured by what was transmitted: by the number of sermons preached, the hours of radio broadcast, and the quantity of tracts and Bibles distributed.

In contextualization formal semiotics assumes that signs in other cultures—such as drama, drums, bowing, and music—are inherently tied to their pagan meanings and therefore cannot be used by Christians. This leads to a widespread rejection of local signs and the importation of Western Christian ones. We sing Western hymns translated into the local language, build churches in European styles, and import our liturgies. If we are Anglicans, we have priests; if Presbyterians, we have presbyters; if Baptists, we introduce voting. The result was a minimal contextualized approach to missions.

VIEW 2. UNCRITICAL CONTEXTUALIZATION

The more deeply we are involved in cross-cultural ministries, the more we realize the reality of social, cultural, and historical contexts; the depth of the differences between them; and the difficulties in dealing with these differences. Early anthropologists and missionaries studied other cultures using Western theoretical frameworks. After the 1930s anthropologists began to realize the importance of understanding the world as the people they studied see it, seeking to understand culture like an insider (the "emic perspective"). This change in perspective led to a profound shift in the nature of anthropological and missiological theories and to an ongoing exploration of the differences between cultures and their mutual intelligibility. Can we truly understand "others"? Can we compare their cultures with our own; if so, on what basis? We start by studying the people we serve, but what starts as a study of other people ends with us studying ourselves and our own assumptions. Our tendency is to pull back from the analysis and dogmatically to reaffirm the rightness of our own world.

The growing awareness of anthropological insights into human contexts leads in missions to a growing awareness of the importance of radically contextualizing the gospel in other contexts so that the people can understand the gospel and become followers of Jesus Christ. This awareness was influenced by two paradigm shifts. The first was the emergence of Saussurian semiotics. F. de Saussure raised the question of the relationship between forms and meanings in signs and came to the conclusion that it was "arbitrary."[4] He argued that signs do not refer to external realities, as formerly thought. Rather, they are mental constructs that create meaning systems in the mind. Signs have forms and meanings, and there are no links between signs and realities other than the conventionalities of human cultures. Meanings are wholly subjective. If this is true, then an accurate literal translation from one culture to another does not guarantee the preservation of the meaning. Rather, we must measure communication not by what is sent by the speaker but by what is understood by the listener. We need translations in which mental meanings are preserved in cross-cultural communication rather than literal references. The result is dynamic-equivalent, receptor-oriented Bible translations. The problem remained; if signs do not have external and objective reference points, then there is no way to test whether the meanings understood in one cul-

---

[4] F. de Saussure, *Course in General Linguistics*, ed. C. Bally and A. Sechehaye, trans. from the French by W. Baskin (New York: McGraw-Hill, 1966), 67.

ture are the same as those found in another culture. There are no objective tests for truth.

The second paradigm shift is in epistemology. Positivism, which was the foundation for the enlightenment, is increasingly challenged as false, arrogant, oppressive, and colonial. In its place emerged postmodern instrumentalism (also known as pragmatism), which sees knowledge systems as the creation of human minds. They are like cultural Rorschach tests, not photographs, of reality. There is no way to test whether they are true, so we adopt those most useful to us. The result is cultural relativism. All cultures are seen as equally good and true. None can judge another. Moreover, the preservation of cultures becomes an unquestioned good.

The introduction of Saussurian semiotics and instrumental epistemology profoundly challenged the fundamental assumptions of the Western mission movement and its colonial attitudes. If there is good in all religions, why should missionaries seek to convert people who are not Christians? If missionaries go, they should go as insiders and identify fully with the people they serve. Local people were encouraged to read the Scriptures for themselves and to formulate their own theologies.

The second phase of this shift to radical contextualization occurred when missionaries, such as E. S. Jones and L. Newbigin, returned to their home countries. They began to look at these as mission fields, and they were shocked at the uncritical contextualization of the gospel in Western context. The Church became a part of the culture, not an outside counterculture community, and it largely lost its prophetic voice. Out of their prophetic calls emerged the Gospel in Our Culture movement.

VIEW 3. CRITICAL CONTEXTUALIZATION

In recent years there has been a reaction to radical contextualization, which brings up a few questions: Is the gospel still the gospel when it is radically contextualized? Or has it become captive to the cultural context? Does the most contextualized gospel lead to the most vital, biblical churches? Out of this has emerged a critical approach to contextualization.

Central to this view is the fact that the gospel cannot be equated with any contextual expression of it. A. Walls notes that

> no one ever meets universal Christianity in itself: we only ever meet Christianity in a local form and that means a historically, culturally conditioned form. We need not fear this; when God became man he became historically, cultural conditioned man in a particular time and place. What he became, we need not fear to be. There is nothing wrong in having local forms of Christianity—provided that we remember that they are local.[5]

Underlying this new paradigm is a rejection of Saussurian semiotics and emergence of Peircian semiotics. C. Peirce, an American mathematician and linguist, proposed a third way of looking at signs. He rejected the dualism of form and meaning introduced by Humboldt and Saussure, and introduced a triadic view of signs.[6] He said that each sign had three elements: (1) the sign or the signifier (e.g., the spoken or written word, the sound of a bell, an arrow); (2) the mental concept or image the sign evokes in the mind (i.e., the signified); and (3) the reality to which it refers (the significatum).[7] For example, the word *tree* invokes a mental image of a tree, and it normally refers to real trees in the forest. In other words, a sign is the linking of mental images to realities by means of words, gestures, sounds, and images. A sign has a subjective dimension and an objective dimension. This means that signs are not simply human constructs but that they reflect the order in reality itself. If there was not a great deal of correspondence between peoples' views of reality and reality itself, life would be impossible. While driving down the road, we need to watch out not only for mentally constructed traffic but also for traffic that is indeed real and deadly.

There is also a growing reaction to postmodern instrumentalism and the emergence of a post-postmodern critical realist epistemology.[8] In this view humans can know reality in part, but their knowledge is not a photograph of reality with a one-to-one correspondence between theory and facts but a map of reality. Maps

---

[5] A. Walls, *The Missionary Movement in Christian History: Studies in the Transmission of the Faith* (Maryknoll: Orbis, 1996), 235.

[6] C. Peirce, *Philosophical Writings of Peirce*, ed. Justus Buchler (New York: Dover, 1955), 91–93.

[7] Ibid., 101–4.

[8] P. G. Hiebert, *The Missiological Implications of Epistemological Shifts: Affirming Truth in a Modern/Postmodern World* (Harrisburg: Trinity Press, 1999), 63.

must correspond to reality in what they claim to affirm, but they are mental images that are schematic, approximate, and of necessity limited and selective. A road map does not make truth claims about property boundaries or economic variables. Moreover, to be useful, it must be simple, not showing every bend in the road or every pothole or bridge. But it must get drivers to their intended destinations.

Given Peircian semiotics and a critical realist epistemology, it is possible to compare human belief systems and to test them against external realities that all humans experience. To do so, we need to develop metacultural grids that enable us to compare and evaluate between two worlds, to translate between them, and to negotiate between them.

In Bible translation Peircian semiotics leads beyond dynamic equivalence to double translations in which the translators seek to communicate ideas accurately while preserving the forms in Scripture as much as possible, often by using footnotes or parenthetical clarifications.

In contextualization the new paradigm calls for critical contextualization or doing missional theology.[9] The Bible is seen as divine revelation, not simply as humanly constructed beliefs. In contextualization the heart of the gospel must be kept as it is encoded in forms that are understood by the people, without making the gospel captive to the contexts. This is an ongoing process of embodying the gospel in an ever-changing world. Here cultures are seen as both good and evil, not simply as neutral vehicles for understanding the world. No culture is absolute or privileged. We are all relativized by the gospel.

A critical realist epistemology differentiates between revelation and theology. The former is God-given revelation; the latter is human understandings of that revelation and cannot be fully equated with it. Human knowledge is always partial and schematic, and it does not correspond one to one with reality. Our theology is our understanding of Scripture in our contexts; it may be true, but it is always partial and subject to our own perspectives. It seeks to answer the questions we raise. This calls for community-based hermeneutics in which dialogue serves to correct the biases of

---

[9] T. Tiénou and P. G. Hiebert, "Missional Theology," *Missiology* (April 2006): 219–38.

individuals. On the global scale this calls for both local and global theologies. Local churches have the right to interpret and apply the gospel in their contexts, but they also have a responsibility to join the larger church community around the world to seek to overcome both the limited perspectives each brings and the biases each has that might distort the gospel.

In this view of contextualization, missionaries are transcultural people—outsider-insiders, people who come to *serve* the local churches instead of being rivals for power and positions.

VIEW 4. DIVINE REVELATION GIVEN IN HUMAN CONTEXTS

While Scripture is divine revelation, Scripture itself was given to humans in their particular historical and sociocultural contexts. This is obvious to Old and New Testament scholars, but it is often overlooked by ordinary Christians. Differentiating between eternal truth and the particular contexts in which it was revealed is not an easy task, but doing so is essential if we are to understand the heart of the gospel that is for everyone.

What then is the relationship between the gospel and human contexts, and how can we communicate the gospel to humans in their contexts? Three principles can help us here: ontology, phenomenology, and missiology.

GOSPEL VERSUS HUMAN CONTEXTS: ONTOLOGY

A full view of the gospel in human contexts must first emphasize that the gospel is indeed divine revelation to humans, not human searches for the truth. This revelation is given in the particularities of history and locality, but it is given by God and reveals God's universal message to all mankind. It is easy, particularly in academia, to ask what humans think about God. We must always remember, as Malik reminds us, that the real question is, What does God think about us?[10]

From this principle it follows that the gospel must not be equated with any particular human context. This is true not only with regard to Western Christianity but also with the Scriptures. The gospel was revealed in the historical and sociocultural contexts of the Old and New Testaments, but those contexts are not

---

[10] C. Malik, *A Christian Critique of the University* (Downers Grove: InterVarsity, 1982), 25.

normative for Christianity around the world. While the gospel is distinct from human cultures, this does not set the two in opposition to each other. Rather they are two separate but interrelated realities. Divine revelation was given to humans in particular social and cultural contexts, but that the gospel is not to be equated with any one of these contexts.

From this principle it also follows that we dare not equate the gospel with any human theologies. Our theologies are our partial human attempts to understand Scripture in our particular contexts, but the gospel transcends them all.

It is difficult in a pluralist world to affirm the truth of divine revelation. But, as E. S. Jones points out, we are called not to be God's lawyers but to bear bold witness to what we know—that Jesus Christ is the only way to God and His kingdom. If we truly believe this, then to affirm other ways is to withhold from people knowledge of the way to eternal salvation.

THE GOSPEL IN HUMAN CONTEXTS: PHENOMENOLOGY

The second principle we need to keep in mind is that the gospel must be put in specific sociocultural contexts for people to understand it. To do so we must study Scripture and humans and build a bridge between them. This process is doing missional theology.[11]

Studying Humans

The first step in doing missional theology is to study humans in their contexts, particularly the issues that concern them and us. Church leaders and missionaries should study and lead the church to study the contexts of the people they serve. To study humans, they need theoretical frameworks. Here they can draw on human studies, such as anthropology, sociology, psychology, history, and the humanities. These must be tested against biblical teachings because these are human methods, just as the philosophical and historical methods we use in doing systematic and biblical theology are human methods.

In this step, leaders and missionaries should avoid criticism of the customary beliefs and practices because the people will not

---

[11] Tie'nou and Hiebert, "Missional Theology," 224–25.

talk to them freely for fear of being condemned and because we are in danger of making premature judgments based on an incomplete understanding of the situation. In either case we will only drive the old ways underground. The result is split-level Christianity.

We must also study our own contexts to see how these have shaped our understandings of humans and of Scripture. This reflexivity is difficult to do, but it is essential to the process. Often Christian leaders from other contexts can see our biases better than we do, so we need to listen to them carefully.

Having studied our own contexts and those of the people we serve, we must develop a transcultural framework that enables us to translate between and compare different contexts. The formation of this mental framework is critical in building bridges of understanding between cultures, and all parties to the conversation must be heard in its formation. In it all must agree that their views have been truly understood by outsiders as best as can be done in outside terms. Anthropology can help because it has sought to develop transcultural frameworks for translating and comparing social and cultural systems around the world. Its frameworks are imperfect, and an ongoing dialogue between spokespersons for different cultures must continue in the construction of a transcultural frame of reference in which all their voices are accurately heard.

Studying Scripture on the Issue at Hand

Having studied humans in their contexts phenomenologically, we then need to study Scripture to discern ontological criteria for evaluating specific human issues in their sociocultural contexts. What does the gospel say about polygamy, divorce, leadership, money, war, and other human affairs? We need to study Scripture carefully to understand the gospel in its three dimensions. First, it has a cognitive dimension; it is about truth. Second, it has an affective dimension; it is about beauty and love. Third, it has a moral dimension; it is about holiness and justice. Contextualization seeks to formulate and communicate universal truth (cognitive dimension), love (affective dimension), and holiness (moral dimension) revealed in Scripture in particular human contexts that are diverse and ever changing. To assume that general rules (once properly determined) remain unchanged and need simply to be applied in later cases overlooks the changing nature of human life and the dynamic quality of theology that must be extended to new situations.

The study of Scripture is the responsibility of the church as a hermeneutical community. We need experts to help us, but as the church we are entrusted with the gospel. If we all do not study it together, we will not be active participants in knowing and living it, and we may be led astray by lone individuals. We must keep in mind that our own interpretations are shaped by our social, cultural, psychological, and historical contexts and that these need to be checked by others from other cultures who can help us see these biases. This is not to say that our interpretations are wrong, but our contexts determine how we see things. By studying our perspectives carefully, we can grow in our knowledge of and obedience to the gospel. Moreover, in the process of contextualizing the gospel, people do not always agree. The effort to find complete agreement before acting is meaningless. It is easy to forget the purpose for which theological reflections must be done, namely, to make known the gospel to humans in their contexts so that it can transform them.

What checkpoints help us in this process to guard against syncretism? All our Christian understandings and life are in human contexts, and therefore they are partial. This does not mean they are necessarily wrong, but we need to be humble in our stance and to seek unity in the church "so that God's multi-faceted wisdom may now be made known through the church" (Eph 3:10). But there is always the danger when we put the gospel in human contexts that the essence of the gospel would be so distorted that it loses its message. God starts with us where we are, and He reveals Himself to us more fully as we grow in the knowledge of our Lord. In one sense syncretism is a message that has lost the heart of the gospel. In another sense it is moving in the wrong direction, away from a fuller knowledge of the gospel.

The checkpoints against both types of syncretism lie in a metatheology—theological reflections on the way we do our theologies. First, we need to take the Bible seriously as the rule of faith and life. This may seem obvious, but we must constantly remind ourselves that biblical revelation is the standard against which our beliefs and practices must be measured. Second, we need to recognize the work of the Holy Spirit in the lives of all believers open to God's leading. Reason in its many forms is important, but the Holy Spirit reveals to us through Scripture mysteries that transcend human knowledge. Third, we need the church to be a hermeneutical community that seeks to understand God's Word to it in its particular contexts. In this community we need Christians from other cultures, for they often see how our cultural biases have distorted our interpretations of the Scriptures. This corporate nature of the church as a community of interpretation extends not only to the church in every culture but also to the church in all ages. Through community hermeneutics, we seek a growing understanding, if not agreement, on key theological issues that can help us test our theologies and our practices. This is an ongoing process in which the church constantly engages itself and seeks to understand what the lordship of Christ and the kingdom of God on earth are about.

THE GOSPEL TO HUMAN CONTEXTS: MISSIOLOGY

The third principle to guide us in understanding the relationship of the gospel to human social and cultural contexts is that the gospel is transformative. It is not simply a message to be affirmed as true but a call to follow Christ throughout life in radical discipleship. Newbigin understands the relation of a church to culture as essentially missional in nature.[12]

Early anthropologists and missionaries often saw other cultures as primitive and uncivilized. Later they began to see that there is good in all cultures, good that can be preserved so that people have a sense of their identity. Now we realize that evil also exists in all cultures, such as oppression of the poor, corruption, and sin. All need to be transformed into the likeness of Christ. A missionary encounter occurs when the church embodies the comprehensive demands of the gospel as an alternative way of life to the culture in which it is set and thereby challenges the culture's fundamental assumptions. In this way the church offers the gospel

---

[12] G. R. Hunsberger, *Bearing the Witness of the Spirit: Leslie Newbigin's Theology of Cultural Plurality* (Grand Rapids: Eerdmans, 1998), 270–71.

as a credible alternative way of life to its fallen culture, calling for radical conversion and issuing an invitation to understand and live in the world in the light of the gospel.

The day of moral neutrality is over. Human contexts are both good and evil. Humans are created in the image of God and are the object of His great love. But they are also fallen, and the societies and cultures they build are affected by that fall. There is both personal and corporate sin and personal and corporate dimensions to God's redemption.

Knowledge is not simply information. It is a power used by the participants in the social, economic, political, and cultural arenas of life. Knowledge of the gospel makes us responsible to share its message of salvation and transformation with all people; to care for the poor, oppressed, and sick; and to bring the gospel to the lost.[13]

In transformation we must start where the people are and help them grow, just as God starts with us where we are but leads us into maturity and faithfulness. Conversion is to turn to follow Christ, as individuals and as churches. It is the first step in spiritual growth and obedience. This transformation must be both personal and corporate. As individuals we need to be "born again" into a new life. As a church we need to model not the way of this world but the ways of the kingdom, and we need to challenge the evils in our societies and cultures.

In transformation we need to involve people in evaluating their own culture in the light of the Bible. They know their old culture better than does the outsider, and they are in a better position to critique it and live transformed lives once they have biblical instruction. We can bring outside views that help them see their own cultural biases, but they are involved in making the decision, and they grow spiritually through learning discernment and applying scriptural teachings to their own lives. The gospel is not simply information to be communicated. It is a message to which people must respond. Moreover, it is not enough that leaders be convinced that changes are needed. They may share their convictions and point out the consequences of various decisions, but they

---

[13] M. G. Cartwright, "Stanley Hauerwas's Essay in Theological Ethics," *The Hauerwas Reader,* ed. J. Berkmanan and M. Cartwright (Durham: Duke University Press), 629–30.

and their people must together make and enforce decisions arrived at corporately. Only then will old beliefs and practices not be pushed underground, subverting the gospel.

In transformation we must deal with the deeper issues involved. Too often we act on immediate cases at hand, and we do not use them to stimulate long-range reflections on the underlying issues. Specific cases should stimulate further reflections in systematic and biblical theologies and human studies that facilitate long-term and well-grounded responses to the personal, social, and cultural contexts at hand.

Transformational theology focuses on mission. It takes humans seriously, in the particularity of their persons, societies, cultures, and their ever-changing histories. It integrates cognition, affectivity, and evaluation in its response to biblical truth, and it defines faith not simply as mental affirmations of truth or as positive experiences of God but as beliefs, feelings, and morals that lead to response and obedience to the Word of God. It rejects the division between pure and applied theology and sees ministry both as a way of doing theology and as a form of worship.

CONCLUSION

This essay has sought to reflect on the PRESENT in missions. Contextualization is clearly one of the most discussed and debated issues in missions at present. The early or pioneer missionaries practiced minimal contextualization. They worked hard to translate the Scriptures into the languages of their people groups, but they generally felt no need to make cultural adjustments in their presentation of the gospel. The churches they planted emulated Western churches in theology, worship, and church polity. In the twentieth century missionaries who were cognizant of anthropology practiced uncritical contextualization. If the early missionaries adjusted too little, these missionaries accommodated too freely, and the result was syncretism. In my writings I have endeavored to advocate critical contextualization. Critical contextualization seeks a balanced approach in which missionary interaction with societies is both true to the Bible and sensitive to the cultures of the particular people groups.

The final section of my essay speaks to the gospel in human

contexts. Jesus was incarnated in a cultural context, and modern missionaries must communicate the gospel in a particular cultural context. In recent years Evangelical missiologists, especially anthropologists, have emphasized the importance of contextualized hermeneutics. A contextualized hermeneutic seeks to interpret the Scriptures in a way that is biblically correct but also culturally appropriate. This approach reflects the importance of the two hermeneutical questions: What did the biblical text mean originally? And what does this text mean for us today? In the essay I call for a contextualized hermeneutic that is informed by the Holy Scriptures, guided by the Holy Spirit, and discerned by the church, functioning as a hermeneutical community. By God's grace this approach will produce contextualized theology, ethics, worship, and polity.

BIBLIOGRAPHY

Cartwright, Michael G. "Stanley Hauerwas's Essays in Theological Ethics: A Reader's Guide." Pages 623–72 in *The Hauerwas Reader.* Edited by John Berkmanan and Michael Cartwright. Durham: Duke University Press, 2001.

Hardy, R. S. *The British Government and the Idolatry of Ceylon.* London: Crofts and Blenkarn, 1841.

Hauerwas, S., and W. Willimon. *Resident Aliens: Life in the Christian Colony.* Nashville: The Abingdon Press, 1989.

Hiebert, P. G. "Form and Meaning in the Contextualization of the Gospel." Pages 101–20 in *The Word Among Us.* Edited by Dean S. Gilliland, Dallas: Word Publishing, 1989.

———. *Missiological Implications of Epistemological Shifts: Affirming Truth in a Modern/Postmodern World.* Harrisburg, PA: Trinity Press International, 1999.

Hunsberger, George R. *Bearing the Witness of the Spirit: Leslie Newbigin's Theology of Cultural Plurality.* Grand Rapids: William B. Eerdmans, 1998.

———, and Craig Van Gelder, eds. *The Church Between Gospel and Culture: The Emerging Mission in North America.* Grand Rapids: William B. Eerdmans, 1996.

Jones, E. S. *The Christ of the Indian Road*. New York: The Abingdon Press, 1925.

Laudan, L. *Beyond Positivism and Relativism*. Boulder: Westview Press, 2001.

———*Progress and Its Problems: Towards a Theory of Scientific Growth*. Berkeley: University of California Press, 1977.

Lyons, John. *Semantics*. Vol. 1. Cambridge: University Press, 1977.

Malik, C. *A Christian Critique of the University*. Waterloo, ON: North Waterloo Press, 1987.

Newbigin, L. *The Gospel and Western Culture*. Grand Rapids: Eerdmans, 1986.

———. *The Gospel in a Pluralist Society*. Grand Rapids: Eerdmans, 1989.

Peirce, C. *Philosophical Writings of Peirce*. Edited by J. Buchler. New York City: Dover Publications, 1955.

Saussure, Ferdinand de. *Cours de Linguistiques General (Course in General Linguistics)*. Translated and edited by Charles Bally and Albert Sechehaye. New York: McGraw-Hill Book Company, 1916.

———. *Course in General Linguistics*. Edited by Charles Bally and Albert Sechehaye. Translated from French by Wade Baskin. New York: McGraw-Hill Book Company, 1966.

Silva, K. M. de, ed. *Sri Lanka: A Survey*. Honolulu: The University Press of Hawaii, 1977.

Small, W. J. T., ed. *A History of the Methodist Church in Ceylon 1814–1964*. Colombo, Sri Lanka: The Wesley Press, 1971.

Tiénou, T., and P. G. Hiebert. "Missional Theology." *Missiology* (April 2006): 219–38.

Walls, Andrew. *The Missionary Movement in Christian History: Studies in the Transmission of the Faith*. Maryknoll, NY: Orbis Books, 1996.

CHAPTER 9

Response to Paul G. Hiebert

"The Gospel in Human Contexts: Changing Perceptions of Contextualization"

MICHAEL POCOCK

INTRODUCTION

It is a privilege to respond to what are essentially the last words of Paul Hiebert on the issue of contextualization. Hiebert was a mentor and friend to so many during a lifetime of missionary and academic ministry. His breadth of expertise was amazing. He could address almost any issue from cultural anthropology to linguistics, from folk religion to philosophical epistemology, and do it helpfully, biblically, and without pomposity.

By tracing four progressive perceptions, orientations, or approaches to contextualization that have marked the modern missionary epoch, Hiebert gives us a brief history of the development of the concept. I do not retrace the entire history of contextualization here, since it is in Hesselgrave and Rommen's helpful *Contextualization: Meanings, Methods and Models*[1]—to which much has been added in the past 20 years. Instead, I deal with Hiebert's three levels of contextualization—minimal, radical, and critical—with

---

[1] D. J. Hesselgrave and E. Rommen, *Contextualization: Meanings, Methods, and Models* (Grand Rapids: Baker, 1989), 12–26.

particular emphasis on the last, which Hiebert develops into a fourth step: "Divine Revelation Given in Human Contexts." This ultimate phase seems most fruitful for contemporary and future adaptation of the Christian message to the cultures in which we find ourselves and avoids a descent into relativistic syncretism.

Hiebert's four levels are reminiscent of the well-known six levels of contextualization, C-1 to C-6, proposed by J. Travis[2] to which P. Parshall and others have responded.[3] Controversy continues over the extent to which contextualization can be carried before basic biblical principles are sacrificed, prompting the *Evangelical Missions Quarterly* to devote most of the July 2004 issue to these questions.[4] Hiebert is aware of the impact context makes on the understanding of communicators and receptors. He is aware of the nonverbal aspects of communication, but he is most concerned about the *communication* of the *message*, whereas Travis's C-1 to C-6 have to do with the shape and texture of the church or Christian community in a non-Christian context. Hiebert is concerned in this article with the *roots* and *process* of what he regards as inappropriate polarities of minimal and radical contextualization.

MINIMAL CONTEXTUALIZATION

Although no one was using the term *contextualization* prior to the 1960s, various attempts had been made to adapt Western Christian conceptions, forms, and practice to the cultures confronting missionary endeavor. Minimal contextualization characterized the opening phase of modern Protestant missions. The strength of Western civilization, its linkage with Christianity and the general acceptance of the empirical-rational approach of positivism, merged in popular attitudes of superiority, frequently shared by missionaries. Missionaries arrived in other cultures as largely unself-critical people who identified the gospel with their general understanding of Western values and Christianity as practiced by Westerners. Western missionaries were correct in their

---

[2] J. Travis, "The C-1 to C-6 Spectrum: A Practical Tool for Defining Six Types of 'Christ-Centered Communities' Found in the Muslim Community," *EMQ* 34:4 (October 1998): 407–8.

[3] P. Parshall, "Danger! New Directions in Contextualization," *EMQ* 34:4 (October 1998): 404–6.

[4] P. Parshall, "Lifting the Fatwa," *EMQ* 40:3 (July 2004), 288–95; J. Massey, "Misunderstanding C-5: His Ways Are Not Our Orthodoxy," 296–307; H. L. Richard, "New Paradigms for Understanding Hinduism and Contextualization," 308–20.

belief in the existence of absolute truth and the exclusive claims of Christianity. Their weakness, as Hiebert sees it, was in their *underestimation* of legitimate values in other cultures and their uncritical assumption that Western civilization, culture, and science were as authoritatively correct as the truth of their gospel. The peoples of receiving cultures had no choice but to conclude that acceptance of the Christian gospel would mean acceptance of everything Western and the disavowal of their own culture. As Hiebert indicates in the popular statement of the Chinese during the nineteenth century, "One more Christian, one less Chinese."

A central characteristic of minimal contextualization, and of the modernity-oriented Western Christians, was their overdependence on *words* to express truths at the expense of feelings, morals, actions, or anything remotely mystical. Western Christianity became what I have come to term an "engineering" faith—in love with schematic truth presented in charts and paradigms.[5] In the minds of many Westerners, there was a direct connection or complete identification between words expressing truth in the sender's language and those of the receiver. Communication of this nature is always incomplete. Ideas in the mind of a communicator never reach the minds of the receptors in the same shape they were sent. Something is always lost in translation.

As the modern missionary era dawned with W. Carey (though he had predecessors in the Pietist movement), one can see the earnest, though incorrect, Western assumption that there is a "one-to-one" correspondence between words in one language and words in another language. Indians were unable to read Carey's heroic early translation of the New Testament into Bengali because it was too "wooden," like reading a Greek interlinear translation. Fortunately Carey absorbed this disappointment. He invested amazing efforts in learning Indian languages, history, literature, and culture. His later translations were far more successful.[6]

But contextualization is always more than a matter of mere words. Shaw and Van Engen said it well:

---

[5] M. Pocock, G. Van Rheenen, and D. McConnell, *The Changing Face of World Missions* (Grand Rapids: Baker, 2005), 115.
[6] S. Neill, *A History of Christian Missions*, rev. ed. (London: Penguin Books, 1986), 224–25.

Communication as translation is more than grappling with ex-egetical issues and their transference into a particular context. Christianity is not about knowing; it is about appropriate living, about being, about each person's relationship to the God who has spoken in Jesus Christ through the revelational activity of the Holy Spirit. It is about incarnation. It is about a life lived today so people can see Jesus in believers.[7]

As Hiebert shows, earlier missionaries during the modern era did eventually learn to value the worldviews and cultural heritage of non-Christian cultures, and so did cultural anthropologists. The pendulum began to swing from *minimal contextualization* to *uncritical contextualization.*

UNCRITICAL CONTEXTUALIZATION

Hiebert's essay is relatively brief in its treatment of the movement toward uncritical contextualization. He dealt with this phenomenon in much greater depth in a previous work.[8] Although postmodernism is usually thought to have originated about 1979 with F. Lyotard,[9] a growing wave toward postmodernity can even be called "pre-postmodernism." The roots of the rebellion against the arrogance of modernity can be traced to S. Kierkegaard's essay: "Concluding Unscientific Postscript," in the mid-nineteenth century.[10] But as Hiebert himself notes, the movement was building from about the 1930s. Secular linguists and anthropologists were already moving toward the idea that, in any culture, meaning is subjective and cannot be accurately transmitted from one cultural setting to another. In other words, they were approaching the postmodern position that all truth is cultural and thus there are no absolutes.

Although evangelical Bible translators have always been committed to absolute truth as revealed in Scripture, they have moved from merely translating *words* to translating *thoughts*, albeit in

---

[7] R. D. Shaw and C. Van Engen, *Communicating God's Word in a Complex World* (New York: Rowman and Littlefield, 2003), 4.

[8] P. G. Hiebert, *The Missiological Implications of Epistemological Shifts: Affirming Truth in a Modern/Postmodern World* (Harrisburg: Trinity, 1999), 63.

[9] F. Lyotard, *The Postmodern Condition: A Report on Knowledge*, trans. G. Bennington and B. Massouri (Minneapolis: University Press, 1984).

[10] S. Kierkegaard, "Concluding Unscientific Postscript," in *A Kierkegaard Anthology*, ed. Robert Bretall (New York: The Modern Library, Random House, 1946), 190–258. For further information on this point, see M. Pocock, "The Changing Basis of Knowledge: From Modernity to Postmodernity," in *The Changing Face of Missions*, 105–28.

as close a correspondence as possible to the intent of Scripture writers. This was the concept of "dynamic equivalence" advanced by E. Nida.[11] Hiebert is dissatisfied with dynamic equivalence because it still implies that there are no "external, objective reference points . . . no way to test whether the meanings understood in one culture are the same as those found in another culture."[12]

Hiebert does not enlarge on the nature and difficulty of uncritical contextualization, but in reality the application and fruit of this method can be seen in the rise of regional theologies and theologies of liberation in the late 1960s and 70s. These movements were legitimate efforts to construct theology from a particular cultural viewpoint. Liberationists intended to address the conditions and concerns of a particular region or class of people, as E. Nunez has shown,[13] but the methodology employed in attempting to contextualize true Christianity in Latin America in particular, while critical of the concrete historical situation, uncritically used Marxist categories to analyze social inequities and only selectively used Scripture to maintain Liberationist positions. For Hiebert, uncritical contextualization leads to applications and theologies that are untethered to the true intent of Scripture. His answer is a form of *critical contextualization.*

CRITICAL CONTEXTUALIZATION

What Hiebert is looking for in the most appropriate form of contextualization is optimum understanding in a receptor culture of the original intent of Scripture that can be tested outside the subjective understandings of individuals by themselves. He understands that one-to-one correspondence between the text in one language and the text or understanding of a person in another culture is not possible. A translation can never have total correspondence to the original, but he maintains that it can have the correspondence we expect between a good map and a particular geographical area. The map does not have every detail of the referent geography, but it can be accurate in terms of the existence and direction of roads, buildings, and other physical features. It

---

[11] Shaw and Van Engen, *Communicating,* 31–32.
[12] P. G. Hiebert, "The Gospel in Human Contexts: Changing Perceptions of Contextualization" (unpublished manuscript, 2007), 11.
[13] E. A. Nu–ez, *Liberation Theology,* trans. Paul E. Sywulka (Chicago: Moody, 1985), 272–74, 275–90.

can get you where you are going. To do this, the map must have *essential* correspondence to the reality it portrays. This correspondence can be tested. If you follow it, does it get you where you are going? If one person, perhaps a poor map reader, uses the map but fails to arrive, was the map inaccurate? The answer would be to check with other people who use it as well as with those already familiar with the terrain.

Critical contextualization is an application of *critical realism.* In several of his works, but particularly in *Missiological Implications of Epistemological Shifts,*[14] Hiebert uses what he calls critical realism as the bridge between the impossibility of truly grasping ultimate reality through "modern" or verifiable empiricism and the gulf of subjectivity represented by postmodernity. The essence of Hiebert's method is the exploration of any given phenomenon, or Scripture, by a community or multiplicity of people who provide checks on the subjectivity of one another. Community consultation reduces the "investigational bias," the unavoidable tendency of a single researcher to affect the results of his or her work due to the element of subjectivity.

In another work Hiebert differentiates between revelation and theology.[15] Revelation, while delivered to people in particular contexts and times, nevertheless has a singular intent that "does not equate with any of these contexts," but rather, "the Gospel transcends them all."[16] The task of the missionary then becomes that of building a bridge between revelation and a given human culture. Hiebert terms this process "missional theology." *Theology* is a human product; it has no claim to infallibility. It is what humans do in arranging and rendering revealed truth in understandable categories. Revelation has a *magisterial* use while theology has a *ministerial* function. Nevertheless, Evangelical believers hope that the theology they construct corresponds as closely as possible with revealed truth and becomes a dependable guide to discovering and living out the gospel.

By dealing with the fundamental or *ontological reality* of the difference between the gospel and culture, the *phenomenology*

---

[14] See p. 63.
[15] Hiebert, "Gospel in Human Contexts," 15.
[16] Ibid., 16.

of the human contexts of the communicators and the receptors, and the Scriptures themselves, Christian workers can construct a transformative understanding of the gospel that leads to a trans-formational *missiology*. For Hiebert, and for all of us, this is the truly exciting yet mystical part: The people on both sides of the communicational bridge are transformed by the reality of what they are studying! This is what is wonderful about Hie-bert. Even though he was a scientist and strove for objectivity, he could easily grasp that the process and point of contextualiza-tion is transformation. No doubt other mundane concepts have changed the lives of communities—sanitation, clean water, and primary health care—but only the gospel changes hearts and motivations.

Hiebert's approach to critical contextualization has the enor-mous benefit of fully involving the recipient culture in the process of understanding God's Word. In Hiebert's approach, local people and those from outside the community sit down to discuss matters that concern them. They discuss how situations have been handled previously in the community; the outsider may share how things were dealt with in his or her community. Together they search the Scriptures to see how God's Word applies to the current situation, and they come to a conclusion that avoids both paternalism on the part of the missionary and syncretism on the part of the new believers. The process also yields the inestimable value of confi-dence in what the Spirit can do through their own local reflection, while connected to the larger community of God's people in other cultural contexts.

THE FUTURE OF CONTEMPORARY
CONTEXTUALIZATION EFFORTS

Resistant cultures—whether secular, Muslim, Hindu, Bud-dhist, or other traditional faiths—draw the Christian worker into deep dependence on the Holy Spirit and prayer. Resistance also prompts us to use everything else in the contextualization kit bag to be sure we have made ourselves as clear and as free from non-essential baggage as possible. At the beginning of this response, I mentioned the controversy over different levels of contextual-ization (C-1 to C-6) that Hiebert's article calls to mind but does not directly address. Hiebert was certainly aware of the categories and the controversy. But he chose to address two extremes, minimal and radical contextualization, and then he expounded a *process* rather than a *degree* of contextualization that he felt was biblically centered and theoretically sound, namely, critical contextualization.

Lively dialogues about contextualization will likely continue. Most seem clear on the validity and scriptural legitimacy of the first four levels. C-5 and C-6 generate the most controversy, though C-6 is really just an observation that some believers remain secret believers, a phenomenon we may understand without advocating. S. Woods works among Muslim peoples in Asia at the level of C-4, in which Christ-centered communities use insider language and biblically permissible cultural and Islamic forms.[17] Woods believes strongly that the practitioners of C-5 contextualization have gone a step too far toward syncretism. In C-5 contextualization, expatriate Christian workers and Muslim background believers identify themselves as Muslims who follow *Isa Al Mesih* (Jesus the Messiah); continue in mosque exercises and daily prayers; recite the *Shehada* (Islamic confession), often while inserting their own quiet attribute of Jesus as the prophet of Allah rather than Muhammad; pay *Zakat,* a form of tithing; and continue to live in the community. He believes they have, in fact, opened themselves to charges of deceit and encouraged new Muslim Background Believers to remain in a spiritually detrimental environment as far as mosque attendance is concerned.

Like Woods, P. Parshall, who has also worked among Muslims for many years, feels most at ease with C-4. He grants that C-5 advocates are well intentioned, as does Woods, but he asks a series of penetrating questions about the various elements of the C-5 position rather than condemning it outright.[18] His article and J. Massey's article[19] are well worth examination and reflection. Parshall concludes with a concern to avoid judgmental attitudes where fellow workers are exerting every effort to minister in

---

[17] S. Woods, "A Biblical Look at C-5 Muslim Evangelism," *EMQ* 36:2 (April 2003): 188–95.

[18] Parshall, "Lifting the Fatwa," 288–93.

[19] Massey, "Misunderstanding C-5," 296–304.

difficult situations. Where progress has been difficult over a long period, there must be room for experimentation and mistakes. Where there have been great awakenings, there have often been ragged edges that appear heretical to some, what R. Winter once called "the silver linings" of otherwise dark clouds.[20]

Missionaries will continue to wrestle with contextualization issues relating to lifestyles, self-identity, church forms, and Christian personal communication in other cultures. Bible translators will continue to search for the linguistic expressions that best communicate the intention of the original Scripture writers. As they do this, it is remarkable to see the impact that Hiebert has had on their thinking. Whether it is L. Owens (pseudonym) discussing the contextualization of Scripture for ethno-linguistic minorities,[21] or R. Brown pleading for understanding of the Muslim cultural understanding of "Son of God" terminology,[22] both employ Hiebert's use of the "hermeneutical community" that compares local understandings with biblical teaching as the best safeguard against syncretism. And both plead for understanding those who are experimenting in new kinds of contextualization with the attendant risks.

CONCLUSION

It is one thing to advocate a particular approach to gospel communication and another to recognize that understandable oddities exist among genuine movements of God. Rigorous biblical reflection by those who are closest to the situation always yields the best answer, and that is truly what Hiebert has advocated in critical contextualization. Where questions remain, we could do a lot worse than Gamaliel, who rebuked his fellow members of the Sanhedrin in their rush to judge the apostles: "And now, I tell you, stay away from these men and leave them alone. For if this plan or this work is of men, it will be overthrown; but if it is of God, you will not be able to overthrow them. You may even be found fighting against God" (Acts 5:38–39).

---

[20] R. Winter, "Do We Need More Heresies on the Mission Field?" *Mission Frontiers* (September-October 1996): 6.

[21] L. Owens (pseudonym), "Syncretism and Scriptures," *EMQ* 43:1 (January 2007): 74–80.

[22] R. Brown, "Why Muslims Are Repelled by the Term 'Son of God,'" *EMQ* 43:4 (October 2007): 422–29.

BIBLIOGRAPHY

Brown, R. "Why Muslims Are Repelled by the Term 'Son of God.'" *Evangelical Missions Quarterly* 43:4 (October 2007): 422–29.

Emilio, A. N. *Liberation Theology.* Translated by P. E. Sywulka. Chicago: Moody Press, 1985.

Hesselgrave, D. J., and E. Rommen. *Contextualization: Meanings, Methods, and Models.* Grand Rapids: Baker, 1989.

Hiebert, P. G. "The Gospel in Human Contexts: Changing Perceptions of Contextualization." Unpublished manuscript, 2007.

————. *The Missiological Implications of Epistemological Shifts: Affirming Truth in a Modern/Postmodern World.* Harrisburg: Trinity Press International, 1999.

Kierkegaard, S. "Concluding Unscientific Postscript." In *A Kierkegaard Anthology.* Edited by R. Bretall. New York: The Modern Library, Random House, 1946.

Lyotard, F. *The Postmodern Condition: A Report on Knowledge.* Translated by G. Bennington and B. Massouri. Minneapolis: University of Minnesota Press, 1984.

Massey, J. "Misunderstanding C-5: His Ways Are Not Our Orthodoxy." *EMQ* 40:3 (July 2004): 296–307.

Neill, S. *A History of Christian Missions.* Rev. ed. London: Penguin Books, 1986.

Owens, L. (pseudonym) "Syncretism and Scriptures." *EMQ* 43:1 (January 2007): 74–80.

Parshall, P. "Danger! New Directions in Contextualization." *EMQ* 34:4 (October 1998): 404–17.

————. "Lifting the Fatwa." *EMQ* 40:3 (July 2004): 288–95.

Pocock, M., G. Van Rheenen, and D. McConnell. *The Changing Face of World Missions.* Grand Rapids: Baker, 2005.

Richard, H. L. "New Paradigms for Understanding Hinduism and Contextualization." *EMQ* 40:3 (July 2004): 308–20.

Shaw, R. D., and C. Van Engen. *Communicating God's Word in a Complex World.* New York: Rowman and Littlefield Pub., 2003.

Travis, J. "The C-1 to C-6 Spectrum: A Practical Tool for Defining Six Types of 'Christ-Centered Communities' Found in the Muslim Community." *EMQ* 34:4 (October 1998): 407–8.

Winter, R. "Do We Need More Heresies on the Mission Field?" *Mission Frontiers* (September-October 1996): 6.

Woods, S. "A Biblical Look at C-5 Muslim Evangelism." *EMQ* 36:2 (April 2003): 188–95.

CHAPTER 10

Response to Paul G. Hiebert

"The Gospel in Human Contexts: Changing Perceptions of Contextualization"

DARRELL L. WHITEMAN

INTRODUCTION

It is fitting that one of the last pieces Paul Hiebert wrote dealt with the challenge of contextualization, a concept and mission practice to which he devoted much of his life. Hiebert, more than any other anthropologist or missiologist, made a significant contribution to the world of Christian mission through his writings, spanning 40 years, on how the gospel can and must relate to diverse people in their varied cultural contexts. His analytically trained mind (mathematics and anthropology), his immense cross-cultural experience starting from childhood (growing up as a missionary kid in India), and his passion for living out the kingdom of God coalesced to provide Hiebert with an unusually helpful perspective on why and how the gospel must be contextualized.[1]

In this chapter Hiebert gives us a helpful heuristic device to

---

[1] For an assessment of Hiebert's contribution to missiological anthropology, see D. L. Whiteman, "Anthropological Reflections on Contextualizing Theology in a Globalizing World," in *Globalizing Theology: Belief and Practice in an Era of World Christianity,* ed. C. Ott and H. A. Netland (Grand Rapids: Baker Academic, 2006), 52–69. The Fall 2009 issue of *Trinity Journal* (vol. 30 NS, no 2) consists of six articles honoring Paul Hiebert.

catalog various attitudes toward contextualization. A harbinger of this important chapter was a brilliant article[2] in which he explained that different eras of mission, anthropology, and theology corresponded with different epistemological assumptions that missionaries, anthropologists, and theologians held at the time.[3] The following is a brief review of his model.

NONCONTEXTUALIZATION

In the colonial era, missionaries tended to equate Christianity with Western culture, leading to a theory of mission that aimed first to civilize and then to Christianize "the natives." Proponents of this theory argued that "natives" were incapable of understanding the complexities of Christian doctrine or living under the ethical codes of Christianity until they were first "civilized." Anthropologists during this same colonial era assumed they were in search of objective truth and attempted to apply evolutionary models to all areas of life and culture. Theologians at the time attempted to mold their discipline into a science, believing their European and North American theology had universal validity for all cultural contexts. In fact, theology at this time was often called the "queen of the sciences." The reigning epistemology of the day was positivism or naïve realism.[4] Scientific knowledge was thought to be an accurate picture of reality. Theologians did not realize their theologies were influenced by their cultural contexts and social locations, and they believed their theology was not culture bound but applied to all people in all cultures at all times. This was the era of noncontextualization. There was little interest in understanding the need for contextualizing the gospel.

We are now vividly aware of the postcolonial reaction to this particular ethnocentric worldview of missionaries, anthropologists, and theologians. One of those reactions was the realization that along with Western imperialism had come cultural arrogance

---

[2] P. G. Hiebert, "Beyond Anticolonialism to Globalism," *Missiology* 19.3 (July 1991): 263–82.

[3] For a comprehensive table that summarizes how missions, anthropology, theology, and epistemology were expressed in the colonial, anticolonial, and present-day global eras, see Hiebert (ibid., 279) or Hiebert (*Anthropological Reflections on Missiological Issues* [Grand Rapids: Baker, 1994], 72).

[4] For a thorough and illustrative discussion of the epistemology of naive realism in both science and religion, see I. Barbour, *Myths, Models, and Paradigms: A Comparative Study in Science and Religion* (New York: Harper & Row, 1974). The other epistemologies of instrumentalism and critical realism discussed below are also covered in Barbour.

and oppression of others, whether in the name of spreading democracy or promoting Christianity. During the colonial era, Westerners often dismissed the perspective or the experience of the "native" as irrelevant at best or at worst as a stumbling block or impediment to progress.

UNCRITICAL CONTEXTUALIZATION

In reaction against this colonial attitude, the era of anticolonialism began in the 1960s, and "contextualization" became more important. The word first appeared in the literature in 1972.[5] However, contextualization efforts were occasionally applied uncritically. In an effort to be relevant and contextual, the prophetic offense of the gospel was sometimes ignored. The good and positive aspects found in other cultures were emphasized, while the evil or dysfunctional elements were ignored. Having lost confidence in any universal claims of theology, local and contextualized theologies proliferated—sometimes in isolation from or in disregard of the wider universal church.

In anthropology, social scientists were so disillusioned with grand nineteenth-century explanatory schemes such as social and cultural evolution that cultural particularities became the focus of ethnographic research, and the doctrine of cultural relativism was hammered out on the anvil of cultural diversity. Anthropology became far more reflexive and much less confident in its ability to understand cultural diversity through any models or theories purporting to have universal validity.

The reigning epistemology of this anticolonialism period was instrumentalism, which argued that since truth was impossible to know, we should judge the value of a particular model or theory solely on the basis of whether it was useful. The epistemology of instrumentalism is still alive and well and is at home in much of postmodernism today. For example, the word *whatever* spoken with an attitude captures this notion. Hiebert says, "The anti-colonial reaction was a necessary corrective. It called into question

---

[5] For a discussion of the term and its brief history see D. L. Whiteman, "Contextualization: The Theory, the Gap, the Challenge," *International Bulletin of Missionary Research* 21.1 (1997): 2–7.

Western cultural arrogance, and it forced Western Christians to differentiate between the gospel and their culture."[6]

Though many people in mission understand the value of this anticolonial corrective, it is interesting to note, but sad to observe, that thousands of cross-cultural witnesses remain who are still steeped in the worldview and epistemology of the colonial period and who have not made the important paradigm shift to postcolonial mission. They are neocolonial in their actions and perspectives and are in need of a truly cross-cultural conversion, much the same as the apostle Peter underwent in his experience of leading Cornelius to faith in Christ after God showed him that Gentiles were just as good and acceptable as Jews (Acts 10). As helpful as the anticolonialism reaction was as a necessary corrective, it left us with huge missiological problems and gives us no theory or foundation from which to work and to relate intimately with people who are culturally different from ourselves.

CRITICAL CONTEXTUALIZATION

Today is the era of globalization and increased connectedness, or as Thomas Friedman puts it, "The world is flat."[7] More than ever we recognize the need for contextualization in mission but not the uncritical approach that sometimes occurred in the reaction against the colonial era. This is where Hiebert's development of the concept of critical contextualization is so appropriate and timely for the present era of Christian mission. His discussion of critical contextualization in this book is some of his best writing on the topic. Readers who are unaware of the original article on "Critical Contextualization" should consult it to discover the three steps or stages Hiebert suggests that Christian communities go through in order to determine how the gospel should relate to them in their specific cultural context, what elements of their culture are counter to the gospel, what elements are compatible with it, and what new forms need to be created to express the meaning of living in obedience to the lordship of Christ in their particular culture.[8] Hiebert's recommended three steps are as follows:

---

[6] Hiebert, "Beyond Anticolonialism," 271.

[7] T. L. Friedman, *The World Is Flat: A Brief History of the 21st Century* (New York: Picador, 2007).

[8] See Hiebert, "Critical Contextualization," *Missiology* 12.3 (1984): 287–96; "Critical Con-

The first step is for the missionary and church leaders working together to lead the congregation in uncritically studying the local culture, gathering and analyzing the traditional beliefs and practices. The goal here is to understand the traditional ways, not to criticize or judge them.

The second step is for the missionary or pastor to lead the church in studying the Scriptures related to the problem area under discussion. What does the Bible say to their particular situation? It is important to distinguish the meaning of the biblical teaching in its original context from the forms used to express that biblical principle.

The third step is for the people corporately to evaluate their own past customs and beliefs in the light of their new biblical understanding. As the Holy Spirit guides them, some of their customs and beliefs will change because they are incompatible with their understanding of what it means to be a follower of Jesus. Much of their culture, however, will remain the same.

In his chapter for this book, Hiebert's fourth view of contextualization, which he calls "Divine Revelation Given in Human Contexts," he discusses new territory for him while drawing on familiar concepts, reminding us that the gospel is God given, not humanly created, and that this divine revelation occurred in specific contexts in the Old and New Testaments. Discerning the difference between biblical principles and their cultural expressions—in cultural contexts that existed 2,000 to 4,000 years ago—is not always an easy task, nor is the biblical principle being expressed always self-evident. For example, Paul argues that it is a disgrace for men to have long hair, and women should not cut their hair (1 Cor 11:14–15). Is that just a recommended cultural practice for that time and place, or is it a universal biblical principle intended for all people at all times? For most North American Christians that's an easy call, and we conclude that this teaching was just cultural, implying that it may not be a transcendent value. But of course it *is* important because of the underlying meaning to which the form (or length) of hair points.

As the center of gravity for the Christian faith shifts from

textualization," *International Bulletin of Missionary Research* 11.3 (1987): 104–12; and "Critical Contextualization," in *Anthropological Reflections*, 75–92.

North America and Europe to Africa, Latin America, and parts of Asia,[9] we should expect to find an increase in contextualized expressions of Christianity. The effects of colonialism are still felt in many parts of the world, but as the decolonization of people's minds progresses, we will see more and more cultures taking ownership of Christianity, practicing and expressing it in ways that are appropriate for their time and place but that may appear quite different from our own forms.

The gospel relates to culture in three ways. The gospel affirms most of culture, it critiques and confronts some of culture, and it transforms all of culture. Let's look at each of these areas. First, the gospel affirms and confirms *most* of culture. For example, we don't have to learn a new language or change our eating habits (unless we are cannibals) when we become followers of Christ. A large part of a culture in every society is usable as people within that culture begin to follow Jesus.

Second, the gospel also critiques or confronts *some* of culture. Because human beings are fallen and sinful people, expressions of this in their culture show that examples of structural evil abound in every society. These aspects of their culture are confronted by the claims of the gospel. For example, although it took us a long time, we now recognize that slavery in any culture is inconsistent with the gospel and therefore must be repudiated. In other words, the gospel is always offensive in some ways. Unfortunately, we too often offend people for the wrong (cultural) reasons so that they never hear the gospel, which offends people by confronting their sins.

Third, the gospel transforms *all* of culture. Cultural forms that were once used for evil purposes can be employed in the service of the kingdom of God. For example, in a Methodist church on the island of Bau in Fiji stands an ancient baptismal font carved out of stone. But it hasn't always been used for baptisms. It was once used to catch the dripping blood when Fijian cannibals decapitated an enemy warrior. This artifact, which was once used for evil purposes, has now been transformed because Fijian Christians today recognize that the blood of Jesus has been shed for their sake and

---

[9] P. Jenkins, *The Next Christendom: The Coming of Global Christianity* (New York: Oxford University Press, 2002).

now gives them eternal life (John 6:56). This new understanding brought new life to them as individuals, but it also has transformed much of their culture.

Today we are in an era of increasing need for contextualization while at the same time great resistance to it still exists. This resistance does not occur only among Western missionaries but is also found in many churches that are the products of Christian mission. They are often autonomous churches, but they are seldom indigenous. This means that they may have local indigenous leaders, and they may even use some aspects of local art, architecture, and music, but they are still perceived to be very foreign in the culture in which they are planted.

RADICAL BIBLICAL CONTEXTUALIZATION

At the other end of the spectrum, some people groups are expressing their faith in what could be considered "radical biblical contextualization." There is nothing foreign about it. John Travis (1998) gave us a helpful pedagogical tool with his C1-to-C6 spectrum,[10] which is a tool for defining six types of Christ-centered communities in Muslim contexts, moving from least contextualized (C1) to most contextualized (C5) but also including communities of secret believers (C6). We are discovering that the C1-to-C6 scale is useful to understanding the form of Christ-centered communities within other religious traditions as well. Those Christ-centered communities that fit within the C5 category are comprised of people who remain legally and socially within their religious tradition, but they are nevertheless true followers of Jesus, confessing Jesus Christ as their Lord and Savior, and experiencing new life in him. In other words, they do not abandon their birth identity in order to affirm their second birth identity as born-again believers in Jesus. On the surface they may not be distinguishable from others in their religious tradition except for the fruit of the Spirit that emanates from their lives. The mission world seems to be deeply divided over this C5 form of radical biblical contextualization, called "Insider Movements."

In a recent article entitled "Muslim Followers of Jesus?"

---

[10] J. Travis, "The C1 to C6 Spectrum: A Practical Tool for Defining Six Types of 'Christ-centered Communities' ("C") Found in the Muslim Context," *EMQ* 34.4 (1998): 407–8.

Joseph Cumming[11] discusses the controversy between missiologists who affirm C5 as a legitimate form of radical biblical contextualization and those who believe this expression goes too far and can slip into syncretism. Cumming acknowledges the legitimacy of C5 contextualization while not assuming that it is appropriate for all situations of Muslims coming to faith in Christ.

How can we understand this conflict? Why wouldn't everyone be happy to see Muslims or Hindus or Buddhists come to faith in Christ? Sadly, some of the greatest opposition to Muslim Insider Movements has come from Christian converts out of Islam. I remember vividly a meeting my colleagues and I had with a group of Muslim followers of Jesus in a South Asian country. After spending a week with leaders of this movement, one of them asked us, "Do you accept us as brothers in Christ?" We responded, "Of course we do. Why wouldn't we?" With tears rolling down his cheeks he said that most of the traditional Christians in his country would not accept them as Muslim followers of Jesus and in fact had severely persecuted them and the movement. We also admitted that there were Christians in our country who would be reluctant to accept them as brothers in Christ.

Is there a parallel between Jews who become "Jews for Jesus" as messianic Jews and Muslims who become followers of Isa (Arabic for Jesus)? One's answer to that question is influenced by one's understanding of socioreligious identity.[12] The debate at the Jerusalem Council recorded in Acts 15 was whether Gentiles had to become culturally Jews before they could become followers of Jesus. Fortunately for those of us who are Gentiles, the decision was that we did not first have to become Jews in order to become Jesus' followers. Unfortunately, we have not been as generous in extending this biblical principle to others who are culturally and religiously different from ourselves.[13]

---

[11] J. Cumming, "Muslim Followers of Jesus?" *Christianity Today* (December 2009): 32–35.

[12] See Rebecca Lewis's helpful article that discusses how Muslim followers of Jesus retain their socioreligious identity but gain a new spiritual identity. "Insider Movements: Retaining Identity and Preserving Community," in *Perspectives on the World Christian Movement,* 4th ed., ed. R. Winter and S. Hawthorne (Pasadena, CA: William Carey Library, 2009), 673–75.

[13] See Dean Flemming's helpful discussion of the Jerusalem Council debate and its implications for mission today. "Contextualization in a Wesleyan Spirit: A Case Study of Acts 15," in *World Mission in the Wesleyan Spirit,* ed. D. L. Whiteman and G. H. Anderson (Franklin, TN: Providence House, 2009), 16–27.

Carl Medearis, in one of the most helpful books in explaining insider movements, notes that

> Truth be told, there is a growing number of Muslims around the world who maintain their cultural identity as "Muslim" but choose to align themselves with the spiritual and moral teachings of Jesus, becoming *his* disciples while becoming what "Muslim" truly means: submitted to God.[14]

One often hears the question, Can one remain a Muslim or a Hindu after becoming a Christian? I think that question needs to be reframed. Perhaps a more accurate way to pose the question is to ask, "Can someone enter the kingdom of God without becoming a follower of Jesus?" To maintain fidelity to the Bible, the answer is unequivocally "No!" (Acts 4:12; John 14:6). But if we ask, "Can someone enter the kingdom of God without becoming a Christian?" that's a more complicated question and deserves a more nuanced response. When the term *Christian* was first used in Antioch (Acts 11:26), it simply meant a Gentile follower of Jesus and was often used pejoratively to describe those who were followers of Jesus. Today, however, 2,000 years later, the term *Christian* has become encumbered with many extrabiblical trappings that are now part and parcel of the Christian religion with all of its religious traditions. Therefore, the term *Christian* today is no longer synonymous with simply following Jesus. Tragically, hundreds of millions of people call themselves "Christian" but have never followed Jesus because it never occurred to them that being a Christian meant following Jesus. If we reframe the question to ask if a person can enter the kingdom of God without joining the Christian religion, then I think we are asking the right question. And here the Bible can help us think through the answer. The lessons from the decision of the Jerusalem Council in Acts 15 that Gentiles did not have to become Jews to follow Jesus, and Jesus' own ministry among Gentiles, point to the fact that one can enter the kingdom of God and confess Jesus as Lord and Savior without necessarily changing one's religion. At first blush this may sound scandalous to us conservative Evangelical Christians. Nevertheless, many Muslims today are attracted to Jesus but turned off

---

[14] C. Medearis, *Muslims, Christians, and Jesus: Gaining Understanding and Building Relationships* (Minneapolis: Bethany House, 2008).

to Christianity, which for them conjures up negative images of the Crusades, colonialism, a foreign religion, and the "Christian" West where we eat pork, drink alcohol, and watch R-rated movies. No wonder they don't want to be identified as "Christians," but they certainly want to follow Jesus and make Him Lord of their lives.[15]

The question is frequently asked, "Where should we draw the line before contextualization becomes syncretism?" Because many of the debates seem to circle around where to draw the line, some are comfortable with a C5 expression of Christianity, but others are uncomfortable with going that far in contextualizing the gospel. As long as we argue over where to draw the line, we will never get far in understanding what God is doing in the world, encouraging people to know and understand Jesus in a wide variety of religious and cultural contexts.

If the debate over where to draw the line before contextualization erodes into syncretism is an unhelpful approach, is there a better way? Hiebert's concept of "critical contextualization" gives us a useful procedure for determining how to distinguish appropriate contextualization from inappropriate syncretism. I want to suggest that perhaps a more fruitful approach would be to look at the underlying meanings that are expressed through contextualized forms. We will find much more common agreement if we focus on the Christian *meanings* being expressed in different *forms*. However, when we focus on the diversity of forms instead of the underlying meanings, it will cause great debates in the Christian community. The global church cannot even agree on the "correct" form of baptism or what elements should be used for the Lord's Supper. Perhaps we would find much more consensus if we focused on the underlying meanings of both ordinances.

Radical biblical contextualization such as we see in C5 expressions of Jesus movements within Islam creates much debate and sometimes dissension because the *forms* used by these Muslim followers of Jesus appear so unfamiliar to us. For example, if we see a Muslim follower of Jesus (Isa in Arabic) praying to Allah[16]

---

[15] See Frank Decker's discussion of this issue in "When 'Christian' Does Not Translate," *Mission Frontiers* 27.5 (September-October 2005): 8.

[16] As Christians we may have an initial negative reaction to the thought of a follower of Jesus

five times a day with forehead touching the ground, it will be hard for us to believe that he or she is praying to Jesus because the form of prayer looks so Islamic and so different to us in the Christian tradition. However, the form of the prayer is not as important as the meaning it expresses. It is the *meaning* of following Jesus that must be maintained to have an expression of vital Christianity. In fact, when the "Christian" *forms* continue but the underlying meanings are lost, the result is that "they will hold to the outward form of our religion, but reject its real power" (2 Tim 3:5 GNB). When this happens, we have classic nominal Christianity. Tragically, we find this throughout the world.

I am convinced that there are no sacred forms, only sacred meanings. This does not mean that forms are not important. They are important, but they are important precisely because of what they point to, that is, the underlying meanings. Some forms are undoubtedly incapable of carrying Christian meanings, but that decision must be made by local believers who understand their culture and who, under the guidance of the Holy Spirit, decide which forms are redeemable and which ones are not. While growing up in a conservative Evangelical church in the 1960s, I was taught that the twang of a guitar and the beat of drums in the church were not forms that could be used to worship God. They were pagan. Today that same church has a praise band, complete with noisy guitars and banging drums, all making music in praise to our Lord. What happened? Did the church go liberal? No, not at all! The people in that church came to realize over time that these musical instruments could be used in acts of meaningful worship to Almighty God.

I have developed the following grid to help us sort through the distinction between forms and the meanings they convey. If we can separate form and meaning in our thinking, it makes it much easier to understand radical biblical contextualization and movements of God's Spirit like the Insider Movements among Muslims. The horizontal axis of FORM at the bottom of the diagram moves from Western on the left to Indigenous on the right. The vertical axis of MEANING to the far left of the diagram moves from Christian

---

praying to Allah, but the name Allah is not a Muslim word but rather an Arabic word for God that was used by Arabic-speaking Christians before Muhammad was born.

on the top to Pagan on the bottom. When you combine these two axes, you get four possible outcomes. In our cross-cultural mission efforts we need to understand the important difference between Indigenous Christianity (which we want to promote) and Syncretism (which we want to avoid).

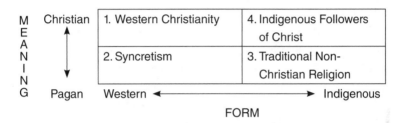

This combination of the two axes, Form and Meaning, gives us four different outcomes as explained below.

Quadrant 1. When Western forms are combined with Christian meanings in other parts of the world, we have nonindigenous (typically Western) Christianity, which is frequently perceived to be foreign in that context. This was one of the consequences of mission in the age of colonialism, and we find expressions of Western Christianity all over the world today.[17] In other cultures this form of Christianity is more prone to becoming syncretistic or nominal over time because of the difficulty people in that culture have in adapting imported foreign Western forms and applying this imported faith to the real issues of their lives.

Quadrant 2. When Western forms are combined with pagan or non-Christian meanings, we have syncretism, which is the combination of Christian and non-Christian beliefs and practices. The resultant form is distinct from both Christianity and the pagan religion. It is neither Christianity nor traditional religion. It is something entirely new and different, as I have explained elsewhere:

> Religious syncretism is essentially a response to the problem of
> meaning. In the interaction between Christianity and animism,

---

[17] In this first quadrant I have used the term "Western Christianity" because historically the missionary movement has been primarily from the West. Perhaps today, however, it is more accurate to refer to this quadrant as nonindigenous forms of Christianity which we find all over the world. For example, we often find Korean missionaries duplicating a Korean style of Christianity wherever they go, which is no more relevant to the people among whom they live than is a typically Western form of Christianity.

if the newly introduced Christian forms are given pagan meaning, then syncretism results—the new belief system is neither
Christianity nor is it traditional primal religion; it is a mixing of
both, and thus the product is qualitatively new.[18]

Quadrant 3. When indigenous forms are combined with pagan
meanings, we have no change at all and so the traditional non-
Christian religion continues.

But how does one encounter traditional religion with the
claims of Christ? Our standard approach has often been to introduce Western Christianity, perhaps because we felt confident that
if potential converts adopted our forms they would also follow our
Christian meaning. Yet this approach is more likely to lead to syncretism because syncretism comes from striving after meaning.
So, if the introduced foreign forms do not make sense to converts,
it will be easy to revert to traditional non-Christian meanings in
order to fill the void left by foreign forms.

Quadrant 4. When indigenous forms are combined with
Christian meanings, we have indigenous followers of Christ, that
is, contextualized Christianity that is appropriate to the context.[19]
Christ-centered communities that fit the C5 category are good examples of those found in this quadrant, where the forms are appropriate to the context, but they are used to communicate Christian
meanings. Far from being the slippery slope that so many neocolonial missionaries fear will lead to syncretism, contextualized
Christianity is the best hedge against syncretism.

I believe the answer to the debate over where to draw the line
in contextualization is better understood if we ask a different question: "Do the forms that are appropriate to the culture of the converts adequately convey biblical meanings?" Forms are easy to
see; meanings are hard to detect. But we must trust the Holy Spirit
to lead followers of Christ into discerning what forms are usable
in a particular cultural context for the sake of the gospel.

Much of Hiebert's writing has been aimed to help us find a
way through the sometimes complex world of contextualization
so that the universal meanings of the gospel can be understood and

---

[18] D. L. Whiteman, *Melanesians and Missionaries: An Ethnohistorical Study of Social and Religious Change in the Southwest Pacific* (Pasadena: William Carey Library, 1983), 414.
[19] See C. H. Kraft, ed. *Appropriate Christianity* (Pasadena: William Carey Library, 2005).

lived out in contexts appropriate to the culture in which followers of Jesus live. To move into this missiological arena of radical biblical contextualization will require that we relinquish our need for certainty in exchange for our quest for understanding. May God give us the wisdom and courage to do so.

BIBLIOGRAPHY

Barbour, I. *Myths, Models, and Paradigms: A Comparative Study in Science and Religion.* New York: Harper & Row, 1974.

Cumming, Joseph. "Muslim Followers of Jesus?" *Christianity Today* (December 2009): 32–35.

Decker, Frank. "When 'Christian' Does Not Translate." *Mission Frontiers* 27.5 (September-October 2005): 8.

Flemming, Dean. "Contextualization in a Wesleyan Spirit: A Case Study of Acts 15." Pages 16–27 in *World Mission in the Wesleyan Spirit.* Edited by Darrell L. Whiteman and Gerald H. Anderson. Franklin, TN: Providence House Publishers, 2009.

Friedman, T. L. *The World Is Flat: A Brief History of the 21st Century.* New York: Picador, 2007.

Hiebert, P. G. *Anthropological Reflections on Missiological Issues.* Grand Rapids: Baker, 1994.

———. "Beyond Anti-Colonialism to Globalism." *Missiology* 19.3 (July 1991): 263–81.

———. "Critical Contextualization." *International Bulletin of Missionary Research* 11. 3 (1987): 104–12.

——— "Critical Contextualization." *Missiology* 12.3 (1984): 287–96.

Jenkins, P. *The Next Christendom: The Coming of Global Christianity.* New York: Oxford University Press, 2002.

Kraft, C. H., ed. *Appropriate Christianity.* Pasadena: William Carey Library, 2005.

Lewis, Rebecca. "Insider Movements: Retaining Identity and Preserving Community." Pages 673–75 in *Perspectives on the World Christian Movement.* 4th edition. Edited by Ralph Winter and Steven Hawthorne. Pasadena, CA: William Carey Library, 2009.

Medearis, Carl. *Muslims, Christians and Jesus: Gaining Understanding and Building Relationships.* Minneapolis: Bethany House, 2008.

Travis, J. "The C1 to C6 Spectrum: A Practical Tool for Defining Six Types of 'Christ-centered Communities' ("C") Found in the Muslim Context." *EMQ* 34.4 (1998): 407–8.

Trinity Journal, "Dr. Paul G. Hiebert in Memoriam." Volume 30 NS, no. 2 (Fall 2009). Deerfield, IL: Trinity Evangelical Divinity School.

Whiteman, D. L. "Anthropological Reflections on Contextualizing Theology in a Globalizing World." Pages 52–69 in *Globalizing Theology: Belief and Practice in an Era of World Christianity.* Edited by C. Ott and H. A. Netland. Grand Rapids: Baker Academic, 2006.

———. "Contextualization: The Theory, the Gap, the Challenge." *International Bulletin of Missionary Research* 27.1 (January 1997): 2–7.

———. *Melanesians and Missionaries: An Ethnohistorical Study of Social and Religious Change in the Southwest Pacific.* Pasadena: William Carey Library, 1983.

Whiteman, Darrell L., and Gerald H. Anderson, eds. *World Mission in the Wesleyan Spirit.* Franklin, TN: Providence House Publishers, 2009.

Winter, Ralph D., and Steven C. Hawthorne, eds. *Perspectives on the World Christian Movement.* Pasadena, CA: William Carey Library, 2009.

CHAPTER 11

A Response to Paul G. Hiebert

"The Gospel in Human Contexts: Changing Perceptions of Contextualization" and to Darrell Whiteman and Michael Pocock

NORMAN L. GEISLER

INTRODUCTION

I count it an honor to respond to Paul Hiebert. The article I was asked to read was one of the last written by him. As one who was trained in theology and philosophy, I shall interact with his essay in light of those academic disciplines, rather than cultural anthropology. My comments on the article are divided into two parts. First, I shall set forth points of agreement. Next, points of disagreement will be stated and discussed. Also, I will interact with two other responders—Michael Pocock and Darrell Whiteman as they interacted with Paul Hiebert.

POINTS OF AGREEMENT WITH HIEBERT

Hiebert's article contains many valuable insights. I begin my response with my agreements with Hiebert on the missionary enterprise.

The Nature and Role of Scripture

Hiebert correctly perceives the Bible is divine revelation,

not simply humanly constructed beliefs. He says the Bible is the conveyor of God-given revelation.[1] Hence, Hiebert correctly understands that the Bible should be taken seriously as the rule of faith and life. He also believes that we must constantly remind ourselves that biblical revelation is the standard against which our beliefs and practices must be measured. Specifically, it should be our basis for belief about polygamy, divorce, leadership, use of money, war, and other human affairs.

However, Hiebert reminds us, as discussed below under Interpretation, that the gospel was revealed in the historical and sociocultural contexts of the Old and New Testaments, and those *contexts* are not normative for Christianity around the world. Only the *content* of the revelation (not its cultural context) is normative for the Christian faith. In brief, the Bible has both divine and human dimensions. It is necessary to understand both if we are to be effective in cross-cultural communication of God's revelation to mankind.

The Interpretation of Scripture

Hiebert rightly distinguishes God-given revelation from a human understanding of that revelation. He stresses that the two should never be equated because our interpretations are shaped by our social, cultural, psychological, and historical contexts. Thus, these contexts need to be checked by others from other cultures, which can help us see our biases. Of course, we should attempt to overcome this limitation by a metacultural perspective (see below). Objectivity is possible (see below) and should be the goal of the interpreter, but we should ever be on guard against subjective distortions of objective truth.

The Nature and Role of Language

Hiebert wisely rejects positivism in its belief that scientific knowledge is an accurate and true photograph of the world that corresponds one-to-one with reality. On the other hand, he warns against postmodern instrumentalism (also known as pragmatism) in viewing knowledge systems as the creation of human minds.

---

[1] The content of this section is a paraphrase or summary of statements in Hiebert's essay, often using his very words.

On the one hand, he correctly perceives the limitations of human language in conveying truth. Nonetheless, he believes that language can communicate objective truth. But when it does, the result is more like a road map than a photograph.

The Translation of Scripture

Hiebert is right when he affirms that in Bible translation one cannot simply find the corresponding words in another language, adjust the grammar, and expect the people to understand the message accurately. Also, he points out that the dynamic equivalence, receptor-oriented Bible translations are misdirected. One should have a more Peircian[2] perspective that rejects Saussure[3] and introduces a view of signs in which a sign signifies some reality (the significatum).

The Role of Culture

As to the important role of culture in missions, Hiebert correctly understands that it needs to be more than monocultural, for by its very nature missions is multicultural. Thus, the missionary should not make new Christians conform to the cultural norms introduced by the missionary. Missionaries should not see themselves as "modern" and others as "primitive" and "backward." To become Christian and civilized, people need not become like us. No culture is absolute or privileged. We are all relativized by the gospel. From this principle it follows that the gospel must not be equated with any particular human context. Not only is this true with regard to Western Christianity but also with the Scriptures.

What is more, Hiebert believes that the heart of the gospel must be expressed in forms that are understood by the people without making it captive to the contexts. For cultures are both good and evil, not simply a neutral vehicle for understanding the world. The good should be accepted and used as the vehicle to communicate the gospel, and the evil should be rejected.

The Objective Nature of Meaning

According to Hiebert, and we concur, feelings and morals,

---

[2] This is named after C. S. Peirce (1839–1914) who coined the word *pragmatism*, a view made into a philosophy by W. James (1842–1910).

[3] F. Saussure (1857–1913) is held by many to be the father of modern linguistics.

as valuable as they are, should be eliminated from the rational process because they introduce subjectivity. Further, he holds that Saussure's conventionalism was wrong in affirming that meaning is culturally relative. He also believes that we must not measure communication by what is understood by the listener but by what is meant by the author. Our mental constructs are not purely subjective. They have a subjective dimension, but they also reflect the order in reality itself. Signs must have external, objective reference points, or else there is no way to test whether the meanings understood in one culture are the same as those in another culture. In this way, Hiebert attempts to overcome the linguistical relativism that has invaded much of Bible translation theory via E. Nida and others.

The Universality of Truth

Hiebert is to be commended for noting that the uncritical contextualization of the gospel in Western context has largely lost its prophetic voice and does not lead to the most vital, biblical churches. Thus, on the global scale, this calls for global theologies. Local churches have the right to apply the gospel in their contexts, but they also have a responsibility to join the larger church community around the world to seek to overcome the limited perspectives each brings and the biases each has that might distort the gospel. Proper contextualization seeks to formulate and communicate universal cognitive truth along with love and holiness.

The Need for a Metamodel Perspective

Hiebert rightly believes that the gospel is transcultural. Thus, the church without the gospel ceases to be the church. He believes we need to develop "metacultural grids" that enable us to compare, evaluate, and translate between different worlds. This is a check against both syncretism and relativism. Without it we cannot overcome cultural relativism in our interpretation of Scripture and its recontextualization in other cultures.

The Need for Realistic Metaphysics[4]

Hiebert contends that there are mental constructs that are not

---

[4] *Metaphysics* means literally "beyond the physical" and is the study of reality. It is also called *ontology*, "the study of being."

purely subjective (as stated above under Objectivity). They have a subjective dimension but are not purely human constructs; they reflect the order in reality itself. Thus, he sees the need for "a critical realist epistemology" that enables us to engage in proper hermeneutics, Bible translation, and the missionary enterprise itself.

The Nature of the Mission Enterprise

Hiebert views the gospel as having three dimensions. The cognitive dimension is about truth. The affective dimension is about beauty and love. The moral dimension is about holiness and justice. This will guide us in understanding the transformative relationship of the gospel to human social and cultural contexts. It is not simply a message to be affirmed as true but a call to follow Christ throughout life in radical discipleship. Knowledge of the gospel is not simply informational; it is also transformational in every area of life. The gospel makes us responsible to share its message of salvation and transformation with all people; to care for the poor, oppressed, and sick; and to bring the good news to the lost. Thus, we cannot measure communication by the number of sermons preached, hours of radio broadcast, and quantity of tracts and Bibles distributed. This can be done only by lives and communities that are transformed.

POINTS OF DISAGREEMENT WITH HIEBERT

As valuable as Hiebert's many insights are, there are some lurking and serious dangers in his views to consider. Space only permits mentioning them with little elaboration. For a more in-depth discussion of most of them, see the "Prolegomena" section in my *Systematic Theology* (vol. 1).[5] The appropriate chapters will be footnoted as the discussion unfolds.

Scripture

While Hiebert believes that the Bible contains revelation from God that should be taken seriously as the rule of faith and life, he fails to note that the Bible is an infallible and inerrant written revelation from God. This is absolutely crucial to the whole mission enterprise. In short, he does not affirm that the Bible is

---

[5] See N. L. Geisler, *Systematic Theology,* vol. 1 (Grand Rapids: Baker, 2002), part 1: "Prolegomena."

the written Word of God. And since God cannot err, then neither can His Word. The Lausanne "Statement of Faith" declares: "We affirm the *divine inspiration*, truthfulness and authority of both Old and New Testament Scriptures in their entirety as *the only written word of God, without error in all that it affirms, and the only infallible rule of faith and practice*."[6] All our words about objective meaning and truth are in vain unless there is a written and infallible Word of God that conveys them. Either the Bible is the infallible Word of God to man (see Matt 5:17–18; John 10:34–35), or it is the fallible words of man about God. Only the former is sufficient for the unique claims of Christianity that are the basis of the Christian mission.

The meaning of the infallibility and inerrancy of Scripture has been spelled out in the "Chicago Statement" (1978) and has been adopted by the largest group of Evangelical scholars in the world, The Evangelical Theological Society. This should be explicitly adopted by any missionary endeavor that calls itself Evangelical.

Meaning

Nowhere does Hiebert spell out just how one can avoid total skepticism in his knowledge of the God whose Word we proclaim to the nations. He does not allow that our mental constructs are totally different from reality (equivocal) or that they are totally the same (univocal), but he does not reveal an understanding that they must, therefore, be analogical—the only alternative left. For either our meaning construct is totally the same as reality (univocal), totally different (equivocal), or they are partly the same and partly different (analogous). A realistic doctrine of analogy[7] is absolutely essential to both objective meaning and objective truth. It is based in the doctrine of man's creation in God's image (Gen 1:27).

Philosophically stated, the effect must resemble (as well as differ from) the Cause. Creation must resemble God since He cannot give what He does not have to give. Being communicates being. But it must also differ because an Infinite Being (God) cannot make another Infinite Being. An uncaused Cause cannot make another uncaused Cause. Hence, only finite beings can be brought

---

[6] See "The Lausanne Covenant," Article 2 on "The Authority and Power of the Bible" (emphasis added).

[7] See Geisler, *Systematic Theology*, vol. 1, chap. 9.

into being. So the creation resembles the Creator in its being (its actuality), but it differs in its finitude (its potentiality). Thus, the Creator/creation relation is the basis for the doctrine of analogy and is also the bridge to similarity between God's Word and the human words in and about Scripture that we employ in recontextualizing it in other cultures.

Truth

Hiebert rightly affirms that there is objectivity in truth, but he does not define or defend either. Truth is correspondence with reality. This position is defendable since it is literally undeniable since one's denial must correspond to reality to be effective. While he appears to believe in some sort of transcendent dimension to the knowing process, he does not affirm that this is possible without a foundationalist view of first principles of knowledge.[8] Indeed, he seems to believe that we can somehow develop or construct this ourselves as a metamodel out of micromodels. But the objective cannot be built out of the relative.

There can be no real knowledge without self-evident and undeniable first principles of knowledge on which it is based. Here are some examples: (1) the law of noncontradiction (A is not non-A); (2) the law of identity (A is A); and (3) the law of excluded middle (either A or Non-A). Without such principles there is no basis for knowledge or any truth claim. None of these principles can be denied without being employed in the denial. Hence, they are literally undeniable.

What is more, his illustration of the incarnation of Christ is problematic. If in the incarnation we have only conditional (relative) and local (not universal) truth, then we are reduced to the liberal accommodation view of the incarnation wherein God condescends not only to human limitations but also to human error and sin. In this sense Christ's incarnation would not be universal truth; neither would what He spoke be absolute truth, for it too would be relativistically conditioned by His human nature. A better alternative would be to affirm that there was no accommodation to error in the incarnation but only an adaptation to finitude. Likewise,

---

[8] See ibid., chap. 5.

what Jesus spoke would all be true—absolutely true—but it would not be all the truth (see John 21:25).

A statement in Hiebert's essay is troubling in this regard. He rejects the approach that "other theologies and religions are false and must be attacked." But if Christianity is true and by the law of noncontradiction the opposite of true is false, then why should one not oppose what is false and is thereby opposed to the truth. Pluralism is the only alternative to this, and it is self-defeating since it claims that pluralism is true and everything opposed to it is false—which is contrary to its view that opposites can both be true. If Hiebert means only that we should speak the truth in love to those who hold false views, then who would object? But truth is truth, even when not spoken in love, and error is error, even when it is spoken in love.

Metaphysics

A realistic epistemology goes hand in hand with a realistic metaphysics. In other words, there is a real world, and it can be known. Hiebert calls his view "critical realism" but does not spell out precisely what this means. If it means, as it usually does in philosophical circles, post-Kantian realism, then it is misdirected since I. Kant's (1724–1804)[9] system has been exposed as self-defeating.[10] For Kant held that we know we cannot know reality. But how can one really know (i.e., know about reality) that reality cannot be known.[11]

Metanarrative and metalinguistical moves are not enough. Missions needs a real metaphysics. Otherwise, we are locked into a Wittgenstinian[12] linguistic bubble in which religion language or God talk is not really talk about God.[13] But in the final analysis, if our language is not truly (though analogously) descriptive of God (an extramental and extracosmic *Being*), then it is really talk about nothing (*no being*). Religious talk, then, would simply be talk by religious people about subjective religious experiences, not any

---

[9] See I. Kant, *The Critique of Pure Reason,* trans. N. K. Smith (New York: St. Martin's, 1965).

[10] See S. Hackett, *The Resurrection of Theism,* 2nd ed. (Grand Rapids: Baker, 1982), part 1.

[11] See Geisler, *Systematic Theology,* chap. 2.

[12] L. Wittgenstein (1889–1951) was an early linguistic philosopher who held a conventionalist (relativistic) view of meaning. He believed religious language (God talk) was meaningful insofar as it is based on meaningful religious experience, but it is not cognitively descriptive of God (an extracosmic Being).

[13] See Geisler, *Systematic Theology,* chap. 9.

objective reality. In short, it would be subjective but not objective. Hiebert's essay does not inform us how he would escape this conclusion, despite his apparent desire to do so.

Doctrinal Truth

Hiebert denies in principle that there are any enduring essential truths of the faith. He declares that "we dare not equate the gospel with any human theologies. Our theologies are our partial human attempts to understand Scripture in our particular contexts, but the gospel transcends them all" (p. 92). As humble and cautious as it may sound, this statement is self-stultifying. For either we know some objective propositional truth in the gospel, or else it is without meaning. If the former, then we do know some transcendent truths of the gospel. It is, in fact, impossible to deny we can know transcendent doctrinal truths without assuming the transcendent doctrinal truth that one claims to know this. And when one unpacks what is meant by "the gospel," he finds some 14 such doctrinal truths that are essential to it. These truths include a theistic and Trinitarian view of God, man's sinfulness, Christ's humanity, His sinlessness, His deity, His sacrificial atonement, His victorious bodily resurrection, and so on; and these can be supported biblically, historically, and logically.[14] This means that they are not only based on God's Word (the Bible); they are also expressed in the early ecumenical creeds of the church and are logically necessary to make the gospel (as defined in 1 Cor 15:1–4) possible. These truths are enduring and transcultural. Although expressed in local languages, they express unchangeable and uncompromisable truths of the Christian faith. Their truth is neither local nor changeable. They are not, to borrow Hiebert's words, "our partial human attempts to understand Scripture in our particular contexts." Of course, like all truths, they are restateable (in different linguistic forms), but their truth is not reformable.

Further, Hiebert appears to deny that we can really know universal truth when he cites A. Walls:

> No one ever meets universal Christianity in itself: we only ever meet Christianity in a local form and that means a historically,

---

[14] See N. L. Geisler and R. Rhodes, *Conviction Without Compromise* (Eugene, OR: Harvest House, 2008), part 1.

> culturally conditioned form. We need not fear this; when God became man he became historically, cultural conditioned man in a particular time and place. What he became, we need not fear to be (pp. 88–89).

But if truth is always conditioned, then how can it avoid being relative, at least as we know it. But here again there is a self-defeating process. For to say we know that we cannot know universal (or absolute) truth is self-contradictory.[15] For this is a universal truth claim that we cannot know universal truth. Certainly his statement that all our theological understandings are a matter of one's own perspective is problematic since this claim contains the implicit claim to be a nonperspective statement that all such statements are just matters of perspective.

Would it not be better simply to claim that we do not know all the truth but that the truth we know is truly known? Simply because we do not comprehend all truth does not mean that we do not comprehend any truth. We must always be careful not to allow contemporary philosophical skepticism and relativism to invade our theological and missiological endeavors. It is better to be skeptical of skepticism than to be skeptical of the things most surely believed among us.

Hermeneutics

Despite his belief in objective meaning, in the final analysis Hiebert has a subjective way of discovering meaning. He proposes a community-based hermeneutic in which dialogue serves to correct the biases of individuals. He fails to note that communities can be as biased and subjective as individuals. Missionaries to Muslims are aware that Islam as a community is no less biased than individual Muslims when it comes to interpreting the Bible.

I am also concerned with Hiebert's statement that legitimate local theologies that differ from other local Christians. He said,

> Local churches have the right to *interpret* and apply the gospel in their contexts, but also a responsibility to join the larger church community around the world to seek to overcome the limited perspectives each brings, and the biases each has that might distort the gospel (pp. 90–91; emphasis added).

---

[15] See Geisler, *Systematic Theology*, chap. 7.

This is confusing at best. How can local theologies have the right to interpret the gospel wrongly, namely, to distort the gospel? And how can there be legitimately different local theologies? Logic would seem to demand that, if there were conflicting views in different local communities, then someone is wrong. All views, particularly contradictory views, cannot be true.

Further, Hiebert claims that "this corporate nature of the church as a community of interpretation extends not only to the church in every culture, but also to the church in all ages" (p. 95). But even in the best sense, this is a *consensus gentium* fallacy (that the majority are right). Or else it implies that it is alright if everything the Christian Church as a whole has taught is not all right. When Evangelicals make claims like this, Roman Catholics smile since such a claim supports their position that even infallible Scripture needs an infallible interpreter. The truth is that this is not so.[16] An objective interpretation is possible apart from any community.[17] Adding more people (a whole community or even the whole Church) using the wrong method of interpretation will not bring us to the truth.

Apologetics and Worldview

One of the greatest failures of modern missions is its failure to see that contextualization is *not* the most crucial problem of communicating the gospel to another culture. Rather, it is the problem of communicating a theistic gospel to those holding a nontheistic philosophical worldview. Missions has come of age with regard to the need to understand different cultures and in learning how to communicate cross-culturally. But it has not yet come of age in the realm of understanding the importance of differing philosophical worldviews and communicating effectively to them. An example is the famous 10–40 Window of unreached people. Why have they been so hard to reach, whereas Africa and South America have not.[18] I suggest that it is because both Africa and South America

---

[16] See N. L. Geisler and J. Betancort, *Is Rome the True Church?* (Wheaton: Crossway, 2008).

[17] See T. Howe, *Objectivity in Biblical Interpretation* (Altamonte Springs: Advantage Inspirational, 2005), which is a masterful tome on objective meaning and interpretation.

[18] See J. Mbiti, *African Religions and Philosophy* (New York: Praeger, 1969). Mbiti demonstrated that the basic belief behind native Africa religions is a theistic view of a High God or Sky God who made the world. W. Schmidt did the same thing in his monumental 12-volume set *The*

had a theistic worldview, and the gospel presupposes that view for it to make sense. Whereas, many of the people (except Muslims[19]) in the 10–40 Window have a nontheistic worldview—largely atheism and pantheism.[20] But it makes no sense to speak of Christ as the Son of (a theistic) God who died for our sins and miraculously rose again (which is an act of a theistic God) to people who do not believe in such a theistic God. In short, missions has been seriously hindered in 10–40 Window countries because they have not known how effectively to preevangelize by showing the viability of a theistic worldview.[21] Thus, the lack of proper apologetic training is a significant hindrance to evangelism in these countries. Most academic programs in missions in the past generation or so have not even required a course, let alone a minor, in apologetics for graduation.[22] This lack must be filled if we are going to reach the last great populations of unreached people.[23]

RESPONSE TO MICHAEL POCOCK

Michael Pocock finds much to admire in Hiebert's essay and indeed in the whole body of Hiebert's work. He enthusiastically

---

Origin of the Idea of God (1912–1955) and in *High Gods in North America* (Oxford: Clarendon, 1933).

[19] While Islam is technically a theistic religion, it is a rigid unitary type of theism that does not allow for God to have a Son. Hence, Muslims also need special preevangelism on the nature of God in order for the gospel about the Son of God to make sense to them.

[20] The current revival in China (a nontheistic culture) may seem to be an exception to this rule. However, on closer examination it is not. For Marxistic atheism has broken many of the previously religious barriers to theism and allowed the theistic light of general revelation (Rom 1:19–20) to shine through, thus paving the way for the gospel.

[21] We have attempted to overcome this difficulty in our book, which offers techniques for preevangelism in the postmodern world, no matter what their worldview may be. See N. L. Geisler and D. Geisler, *Conversational Evangelism* published in early 2009 by Harvest House. D. Geisler is a missionary to Asians based in Singapore.

[22] This is not to say that the Holy Spirit has no role in evangelism. His role is absolutely crucial since no one can be saved apart from His work (John 3:7; 16:7–8). But the Holy Spirit does not work in a vacuum; He can and does work through evidence. Indeed, it is the evidence of God's existence seen through general revelation that brings the truth of God to unbelievers (Rom 1:19–20; 2:12–14; Acts 14; 17). It is certainly unreasonable to conclude that the God of reason (Isa 1:18), who created creatures in His image who have reason (Gen 1:27; Col 3:10), would bypass reason to reach these rational creatures. Indeed, Peter exhorts us to give "a reason for the hope that is in [us]" (1 Pet 3:15), and Paul "reasoned" with the Jews in the synagogues and the Greeks on the Areopagus in Athens (Acts 17:16–34). God wants to reach the heart, but He does not bypass the head on the way to the heart.

[23] I am aware of the claims of the signs and wonders movement to penetrate these unreached areas, but I would counter with the following observations. First, I believe that their scriptural claims are dubious. See my book *Signs and Wonders* (Eugene, OR: Wipf and Stock, 1988). Second, it is logically impossible to have an act of (a theistic) God if no such God exists to perform the act. Third, I know of no evidence of mass conversions as a result of "signs and wonders" in lands among people who do not believe in a theistic God, either via general or special revelation. And it can be argued (though I have no space here) that "conversion" to anything less than a theistic God is not a truly Christian conversion (see my *Systematic Theology*, vol. 3, chap. 17).

affirms Hiebert's critical contextualization approach. It seems to me that he is so positive about Hiebert that he cannot see the weaknesses in Hiebert's position. With both Hiebert and Pocock the cultural context has more influence than it should, and the biblical revelation has less than it should.

To illustrate how Hiebert's approach might be applied in modern missions, Pocock mentions the C1-C6 controversy. Strangely, he raises the issue, but he does not render an opinion. Surely, the C5 approach leads to syncretism, as field research has shown. While the passion of the C5 proponents is understandable, even commendable, their willingness to tolerate syncretism, even heresy, is not. Rather, true Evangelicals must point them to biblical fidelity and theological orthodoxy.

RESPONSE TO DARRELL WHITEMAN

Darrell Whiteman is an anthropologist by training, and that shines through his response to Hiebert. He affirms Hiebert's critical contextualization model and provides several examples of how it can be applied by missionaries. In Whiteman's view theology is naturally "culture bound." By this he means that theology reflects the culture of the theologian. While there is some truth to this, especially in regard to systematic theology, biblical theology is supracultural. It transcends culture. Thus, the triune nature of God is a truth for all cultures, not one that can be disregarded by those who work with Muslims.

In his response Whiteman criticizes "neocolonial" missionaries. In his view these are missionaries who believe the Western church's theological and cultural forms are superior. While modern missionaries should avoid the cultural superiority and paternalism of the past, Whiteman extends this to theology as well. He makes the same mistake as Hiebert, elevating human culture over propositional divine truth.

Whiteman repeats and affirms Philip Jenkins's thesis that the locus of Christianity is shifting from Europe and North America to Asia, Africa, and Latin America. This, Whiteman writes, will produce a wide variety of contextualized expressions of Christianity. Undoubtedly, this is true, but all of these contextualized expressions must be evaluated by and according to their fidelity to the Scriptures and the accepted tenets of the Christian faith. Whiteman holds that the gospel affirms most of culture, confronts some of culture, and transforms all of culture. Could we not apply that template to the contextualized expressions of Christianity?

Finally, Whiteman also mentions the C1-C6 controversy. However, he embraces the C5 approach and argues in favor of it. He denigrates concerns about its syncretistic tendencies. Instead he proposes that missiologists consider cultural/religious forms and meanings. In his view there are no sacred forms, only sacred meanings. I would hold that the biblical revelation contains both. Surely forms communicate meaning. The pattern of Muslim prayer, praying five times each day facing Mecca, is a form that contains meaning for the Muslims who do this. Those observing them see a form, kneeling on a mat and prostrating, and they attach a meaning to it. They conclude these people are Muslims who are praying to Allah. In the same way the Lord's Supper is a form that communicates a meaning to those who participate and to those who observe, though the meaning might need to be explained. Whiteman writes that "contextualized Christianity is the best hedge against syncretism." While it may be granted that the noncontextualized approach of the pioneer missionaries did lead to syncretism, in a similar way the radical contextualization advocated by John Travis and Darrell Whiteman has led to syncretism. This radical contextualization is not a hedge against syncretism; it is a cause of it. We should pray that today's missionaries will find a moderating position between the two extremes.

CONCLUSION

There is much to commend in Hiebert's essay and in his career as well. However, his essay raises some significant concerns. Hiebert understandably makes much of critical contextualization. Contextualization is helpful, but he and we should be more concerned about biblical fidelity. Indeed, Hiebert does not emphasize sufficiently biblical inerrancy and infallibility.

Hiebert correctly asserts that truth is both objective and transcultural, but he does not adequately explain how and why this is so. He also seems to denigrate propositional truth. Surely, missionaries need to believe and proclaim a gospel that is propositionally true in order to evangelize effectively.

I am also concerned about Hiebert's approbation of con-textualized hermeneutics. Contextualized hermeneutics seems to bring into question the propositional truth of Scripture. Beyond that, a local Christian community's assertion of a particular doc-trine does not prove the doctrine true. A group of Christians can err just as an individual believer can.

Finally, while contextualization may profit missionaries in training a little, instruction in worldviews and training in apolo-getics would profit them much more. This training would enable them to proclaim the theistic gospel to those who hold a nonthe-istic worldview.

BIBLIOGRAPHY

Geisler, Norman. *Systematic Theology,* vol. 1: *Introduction/ Bible.* Bloomington, MN: Bethany House, 2002.

————, ed. *Inerrancy.* Grand Rapids: Zondervan, 1980.

————, and Peter Bocchino. *Unshakeable Foundations.* Minneapolis: Bethany House, 2001.

————, and Win Corduan. *Philosophy of Religion.* Eugene, OR: Wipf and Stock, 2001.

Howe, Thomas. *Objectivity in Biblical Interpretation.* Altamonte Springs, FL: Advantage Books, 2005.

Radamacher, Earl, and Robert Preus. *Hermeneutics, Inerrancy, and the Bible.* Grand Rapids: Zondervan, 1984.

CHAPTER 12

Response to Hiebert's Article

"The Gospel in Human Contexts" and to the Responses of Pocock and Whiteman

AVERY T. WILLIS JR.

INTRODUCTION

Paul Hiebert left us an excellent scholarly analysis of the contextualization of the gospel in human contexts. His insightful historical account of the development of contextualization uses the scholarly disciplines of philosophy, theology, and the sciences. Michael Pocock and Darrell Whiteman have summarized and expanded on his arguments, so I have refrained from repetitious comments. I basically agree with all three of them relative to their theses, presuppositions, and constructs. I am grateful for all their invaluable contributions to the field of missiology. I have commented on particular points of their arguments where appropriate.

HIEBERT'S MODEL OF CONTEXTUALIZATION

I would like to begin by pointing out some differences I have with Hiebert. His thesis is, "In this sense this essay addresses the PRESENT of what has traditionally been termed 'missions.'" I believe that missions is much more than contextualization, but I will not spell out the differences here. Although contextualization has been debated the past 50 years and even longer than that under the term *indigenization*, it is still a live topic today in this age of globalization and the expansion of missions.

Another difference I would like to address is the starting point for the discussion. Because missions groups historically practiced minimal contextualization and then overreacted to uncritical contextualization, Hiebert feels obligated to start with the poor examples of colonial missions. He then addresses the slippery slope of relativism before arguing for critical contextualization. His conclusion is a fourth view that he calls "divine revelation given in human contexts."

It is appropriate to address the problem from his perspective for scholars who are wrestling with the inherent conflicts between theology and anthropology in a postmodern world. However, I want to begin at the other end of the argument with God's revealed truth (where Hiebert ends up) and to apply the insights that Hiebert and the responders provide for us to the practical world of the cross-cultural missionary and the missional church. Both the missionary and the missional church will applaud the conclusions in these articles, but they might have difficulty in applying them.

Therefore I shall address how long-term missionaries and the missional church (with its short-term volunteers and cross-cultural indigenous missionaries) can utilize contextualization for maximum transformation without succumbing to syncretism. I begin the discussion with Jesus' model of contextualization and move toward a missionary model that includes specific steps for application.

JESUS' MODEL OF CONTEXTUALIZATION

Jesus fulfilled the ideal of contextualization when He left heaven to be incarnated into the Jewish culture. Although Jesus is "the radiance of His glory, the exact expression of His nature" (Heb. 1:3), He also has "equality with God" and "emptied Himself by assuming the form of a slave, taking on the likeness of men" (Phil 2:6–7). Further, "though he was rich, yet for your sakes he became poor" (2 Cor 8:9 NIV). Jesus' incarnation was the consummate example of contextualization and still is the ideal for cross-cultural missionaries. Jesus gave up everything from His home "culture" of heaven and totally immersed Himself into the Jewish culture of His day. He participated fully in the Jewish culture. No one in the Bible ever questioned whether He was a Jew. His example challenges us to become incarnate in the culture to which we go as much as possible. Jesus commissioned His disciples and us to follow His example when he said, "As the Father has sent me, I am sending you" (John 20:21 NIV).

That being said, we find it impossible to follow His example as cross-cultural missionaries! None of us can be reborn into another culture. Missionaries have not found a way to divest themselves of their culture of origin. Even though some have adopted the host culture to the exclusion of their sending culture, they still experience cultural overhang. Their brains and bodies cannot free themselves totally from the cultures where they have developed and have been socialized. For example, if we work cross-culturally as adults, our brains are already structured by the language(s) we learned while we were children, and all new languages must be learned through the filter of the structure and syntax of our mother tongue. No matter how hard we try, we remain "foreign" to that culture by virtue of our inherited makeup and by the way we were socialized. So should we just give up because we can't be born into the host culture as Jesus was? Absolutely not. We are obligated by Jesus' command and His example to enter a culture completely and to contextualize truth in the culture.

We can learn lessons from Jesus' example. Although He was a Jew, He made a distinction between God's revelation and Jewish culture. Jesus was truly a Jew, but He was also "the truth" (John 14:6). He was able to incarnate truth into culture by always watching and listening to the Father. He said, "The Son is not able to do anything on His own, but only what He sees the Father doing. . . . I can do nothing on My own. I judge only as I hear, and My judgment is righteous, because I do not seek My own will, but the will of Him who sent Me" (John 5:19,30). God had revealed Himself and truth to the Jewish people, but as a fallen culture they developed elements that were not true.

Jesus used truth from His Father and the Scriptures to judge culture. He challenged Jewish cultural beliefs, values, and behaviors. He particularly challenged the religious system and its beliefs. The Jewish culture had drifted from God's revelation, as all cultures do. The Jewish religious leaders, in their attempt to return to the revelation of God, had gone to the other extreme and locked in behaviors and beliefs according to their interpretation of the law. Matthew 23 records Jesus' judgment against the scribes and Pharisees. In the Sermon on the Mount, Jesus reinterpreted their religions beliefs and practices according to the Father's intent. So, while we should make ourselves at home in the host culture as much as possible, we should communicate the revelation of the Father to that culture and let it judge the culture.

A MISSIONARY MODEL OF CONTEXTUALIZATION

Hiebert, Pocock, and Whiteman help us acknowledge the conflicts inherent in the contextualization of truth in a culture. Before I offer a model of contextualization for the missional church and the cross-cultural missionary, I must point out the difficulty in maintaining an appropriate balance between biblical truth and culture in order to contextualize correctly without becoming either relativistic or paternalistic.

Theology dominated what pioneer missionaries believed, how they behaved, and what was communicated during the minimal contextualization period. Anthropology was on the ascendancy and became the dominate force over theology during the uncritical contextualization of the succeeding period. Both theology and anthropology are creations of man. Theology is man's reasoned response to revelation, and anthropology is man's reasoned response to the social sciences. In both, man's reason attempts to become the judge over God's revelation.

Hiebert calls our attention to a second conflict: that of reality versus words/signs. Most philosophers have become agnostic about revelation as reality and settle for dealing with reality in this relativistic age by philosophizing about words and signs.

Whiteman helps us deal with the conflicts between meaning and form. His Johari window adaptation to meaning and form helps us understand how various approaches to conceptualization can reap different results.

In summary, all three essays are cognizant of the battles between the sciences and religions and seek to address the issues raised by this dichotomy.

My response seeks to help the missional church and cross-cultural missionaries both from the West and from indigenous cultures. With this in mind, I have provided nine steps toward the contextualization of truth.

1. *Begin with the supremacy of Scripture.* We should start where Hiebert ended—with truth (or gospel as Hiebert calls it). God has revealed Himself and truth to us through the general revelation of creation and through His specific revelation of Himself in His Son and Scripture. God's revelation is both personal and relational, and we know Him through our personal relationship with Jesus and through His written record of truth—the Bible. The missionary must start with God's revelation of truth.

However, we humans have difficulty separating revelation from reason. Reason is a gift from God to help us understand His revelation, but if reason becomes the master, it moves us from divine revelation toward human interpretation guided by the scientific approaches of the age. Theology is a human interpretation of divine revelation. How else could divergent theologies all sell themselves as the true interpretation? As Hiebert says, "We dare not equate the gospel with any human theologies. Our theologies are our partial human attempts to understand Scripture in our particular contexts, but the gospel transcends them all." So our first task is to understand the truth apart from our culture.

Jesus approached culture from the perspective that there was absolute truth. Truth had been revealed to the Jews as recorded in Scripture, and He interpreted Scripture through direct input from His Father. We recognize that our modern missionary forefathers, with their minimalist contextualization, took their interpretations of that revelation in the form of their theologies and imposed them on the cultures they engaged. But that does not excuse us from starting with God's revelation.

2. *Understand the biblical culture.* Although we start with revelation, we must understand the biblical culture and its influence on God's revealed truth in Scripture. The new missionary and the missional church with its short-term volunteers could miss the importance of understanding the role of culture in Scripture. They may

see themselves as new or amateur missionaries, but that does not excuse them from studying the Scriptures to see what is revealed truth and what is culture. Only in this way can they truly understand God's revelation through Scripture. Hiebert correctly says, "Differentiating between eternal truth and the particular contexts in which it was revealed is not an easy task, but it is essential if we are to understand the heart of the gospel which is for everyone" (p. 91).

3. *Understand your own culture.* All three writers make the case for understanding one's own culture. I first recognized this when I started a church in the United States. I wanted to build it on the Bible instead of on my denomination and theology. I would always refer the members to the Bible to answer their questions about what we believed and practiced. But when I recommended some ways of doing things as our denomination practiced, they asked, "Where is that in the Bible?" Only then did I realize that much of what I had believed to be truth had been influenced by my own culture and tradition. My next insight came from my theology professor in seminary. He helped me realize that I received much of my theology from my parents, peers, churches, and teachers in addition to the Bible. When I became a missionary, I had to distinguish more between my understanding of the truth and my culture.

4. *Understand the receptor culture.* All three of these essays address the contextualization of truth in culture, so I don't need to belabor it here. In light of that, the question remains, "How can short-term volunteers or new missionaries communicate the gospel without spending years to understand different cultures?" These volunteers and new missionaries must be aware that their theologies are shaped by their cultures and that all cultures have both truth and error embedded in them. They should understand that their understanding of the gospel is always colored by culture but that their task is not to change the gospel to conform to culture. Nevertheless, the more they understand the culture and the Bible, the better they can communicate the gospel.

Here are some specific suggestions on how volunteers and new cross-cultural missionaries can witness even without years of studying theology and anthropology. They can start by reading what anthropologists have learned about the particular culture they visit. They can ask long-term missionaries living in the culture how to communicate the gospel in that culture. They can ask local people the key questions of life to see how that culture relates to or contradicts the gospel.

But in this age of globalization, we cannot assume that international communication through the subculture of the Internet and digitalized communication allows us to ignore a studied approach to the culture of the recipient. It is an ongoing process in which the misssional church and its missionaries must constantly engage themselves in seeking to understand the truth, specific cultures, and how they relate to each other. Eternal truth transcends culture.

5. *Use oral communication of Scripture.* The emphasis on contextualization has caused many to question whether volunteers from missional churches or new missionaries from the West or to a nearby culture can effectively witness without years of study. The testimony of Acts shows it can be done. One's personal testimony is always effective in any culture. Of course, it communicates better if the cultural elements are downplayed in one's testimony.

A second method has been recovered in recent years—communicating truth orally through the stories of the Bible. More than two-thirds of the world's population are oral communicators and do not comprehend literate presentations of the gospel commonly used by Westerners and indigenous leaders who were influenced by Western missionaries. They comprehend truth better when they are told the stories of the Bible and are led in exploratory discussions. By telling the stories of the Bible chronologically, one can bypass much of one's own cultural overhang. By asking questions of the people about what the story says (observation), what it means (interpretation), and its relevance to life (application), they have an opportunity to apply the truth to their own culture without going through the filter of the culture of the witness.

To be more effective the cross-cultural witness should learn the bridges, barriers, and gaps to the host culture's understanding and acceptance of the gospel. These are steps or stages Hiebert wants Christian communities to go through in order to determine how the gospel should relate to them in their specific cultural context. Bridges relate to elements that are compatible with the gospel. Barriers are elements of the culture that are counter to the gospel. Gaps are new forms that need to be created to express the meaning of living in obedience to the lordship of Christ in their particular culture.[1] By understanding the bridges, barriers, and gaps in a culture, they can choose the best Bible stories to address those needs.

By using bridge stories, witnesses can help the people identify with the Bible story because it affirms a story in their culture or values or beliefs they hold. By using stories that address barriers in beliefs, values, and behaviors, missionaries can overcome obstacles that hinder people from receiving the gospel in that culture. The bigger the barrier, the more stories are needed to address the barrier. For example, you would not need many stories to affirm that there is only one God for Muslims since they are monotheists, but you would need many more Bible stories on that truth for Hindus since they are polytheists and believe there are over 330 million gods. For Muslims, Jesus as the Son of God is a barrier so many more stories are needed to demonstrate His divinity. Gaps about truths that are not held or applied by people in that culture can be filled by telling more Bible stories to address those issues.

Oral methods work not only for volunteers and new cross-cultural missionaries but also for anyone communicating to oral learners. Bible stories provide the local believers a basis for interpreting the Scriptures in their culture and applying them to their lives.

6. *Aim for spiritual transformation.* The primary job of the missionary is to communicate the gospel in the culture in such a way that it transforms the people. The purer the gospel is communicated, the more likely it will transform the people. The more the gospel speaks to the particular culture, the more the people and the culture will be transformed.

Pocock summarizes Hiebert's argument by saying, "Christian workers can construct a transformative understanding of the gospel which leads to a transformational *missiology*. For Hiebert, and for us all, this is the truly exciting yet mystical part: The people on both sides of the communicational bridge are transformed by the reality of what they are studying!"

7. *Honor indigenous interpretation.* Cross-cultural communicators must recognize that as outsiders they are midwives but the

---

[1] Paul G. Hiebert, "Critical Contextualization," *Missiology* 12 (July 1984): 287–96; idem, "Critical Contextualization," *International Bulletin of Missionary Research* 11 (July 1987): 104–12; idem, *Anthropological Reflections on Missiological Issues* (Grand Rapids: Baker, 1994).

children must be raised by the culture's fathers and mothers. The outsider misses many nuances in the culture and is open to wrong interpretations. Even if the outsider evaluates the culture correctly, the local believers need to wrestle with the truth and apply it to their cultures. Only when they "own" the truth by interpreting it in their culture will it become real to them. Pocock correctly states, "In Hiebert's approach . . . together they search the Scriptures to see how it applies to the current situation, and they come to a conclusion that avoids both paternalism on the part of the missionary and syncretism on the part of the new believers."

None of us hold to pure truth without some cultural bias. Therefore, God has allowed many cultures to develop to challenge us to interpret truth together. Contextualization in the best sense is an attempt to let the truth be seen through the cultural lens of those receiving it.

8. *Practice dynamic equivalence translation and application.* We cannot be content with only a superficial interpretation of the gospel in a culture. We must have Scriptures that speak in every language to every culture. This takes long-term missionaries living in the culture.

Evangelical Bible translators have always been committed to absolute truth as revealed in the Scriptures. However, as Pocock points out, "They have moved from merely translating *words* to translating *thoughts*, albeit in as close a correspondence as possible to the intent of Scripture writers." Although truth may be contextualized in a given culture, the meanings must have objective reference points in Scripture. We need scholars in all cultures who are committed to the truth and who understand the culture so they can help us make truth incarnate in every culture.

Using a dynamic equivalence translation that is more in line with the culture makes it easier for the locals to apply the eternal truths in a relevant way.

9. *Promote continuous adaptation to the culture.* Cultures and languages are always changing. A correct interpretation and contextualization at one time does not mean that it is for all time. Whiteman says that it is

> the Christian *meanings* that must be maintained to have an expression of vital Christianity. In fact when the "Christian"

forms continue but the underlying meanings are lost, we have the "form of religion denying its power" (2 Tim 3:5). When this happens, we have classic nominal Christianity that we find throughout the world.

CONCLUSION

To be effective cross-cultural communicators of the gospel, we involve both the receiving and sending cultures in the contextualization process. We seek to guide the recipients to make critical decisions related to contextualizing revealed eternal truth in their diverse and ever-changing cultures. In order to steer the ship of contextualization, we affirm the truths in culture, and we allow the eternal truth of Scripture to be supracultural in order to maintain the integrity of the gospel when there are conflicts. We commit ourselves to a method of contextualization that does not compromise revealed truth, that does not subjugate a receptor culture by the sending culture, that interprets truth in culture so the value of both is recognized, and that applies truth to culture so that the culture and individuals in it are transformed.

BIBLIOGRAPHY

Bevans, Stephan B. *Models of Contextual Theology.* Maryknoll, NY: Orbis, 2002.

Dilliland, Dean. *The Word Among Us: Contextualizing Theology for Mission Today.* Eugene, OR: Wipf and Stock, 2003.

Flemming, Dean. *Contextualization in the New Testament: Patterns for Theology and Missions.* Downers Grove: InterVarsity, 2005.

Hiebert, Paul G. *Anthropological Reflections on Missiological Issues.* Grand Rapids: Baker, 1994.

_____. "Critical Contextualization." *Missiology* 12 (July 1984): 287–96.

_____. "Critical Contextualization," *International Bulletin of Missionary Research* 11 (July 1987): 104–12.

Hesselgrave, David, and Edward Rommen. *Contextualization: Meanings, Methods, and Models.* Pasadena, CA: William Carey Library, 2003.

CHAPTER 13

Responding to "The Gospel in Human Contexts: Changing Perceptions of Contextualization"

ED STETZER

INTRODUCTION

I have an advantage in writing since I get to read *all* of the comments before making my response. Apart from my esteemed colleague and coeditor David Hesselgrave, I have the last word. Perhaps that's not fair to the contributors who have no opportunity to respond to others' comments, but that's the nature of this kind of book. Since I asked these scholars to write and assigned them their subjects, I guess it is fair that I get to comment on all of them. And all of these contributors deserve comment.

Several respondents noted that this grand essay was Paul Hiebert's last word on the subject of communication. He died shortly after submitting his essay, finishing a life of consummate scholarship and genuinely Christlike relationships with others. Both qualities contributed much to his focus on contextualization. He wanted to build bridges from the gospel to the world so that the world could understand the gospel. Rarely in his writing did he feel the need to defend the gospel or the need to defend his understanding of the gospel. His goal appeared to be moving the discussion of contextualization *past* the point of relativism, or what he called "uncritical contextualization." Keith Eitel's response in the first section of this book against the apparent worship of Shiva by a Christian missionary would certainly fall into the category of this "uncritical contextualization."

As several of these respondents have mentioned, major debate takes place in missiological circles concerning the C1-to-C6 models of evangelism to the Muslims—a debate about "where to draw the line." Hiebert wanted to bypass the *debate* about line drawing. This wasn't because he saw no lines concerning the basic truth of the gospel. Rather, his main focus was consistently reminding Western missionaries of their arrogance and their failure to effectively communicate cross-culturally because of an arrogant assumption about religious truth.

As Avery Willis points out, both Darrell Whiteman and Michael Pocock give excellent summaries of Hiebert's main points. Assuming you have read these chapters, I am not going to summarize Hiebert. Instead I attempt to react with Hiebert and then respond to those who replied to him. The most challenging and thoughtful encounters might be found through that exchange.

Semiotics might be a new word to some who are reading this book. Recently established within the field of the social sciences, this stream of thought deals with how people in cultures gain meaning from signs and symbols. While essentially dealing with the communication of concepts, semiotics is so subjective that one well-known writer has called it "the discipline studying everything which can be used to lie."[1] While his comment might be taken as tongue in cheek, it is both one of the most highly debated and the most studied subjects of our present age, especially given the way we get our information these days.[2] In an age when segments of the church are doing everything they can to grab the attention of the world through advertising and videos—while other parts of the church seek to shield the truth from those kinds of things—this is obviously an important topic.

Hiebert addresses but does not explain semiotics since he apparently assumes his readers will understand the concept and the

---

[1] U. Eco, *A Theory of Semiotics* (Bloomington: Indiana University Press, 1976).

[2] Think of a magazine or the Internet. This is the science of where to place pictures or video clips in relation to main stories or how to use images to sell products. This is the art of "branding."

problems it addresses. He does dip into the subject enough to help us see the difference in Saussurian semiotics and Peircian semiotics, which is an important distinction. Saussurian semiotics is relativistic: the meanings assigned to signs and symbols (including language) are entirely subjective. We may perceive quickly how this view has impacted our society, especially our media. Saussarian semiotics has had a negative impact on the concept of absolute truth—really, absolute *anything*.

At this point many churches are going through internal struggles. Some Christians feel that any yielding toward what they perceive (often rightly) as compromise with the culture will result in an immediate slide into heresy and pluralism. Hiebert identifies this wholesale acculturation with the "uncritical contextualization" of certain missionaries. This kind of contextualization is likely what Eitel is reacting to in the story about the missionary to India. Hiebert (who grew up in India) can see clearly the inadequacy of the uncritical viewpoint, and he wants no part of it.

In addition, Hiebert was more concerned with reaching out to the world than pleasing conservative Christians. Moreover, reaching out to the world obviously meant becoming more aware of the peoples of the world, especially how they communicate and (behind that communication) the way they *think*. Contextualization has this key value: it recognizes that people from other cultures don't think like Westerners do and seeks to translate the gospel in ways that can *help* them understand and grasp that message. What Hiebert calls "critical contextualization" is not a matter of accommodating the culture so that the gospel means whatever the hearers want it to mean or choose to understand. Rather, the issue is a *communication* problem, which does not have a logical, rational solution—although that is part of the equation. Also, this includes a relational aspect that requires that people of other cultures have an opportunity to speak and reason in their own way toward the gospel, as well as to decide within their context how they will respond to the gospel.

Contextualization does not seek to remove new Christians from their culture—as in "One more Christian, one less Chinese." Instead, it seeks to interact with the individual *in* relation to his culture because his culture is not inherently evil; rather, it is a human construct of inherited values and personal decisions (e.g., cultural rituals, social traditions). These subjective tangibles are so engrained that many don't even realize the culture's influence—especially if the individuals are monocultural. We can speak (and Hiebert does) of our own Western monoculturalism, but we need to remember that those we address in other cultures are monocultural as well—perhaps more than we are. If we step across the bridges of God to engage people of other cultures, we really can't expect them to meet us halfway. We cannot expect them even to know what that would *mean*.

Most missionaries who seek to do cross-cultural evangelism have these basic understandings. Many examples can be given of this type of activity in Scripture. In fact, one could argue that the book of Acts is one long example of the contextualization of the gospel into the Gentile world of the Roman Empire. Furthermore, it contains one long example of some Christians being offended as this contextualization takes place and, when possible, *blocking* that process from taking place. As I read about the Judaizers, I sometimes think, *They just didn't get it.*

They had this wonderful good news about the kingdom of God, free to all and extended to all. Instead of reaching out with it, they hoarded it, sought to control it, and sought to *possess* it. Doubtless, they were loving, caring, well-intentioned individuals in their own way. But the book of Acts indicates just how distant they were from God's purpose. I like Pocock's reflection on the attitude of Gamaliel, a man who was capable of questioning his own beliefs when needed in order for God to be truly heard. (On the other hand, did some of the Judaizers look at Paul and blame his "heresy" on *his* teacher? "Look! That's what happens if you follow the teachings of that liberal *Gamaliel!*")

So here is the problem as Hiebert sees it. We have been commanded to take the gospel to the world. Paul models for us that we need to stretch as far into the culture as we can, without yielding on the stumbling block of the cross. The cross is going to be hard enough for people to accept. Why block people from receiving the gospel by insisting that they accept *our* cultural eccentricities?

The description of the actions of the Holy Spirit in the book of Acts ought to be enough to make us realize that God works in different ways in different situations with different people. This task of reaching out to other cultures is under the Holy Spirit's direction. That task requires being humbly certain of our beliefs and methods, rather than arrogantly being so sure that we know what God would do and have us say in any situation. "Drawing the line," then, is not our primary concern. Crossing the barriers is more important if the world is our focus. We don't accomplish this by throwing away the truth; we achieve this by holding the gospel close and climbing the fences with it in order to share it on the other side. That is a description of critical contextualization. Hiebert sums up the problem near the beginning of his essay when he says that the church without the gospel ceases to be the church, but he also asserts that the gospel without humans and social institutions dies.

Of the respondents three of them seem to be on the same page as Hiebert. Whiteman seeks to underscore and explain what Hiebert says by identifying with him and pointing to another article (one that Whiteman wrote) as possibly an even better statement of Hiebert's critical contextualization thesis. Whiteman provides some helpful illustrations of the principle, including the story from Fiji about the baptismal font carved out of stone, which was once used for human sacrifice. While many Christians might balk at the use of such an evil object, critical contextualization has added to the symbolism of the blood of Christ with the font's use.

Whiteman also rightly relates Hiebert's critical contextualization model to the C1-through-C6 debate regarding ministry to Muslims. Whiteman's general view is a hearty endorsement of Hiebert's model. He also appreciates Hiebert's additional thought concerning "Divine Revelations Given in Human Contexts," a recognition of the need for understanding the context in our hermeneutical principles. This is perhaps the beginning point of contextualization studies.

Pocock also relates Hiebert's critical contextualization to the C1-through-C6 argument. Pocock sees that Hiebert's concern was less on defining contextualization for definition's sake and more on the process and difficulties of *communication*. Hiebert emphasized both sides of the bridge—the Christian *communicator* and the receiving *culture*—as part of the process, and he values the participation of the receiving culture. This does not mean that he was comfortable compromising the gospel in order to "get it across." It means that Hiebert recognizes revelation from God and theologies constructed according to man's mental processes as different. Revelation is eternal, objective, absolute truth. Man's attempts to explain it theologically are based in human language. If the history of theological debate teaches us nothing else, it instructs us that God's people can spend inordinate amounts of time and energy seeking to "right" one another's theology, while the world around us advances swiftly toward an eternal, literal, agonizing hell.

Pocock declares, "It is one thing to advocate a particular approach to gospel communication and another to recognize that understandable oddities exist among genuine movements of God." Hiebert's emphasis on biblical reflection as the key is well taken, as is Pocock's reminder to us of the thought of Gamaliel.

Avery Willis is best known in my own denomination for his work on evangelism among oral peoples. In his response to Hiebert, Willis wants to begin where Hiebert ended and work back in a historical direction. He begins from the contextual example of Christ Jesus in Scripture. He says that Jesus is the perfect example of contextualization. He was Jewish yet absolutely concerned with truth. Jesus judged cultures with the truth from His Father, and that is revealed to us in the Scriptures. Willis urges that we must communicate the revelation of the Father to the culture and let it judge the culture. Also, Willis appreciates the limitations this places on the mental processes of theology—"Both theology and apology are the creations of man."

After discussing Jesus as a relevant example of contextualization, Willis gives a nine-point approach to biblical contextualization that in most points meets and affirms Hiebert's. In what follows, I repeat and offer comments on these nine points.

1. *Begin with the supremacy of Scripture.* Willis warns that we humans have difficulty separating revelation from reason. We are pointed to this in Norman Geisler's response and may run into this when dealing with the last respondent.

2. *Understand the biblical culture.* This corresponds with Hiebert's divine revelation given in human contexts.
3. *Understand your own culture.* It is important that we recognize ourselves as cultural beings and our language as a cultural expression.
4. *Understand the receptor culture.* This is the constant task of the missionary in context—trying to correspond between an unknown culture, one's own culture, and the biblical culture—all with the purpose of making Christ known.
5. *Use oral communication of Scripture.* Willis emphasizes the value of storying in other cultures, and he points out the effectiveness of this methodology.
6. *Aim for spiritual transformation.* Emphasizing Hiebert's own emphasis on transformation, Willis underscores again the need for a spiritual change made by the power of the Holy Spirit.
7. *Honor indigenous interpretation.* Here Willis is agreeing with Hiebert's emphasis on the response of the indigenous respondent community.
8. *Practice dynamic equivalence translation and application.* Willis agrees with the need to communicate spiritual meaning, not simply literal meaning.
9. *Promote continuous adaptation to the culture.* Willis advocates the continuing application of biblical culture to every human context. This is different from assuming and determining that we know the truth once and for all.

Of course, we realize that some believe truth is not contextually apprehended in the least. This appears to be the viewpoint expressed by Norman Geisler. No task in this book has been more stressful to me than responding to Geisler's article. That's because I believe his view is an excellent and well-reasoned restatement of what Hiebert called the "colonial" view. I, along with other supporters of contextualization, would resist such views.

With high regard I honor Geisler for his sterling, intellectual encounter regarding the many issues of apologetics. No other writer in this book has published as widely or as effectively about historical theology and its use of and debate with philosophy. He is uniquely qualified to represent the position of Aristotelian certainty, and that he does. He brings us back to what is perhaps the *first* question concerning contextualization—one that most of the other writers here have dealt with and chosen against. Is there an objective truth so humanly understandable and indubitable that it cannot be questioned? Of course there is . . . Jesus Christ.

This question does not bother "missional" types; it is the way intellectual "truth claims" are equated so certainly with God's revelation. What other respondents to Hiebert have identified as the difference between God's revelation and human theology does not appear to be recognized by Geisler. Certainly, it's not that he hasn't heard the arguments. He has chosen to reject them in favor of logic. Perhaps I need to clarify my objections to his objections.

Geisler holds Hiebert's view on Scripture to be dangerous because Hiebert has not stated that it is the infallible and inerrant revelation of God. As a conservative evangelical, I believe in both and want them understood as I write and teach. However, I think Hiebert *does* say this and quite directly. However, Geisler would prefer to hear those words in a formulaic fashion since Hiebert subscribes to the dynamic equivalence view of translation. The reason Geisler suspects Hiebert is because of their disagreement concerning *the way* words convey *meaning*. The problem with this is that some things have inexpressible *meaning* in any human speech but are, nevertheless, understandable through human relationship. How can we relate God's infinite words with our finite words? Geisler disagrees with Hiebert on truth. He asserts, "Truth is correspondence with reality," which leads him into a restatement of the Aristotelian principles of logic: law of noncontradiction, law of identity, and law of excluded middle. Most missiologists have come to the conclusion that there are, indeed, different ways of thinking among other cultures, and these differences do not recognize the black and white of Aristotle's principles as the equivalent of truth. Indeed, these principles are not Scripture and cannot be regarded as "inerrant and infallible."

In the past those who have held Geisler's view have rarely made contact with non-Western thinkers in an effective way. Geisler refers the reader to the beginning of his own book on theology concerning these matters.[3] I would encourage you to read it, but I would also refer the reader to my coeditor's book, *Communicating Christ Cross-Culturally*, specifically chapter 5 on "The Problem of Meaning."[4] I am one who believes in truth, and I believe that truth can be conveyed through language. But I am also concerned that we not equate those affirmations with ways of thinking that are not cross-culturally transferable.

In addition to the meaning of truth, Geisler disagrees with Hiebert (and the other respondents) about theology itself. He takes issue with any dialogue regarding other worldviews, inasmuch as his worldview is true; and noncontradiction means that they must, therefore, be false and subject to attack. He disagrees with Hiebert's critical realism, saying if this is Kantian critical realism, then Hiebert should know Kant has been confirmed as self-defeating. "Kant held that we know that we cannot know reality," which is self-defeating logically. Geisler's argument here appears to become overwhelmingly rationalistic, not in keeping with either the spirit of Hiebert's writing or reflecting the possibility of the intervention of the Holy Spirit.

At last Geisler gets to his disagreement with Hiebert on doctrinal truth: "Hiebert denies in principle that there are any enduring essential truths of the faith." Apparently, this is Geisler reacting to Hiebert's declaration "that we dare not equate the gospel with any human theologies." Geisler has apparently taken offense here regarding the 14 absolute truths that are "enduring and transcultural." Further, he says, "Hiebert appears to deny that we can really know universal truth." This appears to be a response to Hiebert's statement, "No one ever meets universal Christianity in itself."

Hiebert is absolutely correct. Healthy, contextualized churches are faithful to the gospel and appropriately reflect their cultural context. That is, these churches relate to their cultural contexts, but they faithfully teach the supracultural truths of Scripture. Is Geisler, however, affirming that *he* understands perfect universal truth and that his understanding is *not* culturally conditioned but absolutely *true*? Is this not basically the position of the colonial

---

[3] N. L. Geisler, *Systematic Theology* , vol. 1, "Prolegomena" (Grand Rapids: Baker, 2002).
[4] D. J. Hesselgrave, *Communicating Christ Cross-Culturally*, 2nd ed. (Grand Rapids: Bondservant Publishing House, 1991), 55–77.

missionary? Further, Geisler contends that this is true and that the opinion of others, especially a group of others who collectively hold a different view, are simply wrong. By this, is he censuring the entire missiological community? Is he right about contextualization and the rest of us are wrong?

Finally, Geisler disagrees with Hiebert on apologetics and worldview. He asserts, "Missions have come of age with regard to the need of understanding different cultures and learning how to communicate cross-culturally, but it has not yet come of age in the realm of understanding the importance of differing philosophical worldviews and communicating effectively with them." This is what the contextualization issue seeks to address.

At this point Geisler might be demonstrating his aggravation that apologetics has not been incorporated into most missions programs in colleges and seminaries. That's an important point. I would just like to see Geisler concede that most mission programs have valuable insights to offer.

In conclusion, I would like to thank each of these respondents—perhaps Geisler especially—for providing their responses. For me, they have clarified that Hiebert knew his stuff and that his approach may be the best we can do with the imperfect art of contextualizing the gospel.

CHAPTER 14

ESSAY 3: The Future of Evangelicals in Mission

RALPH D. WINTER

INTRODUCTION

The purpose of this essay is to peer into the immediate future and make some educated guesses as to what might be and should be the focus of missions and missionaries in the next generation. A great deal of the future of the Evangelical movement and its mission vision can be deduced by looking closely at its roots, so that is where I begin. In this first section I shall discuss the history of Evangelicalism, explaining what I call First-Inheritance Evangelical and Second-Inheritance Evangelicalism. The essay will demonstrate the difference between the earlier Evangelicalism, which was characterized by both spiritual and social concern, and the latter Evangelicalism, which emphasized evangelism predominantly. I mean to call modern Christians to return to the holistic Evangelicalism of the earlier period.

My larger goal in this is to open conversation about what missionaries, mission agencies, and mission scholars should address next. Evangelical missions in the twentieth century has emphasized evangelism and church planting, but this essay will call for a more balanced approach. In this sense my essay addresses the future of Evangelical missions.

THE MEANING OF THE WORD *EVANGELICAL*

The word *evangelical* in the Catholic tradition refers to those people who take seriously the four Evangelical Gospels and specifically to the members of Catholic orders. Later, in the Protestant tradition, the word came to refer to a political party where the *evangelici* were opposed to the *pontifici*. The idea was that those who were of the *evangelici* party adhered to the authority of the Bible rather than to the Roman *pontif* (the Pope), thus distinguishing two essentially political spheres.

By the time of the Reformation, other things were going on besides the tensions between two parties—Luther and the Pope, or Calvin and the Pope. There were the Anabaptists; later, the Pietists; still later a different kind of "Evangelical," the Quakers; and eventually came the Methodists, who became a world force.

As a broad generalization all of these "third force" movements came to understand the word *evangelical* to mean more than correct belief. It began to refer to those individuals who had had a personal "evangelical experience," by which they meant that something real had happened in a person's heart and life, not just a purely mental assent to some sort of intellectual creed.

Thus, a major concern in the various streams of this "third force" was a wide variety of personal and emotional experiences, which were regarded as manifestations of the Spirit's power in a person's life. The Quakers actually got their name from a characteristic of their meetings in which they "quaked" with emotion. The concept of a "born again" experience was almost entirely unknown at the time of the Reformation. But in 1738 John Wesley, a university-trained Anglican, in a little Moravian chapel on a street called Aldersgate, sensed the *warming of his heart* as he listened to a verse being read out loud from the book of Romans in a commentary by Luther. The verse spoke of people being "saved by faith."

It was not long before the idea of a need for a heart-warming *experience* was followed by a concept of an even deeper work of grace or "second blessing," also called "entire sanctification," "infilling of the Spirit," and "baptism of the Spirit." In fact, other things like falling, groaning, howling, women whipping their hair, and speaking in tongues eventually were added, each new tradition tending to canonize particular aspects of *experience* with a specific phraseology to match. For example, there were, and still are, people who make a big distinction between "the baptism of the Spirit" and "the infilling of the Spirit." Yet there is no question that many people have been significantly affected by these movements.

PART 1: AN OVERVIEW OF FIRST-INHERITANCE AND SECOND-INHERITANCE EVANGELICALISM

Evangelicalism presents a complex picture. But as we enter the period beyond 1700, it may be of value to distinguish between First-Inheritance Evangelicalism (FIE) and Second-Inheritance Evangelicalism (SIE), both my terms. For this chapter we can define the FIE as that which was characterized by a broad social and spiritual spectrum of concern ranging from foreign missions to changing the legal structure of society and even war. This spectrum is seen in the heady combination of *earthly and heavenly* perspective in the Evangelical Awakening in England as related to Wesley. It is seen in America where a simultaneous awakening occurred called the Great Awakening, which both increased church membership and led to the Revolutionary War, and where a Second Great Awakening brought thousands more into the churches, drastically transformed society, and led to the Civil War. These major "awakenings" are far more significant in American history than our secularized schoolbooks reveal. Even R. Fogel (a secular Nobel Prize winner) wrote a book called *The Fourth Great Awakening*, which recognizes the foundational importance of four spiritual awakenings in American history.

To generalize, FIE ran from about the earliest glimmers of the Great Awakening with T. Frelinghuysen in 1721 in the Raritan Valley in New Jersey to the onset of D. L. Moody's enormous influence around 1875. This period was significantly characterized by Evangelicals *in positions of civil leadership.* This is the reason they could readily believe not only in an emotional transformation of individuals but also in a wide range of different aspects of social transformation and God glorification. Nevertheless, this was an inheritance that in later generations after 1875 suffered two gradual reductions, each concentrating on one of the two formerly united emphases.

One of the reductions after 1875 continued to be social concern, and the other continued the emphasis on sin and salvation, and, specifically, on the necessity (and supposed sufficiency) of a personal *experience* coupled with an otherworldly focus. The followers of the first reduction, being college people, became a relatively small stream outnumbered greatly by a surge of noncollege people.

The followers of the second reduction became the mainstream I am calling SIE. They were mainly noncollege masses swept into faith by popular evangelists—Moody, Billy Sunday, and many others. But they were *not in positions of social influence* and tended to turn away from the idea of transforming society at a macro level. This, to me, is a key point.

This new and soon dominant SIE was itself the result of two forces. One was the impact of massive immigration from the Catholic parts of Europe. The population of the USA jumped from 44 million to 106 million between 1875 and 1920. Many leading families of FIE influence gradually slipped in both faith and political standing. At the same time Moody and others impacted millions of noncollege Americans who, even after conversion, were almost completely isolated from both civic leadership and college education.

This new Evangelicalism of the masses, characteristic of SIE, significantly boosted church attendance in the USA and created 157 Bible institutes. However, it had little stake in politics or social action and tended to suspect the smaller number of continuing, socially upscale college-educated Evangelicals from the FIE as being "liberal" (which by then they often were). As a result, the post-Moody Evangelicals in the noncollege stratum tended to react against social schemes and even to banish the word *kingdom* from their vocabulary, thus tending to undergo their second type of reduction of the gospel to a theology of "this world is not my home, I'm just a passin' through," producing an opposite pole from the other reduction to social action alone.

My prediction in this chapter is that in the twenty-first century the mainstream of Evangelicalism in the USA, and of Evangelical missions in particular, will recover a broader perspective, moving from what has been dominantly SIE to a rediscovery of the earlier full spectrum of the FIE tradition. The latter possessed a theology that combined both personal salvation with vast social responsibility, thus uniting concern for the glorification of God in both individual and social transformation.

We can see that kind of integrated strategy in the character of all truly effective mission history. This unity is in the Bible itself since Jesus validated, illuminated, and empowered His words by His deeds. This type of virile wide-spectrum faith, without being given much credit, contributed enormously to the earlier development of America. I hope it will become the new mainstream of global Evangelicalism with the same effect.

Undoubtedly not everyone will embrace the healed polarization. Two dangers can be anticipated. One danger is that the avoidance of social transformation in SIE may endure in some circles. The opposite danger is a continuing focus on social transformation stripped of an adequate emphasis on individual transformation that is, ironically, so essential to any significant social transformation.

The full spectrum of FIE I am talking about is not a "holism" that often merely adds many good things but leaves a "hole" where evangelism should be. Holism sometimes seems to assume that our "battle" is merely to benefit humans, a suspiciously anthropocentric or even humanistic point of view.

In heaven's war against Satan, our priority is to recruit soldiers, freeing them from "the power of Satan" (Acts 26:18) by winning their allegiance to Christ. But even that is merely *prior* if we are going to gain *effective* soldiers. Obviously, recruitment before battle is a *priority*, but merely a priority. As these new soldiers in their transformed lives seek through Christ's power "to destroy the Devil's works" (1 John 3:8), their good deeds will "give glory to [their] Father in heaven" (Matt 5:16). These new deeds will then validate and empower further evangelism that will gain still more recruits for the battle of the kingdom. *But merely recruiting and not battling does not win wars.*

This perspective is no longer a tension between God and man, as our Reformation heritage tends to portray it, but it is a war between God-plus-His-people against the kingdom of darkness. But seeking to destroy the dominion of Satan must not be confused with the tendency to seek dominion in society through the saints holding worldly power, which is called Dominion Philosophy. The next three sections look more closely at these issues.

PART 2: FIRST-INHERITANCE EVANGELICALISM

Romanticized histories of colonial America portray the American colonies as highly religious. That was true of the early settlements in New England—the Pilgrims and Puritans—but most who came to the new world were fortune seekers. They had little time for worship; they were concerned with earthly riches. For example, many settlers at the Jamestown Settlement in Virginia spent their time digging for gold rather than cultivating crops and gardens. Because of this and a paucity of pastors and churches, the American colonies became degenerate morally and religiously. A spiritual awakening was needed. This awakening began in the early eighteenth century and profoundly changed the religious landscape in North America.

The Great Awakening

In the USA J. Edwards in Massachusetts and T. Frelinghuysen in the Raritan Valley in northern New Jersey—the latter bringing over some of Pietism from the old country—have been identified as the precursors of the widespread and powerful Great Awakening of the Middle Colonies in the early 1700s. This profound movement was then stirred up further by G. Whitefield, a friend of Wesley, who came from England to do powerful outdoor preaching. His major impact from Boston to Charleston built on those earlier events. Whitefield had emerged alongside the Wesleyan movement in England, the Evangelical Awakening that transformed English society more than any other movement in English history.

This new form of personal-experience Christianity was so significantly different that, in the colonies, it split the majority group, the Presbyterians, right down the middle for a number of years—one side reflecting the more intellectual Reformation requirements and the other side emphasizing an experiential and identifiable "work of grace." This kind of emotional evangelical experience came early to be considered essential to salvation among Evangelicals, just as "speaking in tongues" was considered essential to salvation at a later time in much of the Pentecostal sphere.

However, as surprising as it may be to most Evangelicals in the twentieth and twenty-first centuries, the key point of this chapter is that this FIE of the eighteenth and nineteenth centuries was by no means oriented only to personal experience and the next world. In contrast to the almost exclusively personal salvation orientation of SIE, the mountain of social reforms connected with Wesley's profound social impact in England were also powerfully present in America.

In America it is said that 100 colleges were born as a result of the Great Awakening of the Middle Colonies. Also, one of the characteristics of this Evangelical mutation in this early period was that accusations abounded of "unconverted pastors." This new spirituality resulted in the founding of what was condescendingly called the "Log College" in Neshaminy, Pennsylvania, which eventually became a major contributor to the founding of Princeton University. There W. Tennent and his sons were vitally involved in ordination training for the first time on American soil, and through this the Great Awakening instigated a new movement within the Presbyterian Church called (again derisively) the "New Sides." This movement was at first rejected but eventually took the lead in healing the breach with the older group as the new group rapidly became far larger.

The Great Awakening in the Middle Colonies was a powerful movement that actually forged a democratically governed church structure ranging from Boston to Charleston and gave crucial impetus to the Declaration of Independence, the Constitutional Convention, and a single government for the colonies. Without this democratically governed intercolonial model, the birth of the new nation wouldn't have occurred the way it did. The crafting of the American Constitution was done one block away from meetings redrafting the Presbyterian Constitution. Many of the same men were involved in both meetings.

Just as Evangelicalism today is becoming more politically aware and active, so in the Great Awakening the whole idea of breaking away from England derived in part from the religious individualism of the Awakening. Indeed, the emphasis on individual decision and the rights of individuals influenced many people (such as T. Paine) who had no formal connection to the church at all. Indeed, the secular concept of individual freedom and rebellion against authority became so strong that when carried to France, in the total absence of grassroots democratic church structure, the French Revolution became a stridently secularist and even anti-Christian phenomenon as well as a ghastly bloodbath. Forget the guillotine. It was too slow. Thousands were killed at a time, Rwanda style, not with machetes but by chaining people together on large barges that were then sunk in major rivers.

Among America's leaders, the initially Christian vision for wholesale social change became so widespread that it was easy for many (whether, as with Paine, spiritually alive or not) to be enthusiastic about this world cause. Thus, by the time of the American Revolution, the spiritual roots of the Great Awakening became paradoxically overshadowed in public life—virtually snuffed out—by the political and military events going on between the Declaration of Independence in 1776 and the conclusion of the War of 1812 in 1815.

Thus, the idea of revolutionary power sufficient to make wholesale change in society, although spiritually rooted, became such a heady experience—some 75 years before Marx—that by 1800 it is said that you could hardly find a single student at Yale or Harvard who would admit to being a Christian. Students were even calling each other by the names of leaders in the French Revolution, such as Robespierre, Marat, and St. Just.

This anti-Christian spirit, picked up to some extent from the French, ruled in other colleges as well. In western Massachusetts at Williams College, due to severely antagonistic student opposition, the famous Haystack Prayer Meeting took place outdoors. Those five young men did not lack the intelligence to come in out of the rain. They simply could not hold their prayers in the college dorms because the bulk of the students were violently opposed to any religious behavior. This handful of believers couldn't even keep their personal diaries in anything but code. It is a surprising thing that the American foreign mission movement was born in the icy cold crib of the context at that time. At Yale the few students who wanted to pray together had to take refuge in the president's office.

In contrast to both this mood and to the frightening aftermath of the French Revolution was the Cane Ridge Revival of 1801 and other revival movements of that kind. They became especially significant in the first half of the 1800s.

The Second Great Awakening

Many scholars refer to certain events of roughly 1815–1840 as the Second Great Awakening, which was at least a renewal of the earlier Great Awakening. This era saw the contribution of C. Finney, an attorney who found Christ and definitely believed in a "second work of grace." The impact of his ministry, camp meetings, other itinerant preachers, and many local revivals were to be seen in much of America. These spiritual events did not ignore social transformation but fueled it.

Just as the Great Awakening of the Middle Colonies in the 1700s made a great contribution to both the Declaration of Independence and the subsequent Revolutionary War, so toward the middle of the 1800s the Second Great Awakening (and some of its precursor events like the Cane Ridge Revival) provided the moral outrage that underlay the events leading to the Civil War.

In many respects the most prominent event of the early 1800s in America was the unexpected outcome of the War of 1812. Between the time of the Declaration of Independence in 1776 and 1815—quite a lengthy period—the rebellion of the colonies against the British government was considered by many a risky and shaky and perhaps only temporary achievement. Indeed, in 1812 the New England states wouldn't even contribute troops to help the other former colonies fight that war. Thus, when Napoleon headed for Russia and the British turned their full military force against the USA in the War of 1812, many assumed this would be the end of the "glorious experiment" of the American nation.

Unexpectedly for the Americans, when the war was not lost but went to a draw, this amazing turn of events popped the balloon of fear of British reprisal. This miracle—along with the recently acquired Louisiana Purchase, which doubled the landmass of the new country—unleashed a truly massive migration to the West, which was part of the major shakeup in which ongoing revivals took place. It certainly increased the sense of freedom, vision, purpose, and promising future of the new nation, particularly among Evangelicals.[1]

This euphoria of freedom—this sense of ownership for the first time of a vast land of their own (never mind the Native Americans)—gave life to all kinds of radical experiments in the social, political, and religious arenas; and it dynamically sparked the imagination, vision, and even the rethinking of the Christian religion itself. In one case, the Shakers, no one married anyone. In another case, the Oneida Community, everyone married everyone. The pendulum swung on the college campuses, and the Greek and Roman classics were banned from schools on the grounds that they were pagan. Hebrew became a major study. For many decades college presidents were expected at commencement to deliver an oration in Hebrew because it was (supposedly) the language of heaven.

Oberlin College, established with the encouragement of Finney and the financial resources of the wealthy Tappan brothers, was both a fruit of the revival temperament and also socially upscale. Oberlin was the first interracial school, the first coeducational school, the first vocational school, the first school to teach music, the first antislavery school, the first temperance school, and so forth. No holy reform was outside their purview. Students prayed that God would help them improve the efficiency of the Franklin Stove, and so was invented the Oberlin Stove. The entire period represented incredible ingenuity, innovation, and—more specifically—attention to what today we would call social transformation. In this mix Evangelicals were the main leaders—not the reluctant followers of secular initiatives.

It would be impossible to overstate the significant changes of

---

[1] Enough religious people still ran things to keep alive the larger social vision of First-Inheritance Evangelicalism.

direction of both the Christian movement and our nation between 1815 and 1850. By 1850, for example, virtually all of the states had banned alcoholic beverages. In fact, vast numbers would not drink tea or coffee, so extensive was the application of Christian faith to everyday life. Dozens of reform movements sprang into life—the temperance movement, the movement for the abolition of slavery, a movement to use whole grain in wheat flour, which was called Graham Flour because it was preached by a minister named Sylvester Graham.

Both the Mormon and the Adventist groups emerged at this time. They differ greatly in theology but today equally represent museum pieces of the concern for food and health, which had become part and parcel of the mood of that revival period.

All this ferment was the forerunner of mood, morale, and morals, which fueled both aspirations of national unity and the elimination of slavery, which in turn prompted the Civil War. At one point, it is widely reported, President Lincoln met Harriet Beecher Stowe—the Oberlin-related Evangelical author of *Uncle Tom's Cabin* (which sold over six million copies). He said, "So you are the little lady who started this great war."

T. Smith's dissertation at Johns Hopkins University was published as a book titled *Revivalism and Social Reform.*[2] This book blew the lid off the tremendous ignorance of SIE advocates concerning the intimate relation between evangelism and social reform that held in this earlier FIE period. Many other authors have followed along to point out and confirm the same thing. But what these scholars are saying about the startlingly wide spectrum theology of that period is still not well understood today.

In the early twenty-first century, serious polarization still continues regarding linkages between evangelism and social action. C. Little helpfully sums up the background and varying points of view and suggests an alternative: "Doxological mission . . . [in which] the chief end of mission is the glory of God." He rightly bewails the success of the Enlightenment in "dislodging God and placing humankind's dignity, aspirations, values, and needs at the center of the universe."[3]

---

[2] T. L. Smith, *Revivalism and Social Reform* (San Francisco: Harper, 1957).
[3] C. Little, "What Makes Mission Christian?" *EMQ* 42:1 (January 2006): 78–87.

Gaining a new relationship with God for as many humans as possible—or, as one mission leader put it, "peopling the kingdom"—can logically be claimed to be the "priority," that is, what to do first, as has already been mentioned. But that is only a first phase in glorifying God. Those once reconciled to God are expected to proceed to glorify Him by their good works (Matt 5:16). However, for globally minded people, good works must go beyond just personal good deeds to *organized* good deeds that will include such matters as the deliberate discovery and exposition of the glories of God's creation (Ps 19:1–4) as well as serious concern for global poverty and disease. Otherwise, we misrepresent the character of God, and our proclamation activity lacks both credibility and authenticity.

Universities commonly have two major foci: arts and sciences. Art is the study of the handiwork of man. Science is the study of the handiwork of God. Both can be studied for the wrong reasons. In the world of art, we see the praise of man for works of art. In the world of science, we see the praise of man for Nobel Prize-winning discoveries of science or for the technological or humanitarian utility of such discoveries. However, both can also be pursued as a means of pure joy and a demonstration of God's glory.

PART 3: SECOND-INHERITANCE EVANGELICALISM

Remember that, as defined, the period of FIE can be seen as a time when Evangelical leaders at levels of national influence (as well as common people who followed them) briefly and uniquely worked within a window of awareness that made the transformation of society feasible—*something that was within their grasp.*

But what happened after the FIE period? What happened to that kind of socially active Evangelicalism? There are at least two factors. First, as mentioned earlier, European immigration became significant during the latter part of the 1800s. So many Catholics flooded into Protestant Massachusetts that by 1880 there was hardly a city or town in Massachusetts that was not predominantly Catholic. Second, Moody came into the picture from the backwoods of Massachusetts. He was a man who was extremely overweight, impulsive, had dyslexia to the extent that he could not even spell the simplest words. Worst of all—to some—his rural upbringing did not prepare him to speak the right kind of English. But he diligently sought the empowerment of God for ministry, as Finney had urged Christian leaders to do earlier. Moody reportedly said, "The world has yet to see what God can do through one man wholly committed to him." Perhaps no one in American history has come closer to that ideal. When God raised up this seemingly unlikely minister, Moody won millions of non-college people (and a few college students). Through his ministry Evangelicalism became, for the first time in America, a predominantly lower-class movement.

The people who were Evangelical leaders in the earlier days, both before the colonial period and after the War of 1812, were by comparison well educated. They tended to be the ones who ran things in the public sector. America, unlike England, could not boast of a Clapham Sect—a politically powerful group of wealthy Evangelical leaders in England with whom W. Wilberforce bloodlessly took down the slave trade in England. Although America had in many ways possessed a functional equivalent, things had massively changed 100 years later. The American population had exploded from 7 million to more than 90 million by 1910; it was a different country. Leading citizens of the Second Great Awakening were now a tiny minority. But the Evangelical movement had burgeoned marvelously both within the ranks of the immigrants and the uneducated stratum of society. *Yet it was no longer true that people of faith ran the country.*

It was somewhat of a lingering anomaly that 100,000 upscale college students could be caught up in the Student Volunteer Movement for Foreign Missions and provide leadership to the World Missionary Conference in Edinburgh in 1910. Few of these student volunteers came from the mainstream of Moody's converts even though Moody himself, somewhat accidentally, had helped to spark both the Cambridge Seven in England and the Student Volunteer Movement in America.

The last fling of wide-spectrum FIE advocates was arguably the Prohibition era, but the cleavage between college people and Bible institute people, already emerging by 1900, had by the 1920s unfortunately become a major feature of the Evangelical movement—a culture war within Evangelicalism. Upper-class people who were still thinking in terms of social reform were more and more often labeled liberal due to their social reform concerns, whether or not they were liberal in their theology.

Meanwhile, the newer lower-class Evangelicals had never had a chance to elect one of their own as a mayor. Their Bible institute graduates did not pursue the professions or the universities. They were for the most part not college people at all. They sometimes assumed that elite, influential believers must have something wrong with them, and to some extent they were right. To the noncollege people—as with slaves and their "Negro spirituals" that focused on heaven—the idea of reforming society seemed utterly impossible, theologically unexpected, and therefore evangelistically objectionable. The Civil War itself, to this day the bloodiest in American history, had caused a loss of faith in the theory of progress—even though a college teacher in 1895 wrote the words to "America the Beautiful," which describes a vision of the impact of the gospel where "alabaster cities gleam" and in which "thy good is crowned by brotherhood . . . undimmed by human tears."

Soon within the SIE we see a diminishing of the goal of reforming society and in its place a belief in a coming tribulation preceded by a pretribulation rapture. The goal of reforming individuals, while properly considered basic, was often improperly considered all that was needed, despite commendable "intuitive" good works lacking theological guidance. The Moody Bible Institute tradition, including the 157 Bible institutes following in this new perspective, to a great extent typified the SIE type of Christianity that was generally antagonistic to the earlier FIE brand. The remnants of FIE soon became regarded simply and objectionably as "liberal."

Thus, the dominant force of SIE essentially went socially underground for 60 or 70 years, while those Bible institutes, one by one, became Bible colleges, then Christian colleges, and eventually Christian universities. However, as a result of this gradual reemergence of culturally standard educational patterns, even Congress and the White House itself became once more populated by people of Evangelical convictions. But increased social influence was unaccompanied by a theology corresponding to such new opportunities.

The Bible institute stream thus constituted the backbone of the Evangelical movement for a lengthy period, and its eventual marriage with the ethos of the college cultural stream was a long time in coming. During that long transition it was possible for such definitive books to be written, such as C. F. H. Henry's prophetic *The Uneasy Conscience of Modern Fundamentalism* and later M. Noll's *The Scandal of the Evangelical Mind.*[4]

The delay in a recovery of the FIE's wide-spectrum sense of mission was not so much because twentieth-century Evangelicals couldn't think. They may not have continued to think of major reforms in society, but they did develop all kinds of new and creative understandings of the Bible. A typical example was their emphasis on eschatology, the rapture, and the second coming of Christ. Such ideas for many years characterized this SIE brand of Evangelicalism, to some extent following J. N. Darby. Moody Bible Institute may have led the way, but virtually all Bible institutes took part. Prophecy conferences abounded. Social reform seemed illogical if only because the world was predicted to get worse and worse until true believers were raptured out of it. A social gospel was anathema.

PART 4: THE RECOVERY OF FIRST-INHERITANCE EVANGELICALISM

As Evangelicals work their way into social and even political influence, many other changes will take place in the context of mission. Discussion of all such new developments could occupy many pages, but some of the issues include the following:

- There is the shrinking of the globe and the tendency of local churches in the West to have a more direct hand in what happens at a distance. The urgent value of veteran mission agencies will tend to be overlooked.
- The massive trend to send out young and old for two weeks will continue to drain money from more serious mission,

---

[4] C. F. H. Henry, *The Uneasy Conscience of Modern Fundamentalism* (Grand Rapids: Eerdmans Publishing, 2003) and M. A. Noll, *The Scandal of the Evangelical Mind* (Grand Rapids: Eerdmans, 1995).

adding helpful education to the local sending churches but little direct or indirect contribution to missions.

- An unexpected but growing trend is "Insider Movements," which requires us in the West to recognize modern parallels between (1) the much-disputed decision of the Jerusalem Council in Acts to allow Greek culture to become another "earthen vessel" for the gospel, and (2) the decision of millions of Chinese, Hindus, and Africans who have already chosen to follow Christ within their own cultural traditions without identifying with formal Western Christianity. This new appearance of biblical faith is already a phenomenon as large or larger than formal Christianity in those three continents.
- The special challenge of cities will continue to be studied.
- The challenge of nonliterate masses will continue to grow.
- The need to do something about poverty, human slavery, and the eradication of disease (much exacerbated by globalization) will increasingly occupy everyone, but more specifically emboldened and wealthy Evangelicals.

This list could go on and on. However, only the last item is directly related to the thesis of this chapter, namely, that mission theology will follow upon the growth of the civil stature of the Evangelical movement, forcing into existence new interpretations of the Bible in regard to the use of that vastly increased influence. That is what this chapter continues to pursue in view of the far-reaching and novel implications it will have.

Thus, the future of Evangelicalism and Evangelical missions is likely to involve a difficult and painful shift away from decades of polarization between "social action" and "the pure gospel." This shift, which is already taking place, has brought new opportunity and responsibility, but it shares the dangers to which the children of FIE eventually fell prey. As the twentieth century wore on, many outstanding Evangelicals ranging from J. R. W. Stott and others in the Lausanne movement tried hard to point out that there can be no real dichotomy between faith and good works, despite a continuing Reformation-triggered bias in that realm.

As already seen, one example of this is the simple fact that the word *kingdom* was almost totally banned from Evangelical literature for at least 50 years. Only recently has this word, so prominent in the NT, been recovered as some expositors have written books about the kingdom of God and tried to bring it back into the fold.[5] But the word is still suspect in many Evangelical circles.

In missions the polarization is reflected by the fact that on the social action side there is one entire association of over 50 agencies, the Association of Evangelical Relief and Development Organizations (AERDO), which includes a number of strong Evangelical mission agencies, such as World Vision, World Concern, the World Relief Department of the National Association of Evangelicals, and so on. Their social action has gained quite a following; otherwise, it wouldn't be possible for World Vision to achieve an annual half-billion-dollar budget.

Yet, until recently in books by B. Myers, World Vision has not vigorously advanced a theological basis for what it is doing. Fortunately, many Evangelical donors have obviously felt intuitively that things World Vision was trying to do were worth supporting. This is in some way a nontheological, intuitive recovering of one part of FIE focused primarily on helping human beings even though it is not as yet as concerned for social transformation in general (e.g., eradicating disease and rehabilitating science as declaring God's glory).

Meanwhile, in the first five years after the Second World War, when 150 new mission agencies were founded, most of the new agencies were characterized as "service agencies" that added muscle to existing missions—technology like airplanes, radios, or literature to the already existing mission movement. This meant that all of this new vigor almost entirely emphasized what was already going on, that is, the preaching of an intellectual and emotional gospel plus an emphasis on a restoration of individual fellowship with God. If it had not been for the informal theological *intuition* of loving missionaries, it would not have resulted in such extensive "good works" but merely in the evangelism of still

[5] E.g., A. Glasser, *Announcing the Kingdom* (Grand Rapids: Baker, 2003).

others mainly oriented toward the next world—an emphasis on the eternal not the temporal.

In other words, the reason SIE is a complicated phenomenon is that the most extensive and the most influential social transformation-as-mission activity (even in the twentieth century) was actually accomplished (though much was not reported to donors) by the Evangelical mission agencies established before 1900. Evangelical momentum in the mainline denominational missions, the work of the great interdenominational mission agencies like Sudan Interior Mission or the Africa Inland Mission, plus the work of the smaller Evangelical denominational missions—all of these employed *an intuition not undergirded by formal theology* but still made tremendous contributions to the entire educational framework of whole countries like China and Nigeria. The world's largest technical university was founded by missionaries in Sao Paulo, Brazil. Asia's largest agricultural university was founded by missionaries in North India. The university system itself was taken to the field explicitly by Evangelical missionaries in the first half of the nineteenth century. We think of projects like Yale in China. This was in part the final momentum of the FIE wave, some of it carrying over into the twentieth century. It also reflected the keen intuition of socially sensitive missionaries.

It was understood back in the nineteenth century and in these major missions that there was no rift whatsoever between learning and gospel, or good works and gospel, or schools, hospitals, vocational schools and the planting of churches. Nevertheless, today, as far as donors are concerned, the enormous impact of social transformation arising (intuitively) in the work of standard church planting mission agencies is widely resented and underestimated. Indeed, it is virtually unknown in certain spheres, in part due to an intentional downplaying of this effort in reports to donors who want to hear only of spiritual conversions. This is incorrectly rationalized as a tension between the so-called liberal and conservative perspectives, when in fact it is largely due to the inherently different perspective of socially influential Evangelicals and the era of social impotence among most Evangelicals in the twentieth century. People like C. Colson (who was a civil leader) have no trouble envisioning sweeping changes in the whole world's prison systems, nor in helping to resurrect the powerful social and political example of Wilberforce in England.

Empowered Evangelism

Obviously, there is a theological problem here. We know we must take seriously the fact that Jesus was concerned with handicapped people, sick people, children, women, Greeks, and so on, and that His ministry embraced and encompassed those things. When Jesus responded to John the Baptist, who wondered if he was the one to come, Jesus sent back descriptions, not of the text of his message, but simply a report of good works He was doing. This He did, not only as an authentication of who He was but as a demonstration of God's character. His ministry was congruent with His own statement, "In the same way, let your light shine before men, so that they may see your good works and give glorify to your Father in heaven" (Matt 5:16). In the synagogue in Nazareth Jesus quoted Isa 61:1–2 (see Luke 4:18–19):

> The Spirit of the Lord is on Me,
> because He has anointed Me to preach
> good news to the poor.
> He has sent Me
> to proclaim freedom to the captives
> and recovery of sight to the blind,
> to set free the oppressed,
> to proclaim the year of the Lord's favor.

Does Jesus' declared intention to "free the oppressed" apply to 27 million men, women, and children held as slaves in the world today? This is more than were sold in the four centuries before slavery was abolished. Christians today would do well to emulate the activities of the nineteenth-century Christian abolitionists like William Wilberforce.

It has been said that *because the gospel is a message of hope, the poorest must see some concrete reason for hope before they can understand the gospel.* Words themselves have no power if they do not refer to reality. Jesus' words were constantly accompanied and informed by the things to which His words referred. Thus, just as faith without works is dead, so evangelism without works is dead. Unless words refer to works, to reality, they are worth nothing. Just as it is a Reformation myth that faith can be separated from works, so it is meaningless if words are separated from the reality to which they were meant to refer.

It seems that just as we believe that works ought to follow faith in the life of believing individuals, it is equally true that in our outreach to unbelievers *those works displaying God's glory better come first*. We see this clearly when we recognize that the usual way in which individuals come to faith is primarily by viewing the good works of those who already have faith—that is, by observing Christians' good deeds that reflect the character of God. Immediately after speaking of His followers being salt and light in the world, Jesus spoke the verse we have already quoted, "In the same way, let your light shine before men, so that they may see your good works and give glory to your Father in heaven" (Matt 5:16). *That is how people glorify God and are drawn to Him.* Those who may be drawn by mere desires to be blessed personally will have trouble with Jesus' plain statement, "For whoever wants to save his life will lose it, but whoever loses his life because of Me and the gospel will save it" (Mark 8:35).

Thus, in order for people to hear and respond to an offer of personal salvation or a ticket to heaven, it is paramount for them to witness the glory of God in believers' lives—seeing the love and goodness in their lives and deeds, and their new motives and intentions. This is the reality that gives them reason to turn away *from* all evil and *against* all evil as they seek to be closer to that kind of God and His will in this world.

Personal salvation alone can still be a glorious transformation of people who may never arise from a sickbed or from poverty, knowing that God loves them and wants them to love Him. At the same time many believers are not poor and have time and energy to do things other than simply talk to people about the next world. For them, a concept that is hard to avoid (because it is happening throughout the whole Bible) is that works are necessary to authenticate and demonstrate the true character of God. That is the true basis for *empowering* evangelism.

Further, this potent continuity of word and deed is the mainstream of mission history. It may not have been so large a factor among affluent people in a country like Japan, but in much of the world the stunning achievements of medicine and healing have demonstrated to potential converts not only the love of God for them but also the power of God that is on their side against the forces of darkness. People like Simon the sorcerer may try to emulate that activity without the corresponding concern. Others may gain a different message: one of hope and love, not just power to be acquired.

Defeating the "Works of the Devil"

Jesus spoke to Paul about delivering people "from the power of Satan to God" (Acts 26:18). Peter summed up Jesus' ministry by speaking of "how God anointed Jesus of Nazareth with the Holy Spirit and with power, and how He went about doing good and curing all who were *under the tyranny of the Devil*, because God was with Him" (Acts 10:38). This kind of demonstration of the person and the power of God certainly should not be considered antagonistic to evangelism. In most cases it is, again, the basis of an empowerment of evangelism.

But by taking a quick glance at the current record of missions of good works, it is perfectly obvious that thus far no great dents in world poverty have been achieved by missionaries of Jesus Christ, even though their intentions and even their record is highly respectable. Recently more and more high-minded young people have shown themselves willing to go and live among people in extreme poverty. This is also good, but most poor people need more than another apparently poor and powerless person to come and live among them. The dramatic rescue of a handful of individuals from such situations does not materially change structured poverty. Mother Teresa's gift to the world was not so much the problems she directly remedied but the quality of her concern pled for solutions at the roots of her patients' problems.

Once individuals find faith, they have often pulled themselves up by their bootstraps—through their honesty, abandonment of liquor and drugs, and their ability to build businesses that would succeed. This has gradually lifted them up out of the poverty category into the middle-class category, not just in England but also in America and in many parts of the world. This kind of individual salvation is the primary focus of Evangelical missions today even though it may not be the whole picture.

I went to Guatemala in 1957 with the gospel in my heart, my head, and my ministry, and worked for 10 years among a wonderful and responsive people. Now, almost five decades later, there are not just the three churches in that valley when I left but more than 30. By now there is a high percentage of the indigenous population in that entire valley who are out and out believers in Jesus Christ. But during my 10 years there, the people—both believers and unbelievers—were in desperate straits in terms of poverty. The need was so great that a visiting pastor from Chicago after two days with us sharply criticized me for overlooking the people's poverty and for talking just about spiritual salvation, although I had started 17 small businesses. He offered to raise some money in Chicago and send it down *if I would use it solely for food*. When I informed him that the food necessary for the 70,000 people in that valley would require about $1 million every two months, he practically fainted and went back to Chicago without ever sending a penny.

Thus, it is a fact that most missionaries, and especially their individual converts, rarely have the wherewithal of either knowledge or power to make major, fundamental changes in society. This is why the entire sphere of large-scale social action and social transformation is beyond the reach of less powerful people, who have for a lengthy period been thinking of *personal* transformation rather than *social* transformation. They may also be people whose knowledge of the past is vague or perhaps completely nil. By the past I refer to the tremendous period of Evangelical-led social transformation in the middle of the nineteenth century, what I have called First-Inheritance Evangelicalism.

However, without even studying the past, it is apparent that there is a crescendo of concern for the serious problems of our world. The AIDS crisis has thrown us into a lot of confusion but also into serious contemplation about what can or should be done. Since malaria annually detracts significantly from productive work in Africa, then eradicating malaria might eliminate the poverty of that continent all by itself. Yet malaria is simply not something that can be driven into extinction by the local efforts of individual mission stations or churches.

In view of my first wife's five-year descent into a cancerous death and my own current struggling with the same kind of cancer, I am well known for believing that disease is probably the greatest killer and producer of suffering in the entire world. Yet, in many international development books, the idea of setting out to fight various diseases to a standstill is not even mentioned, although that has been done in the case of smallpox and now soon Guinea worm. Why isn't it mentioned? Perhaps because such challenges may have seemed too big for them to handle, but also because they have probably possessed no theology undergirding that kind of effort.

But nine out of 10 Americans in our wonderfully blessed country die prematurely—and by no means painlessly—because of disease. Yet to the average citizen, church congregation, or Evangelical donor, the idea of banishing malaria entirely from Africa seems to be unthinkable—again, for the simple reason that it really is totally impossible on a small scale. We have banished malaria almost entirely from America, but that was a geographically limited project compared with eradicating smallpox from the face of the entire earth. Significantly, the effort to eliminate smallpox was not theologically driven.

It is embarrassing to me that former President Jimmy Carter—a Sunday school teacher, not a theologian or a mission executive or a missiologist—has actually done more than anyone else in arousing world opinion to the need to *eradicate* diseases, not just extend *health care* after people get sick. Carter is the one who took the initiative to found the International Task Force for the Eradication of Disease. This task force has now attracted funds from the Bill and Melinda Gates Foundation.

It is unfortunate that Carter has not been able to get substantial money from Christian sources for this activity. His sources are almost entirely commercial. What he is doing is something that to my knowledge no theologian, mission executive, or television evangelist has ever had the theology to promote. His efforts have already reduced Guinea worm in West Africa by 99.9 percent. The Carters, in a brief visit to West Africa, had witnessed victims of that disease clearly knocked out of the workforce and in pain for months, suffering from a tiny water-born parasite that grows in the body to 30 inches in length. The last few sufferers today are largely located in nearly inaccessible places in Sudan. President Carter's actions in this regard can serve as a model for Christian agencies to emulate.

Thus, in all of our commendable haste to get to the ends of the earth and to the last group that has never heard the gospel, we may be overlooking the fact that the vast bulk of the Western world no longer believes in the Bible and no longer follows our faith. Does this mean our immense overseas achievements are only temporary? Statistics show that 80 percent of the people in France consider themselves Christians, but only 20 percent believe in God. Further, only a small percentage of teenagers brought up in Evangelical homes will retain their faith after they leave home. Is that the future of Christianity in the Southern Hemisphere?

We hear other similar things about the collapse of the Evangelical awakening in England, where church attendance has dropped to 4 percent. We have been successful to a degree in tracking down the last unreached people on the face of the earth, but we face a considerable shortfall in maintaining our faith among educated people. Is this decline due to an absence of recognized signs of God's glory? Is it because the involvement of missions in eradicating disease is so minor that a Harvard professor can observe, "If the god of the Intelligent Design people exists he must be a divine sadist that creates parasites that blind millions of people"?[6]

PART 5: THE FUTURE OF EVANGELICAL MISSIONS

So what is the future of the Evangelical mission movement? The mission movement—more so than the church movement and considerably more so than the secular world—holds the key to a great new burst of credibility that could win new millions. For example, despite all its secularism and Marxism, the first three of China's "Four Modernizations" promoted by Deng Xiaoping (agriculture, industry, science and technology, national defense)

---

[6] S. Pinker as quoted in D. Van Biema, "Can You Believe in God and Evolution?" *Time* (August 7, 2005): 34–35.

were precisely great emphases of missionaries in China before 1950. Surprisingly, as a result, the Chinese government today, which we have known to persecute the church, may today have a better appreciation of the real impact of the gospel of Christ in their country than do the heavenly minded donors funding the missionaries who, in contrast to many donors, were concerned with both heaven and earth. This is an irony.

The Bill and Melinda Gates Foundation and its concerns—along with Bono and other actors and actresses such as Madonna—would seem to pressure other moneyed people to concern themselves similarly. This is no longer the old interest in getting buildings named after them and so forth but in seeking credit for things like the eradication of poverty and disease and suffering. This unexpected trend of philanthropy clearly indicates the potential of people in high places who grow up in a highly Christianized society, even if they haven't regularly gone to church. They need to understand that their efforts will be dismayingly ineffective without a certain minimum of transformed individuals whose character is essential to these major efforts. In that sphere missions have the monopoly on transformed individuals who can be trusted.

But at the same time, I yearn to see Evangelical missions be able to give more direct, credible credit to Jesus Christ for the impetus behind the social transformation they have been and are doing. Practically none of the major religions, by comparison, has any significant contribution to good works, small or large. Islam has the giving of alms as one of its five pillars, but there is absolutely nothing in the entire mammoth global Islamic movement that compares even remotely to the hundreds of major Christian mission agencies or the thousands of ways in which the Christian movement has reached out with love and tenderness to those who are suffering. Islam has a nearly similar vacuum of nongovernment agencies. The West also has thousands of NGOs that are not explicitly Christian. Islam has only a few.

The work of Christ in the Gospels, Christ's references to the coming of the kingdom of God, and the present outworking in this world of the "Your will be done" in the Lord's Prayer (Matt

6:10) are actually echoed by the Great Commission itself. Looking closely at Matt 28:20, it isn't just the *teachings* that Jesus commissions His disciples to pass on; it is the actual enforcing, so to speak, of *obedience to those teachings*. We hear later in the NT about people who do not "obey" the gospel. Obviously, the gospel is not just mere information in the way of good advice. There is an authority and command from God in the gospel. This is the clear meaning of the Great Commission: Jesus sent His disciples out to teach "all nations . . . to observe everything I have commanded you."

As I have suggested, the older missions with roots in the nineteenth century have in actual fact been doing exactly what Jesus did, both demonstrating the love of God and inviting into eternal life all who yield to that love and that authority. The trouble is that the fact of this breadth hasn't been as clearly theologized to the point where we would plan to tackle some of the bigger problems such as the wiping out of Guinea worm, problems which have existed for over a century under the very noses of missionaries. *Such extra breadth must not be seen to be a divergence from the preaching of eternal life but rather an empowerment of the message of a gospel of a kingdom, which is both here and hereafter.* This is the gospel of Jesus Christ. It is the gospel of the kingdom, the announcement of a rule and reign of God that must be extended to the whole world and all of creation. We must stand up and be counted as active foes of the world's worst evils. This is the biblical way, the way more than any other in which missions have in the past and can now more powerfully and extensively than ever demonstrate who God is and what His purposes are.

The Great Commission is great in part because it does not refer merely to the communication of a message such as "teaching them . . . everything I have commanded you." No, it precisely says, "Teaching them to *observe* everything I have commanded you." This implies the conquest of evil when the Lord's Prayer is read in this light: "Your will be done *on earth*" (Matt 6:10).

This more extensive influence will come if agencies will simply take the practical conclusions of their missionaries' magnificent local intuition up into national levels and into international campaigns to drive out the things that not only cause hundreds of millions of people to go to bed at night with severe suffering and pain but also cut their lives short. Otherwise, all such unaddressed evil is blamed on God and His mysterious purposes. This new, expanded influence may thus measurably help us rewin the West to a faith that works and to a God who is not doing bad things for mysterious reasons but who opposes the evil one and all his works—and He asks us to assist Him in that campaign.

Evangelicals are increasingly again in a position of social influence. But we are still mainly in the business of sharing the faith, a faith that does not include much of a mission beyond converts converting still others. However, a return to a full-spectrum gospel could mean an enormous change. Doors will open. Attitudes about missionaries will change. It will no longer be the case of missionaries thinking that they have to use adroit language to cover up the "real purpose" of their work. Their real purpose will be to identify and destroy all forms of evil, both human and microbiological, and will thus be explainable without religious jargon. This will provide common ground in almost any country.

In that event there is no doubt in my mind that the future of the Evangelical mission movement will be bright indeed. A. Judson correctly stated, "The future is as bright as the promises of God." We must not forget that God is the one who asked us to pray, "Your kingdom come, *Your will be done on earth* as it is in heaven" (Matt 6:10).

CONCLUSION

The future of Evangelical missions will reflect how this generation of missiologists, missions administrators, and missionaries understand the New Testament and the history of the Christian church. If these missions scholars and practitioners embrace the holistic mission of Jesus Christ, then missions in the future will address both the spiritual and physical needs of the world's population. If the missions scholars and practitioners emulate the example of First-Inheritance Evangelicals, they will seek the transformation of both souls and society. These emphases truly will serve to make the future bright.

BIBLIOGRAPHY

Glasser, A. *Announcing the Kingdom.* Grand Rapids: Baker, 2003.

Little, C. "What Makes Mission Christian?" *EMQ* 42.1 (2006): 78–87.

Unger, M. F. "Rethinking the Genesis Account of Creation." *BSac* 115 (January–March 1958): 27–35.

———. *Unger's Bible Handbook.* Chicago: Moody Press, 1967.

Van Biema, D. "Can You Believe in God and Evolution?" *Time* (August 7, 2005): 34–35.

CHAPTER 15

Looking Backward While Going Forward

A Response to Winter's Vision

SCOTT MOREAU

INTRODUCTION

Ralph Winter's essay provides a wonderful foundation on which to build in exploring the future of missions. The driving philosophy underlying his thinking is well summarized in the oft-quoted phrase of G. Santayana, "Those who cannot remember the past are condemned to repeat it."[1] The main thrust of his argument for the future of missions is that we have a wonderful heritage from the past on which, if we draw wisely, we can remap missions for the future. In the first section of this response, I have summarized the critical components of Winter's thinking and responded to each. In the second I have introduced several additional developments that will impact the future of missions.

RECOVERY OF FIRST-INHERITANCE
EVANGELICALS' VALUES AND ETHOS

The heritage to which Winter refers is the vision, foundation, and integrative approach of Evangelicals in First-Inheritance

---

[1] G. Santayana, *Life of Reason or the Phases of Human Progress: Reason in Common Sense* (New York: Scribner's, 1905), 284.

Evangelicalism (FIE). He argues that if we are to have an ongoing positive impact on the world for Christ, we need to emulate them. He also identifies three elements of that heritage for emulation. The first element was the solid theological undergirding that provided the foundation to support their transformational goals (provided through thinkers such as J. Edwards). The second element was that they—as civil leaders who were deeply Christian—integrated personal and social transformation together as God's purpose for humankind in the world. They had not yet learned to separate them and did not see a need to do so. As Winter sees it, social transformation has positive and negative foci. Positively it incorporates such things as "rehabilitating science as declaring God's glory." Negatively it includes eradicating disease and slavery, as well as battling the systems and structures that keep people poor and marginalized. The third element was the ability to think big—to envision social transformation on a massive scale (as they did in their work of establishing a new republic in the new world).

Fast-forward to contemporary Evangelicals in Second-Inheritance Evangelicalism (SIE). Winter explains that, in contrast to our spiritual forefathers, we have lived out a reductionistic model of missions that focuses on personal transformation and leaves social transformation to the liberal (or secular) world. As he points out, while the intuition of SIE field missionaries has been to work toward social transformation through such things as education and medical work, they tended to do so at a personal rather than a social level, and this work was done as a result of intuition rather than theological grounding.

With this stage set and with his focus fixed on "the need to do something about poverty, human slavery, and the eradication of disease," Winter argues that it is time to recapture our heritage (1) by providing a theological foundation for battling *all* of the works of the Devil; (2) by reuniting personal (word) and social (deed) transformation in ways that demonstrate God's winsomeness to a harassed and helpless world; and (3) by putting before the entire body of Christ visions of both types of transformation that are as big and bold as those of Evangelicals in FIE. We briefly explore each of these in turn.

In regard to providing a theological foundation for battling *all* of the works of the Devil, there are encouraging signs of this happening in a variety of ways. In evangelical circles theologians and biblical scholars—not just practitioners—have been working through related issues. For example, J. C. Thomas explores the role spiritual conflict plays in disease and other afflictions,[2] S. Page examines the biblical accounts of angels and demons (1995),[3] and N. Wright constructs a holistic theology of evil (2003).[4] While not an evangelical, W. Wink's books, which wrestle with the biblical texts in relation to spiritual powers in society, have enjoyed wide influence in evangelical circles, though not without criticism.[5] Even more exciting is what is happening in the Southern Hemisphere. Certainly most contemporary mission statisticians indicate that the majority of missionaries today (and for the future) will be coming from the Majority World or Non-Western World, and that the future of Christian missions will be resting at least as much on their shoulders as on those from the West. For example, in relation to the theological foundation Winter calls for, Christians from Majority World settings have a clearer perception of sources of evil in all areas of life.[6] This bodes well for his hopes that in the future the church will have a better vision of what it means to use the best God has given to us—in theology *and* science—to combat evil in all its forms.

Winter's second prediction is that this next generation of Evangelicals will reunite personal (word) and social (deed)

---

[2] See J. C. Thomas, "Spiritual Conflict in Illness and Affliction" in *Deliver Us from Evil: An Uneasy Frontier in Christian Mission*, ed. A. S. Moreau, T. Adeyemo, D. Burnett, B. Myers, and H. Yung (Monrovia: MARC, 2002), 37–60.

[3] See S. Page, *Powers of Evil: A Biblical Study of Satan and Demons* (Grand Rapids: Baker), 1995.

[4] See N. G. Wright, *A Theology of the Dark Side: Putting the Power of Evil in Its Place* (Downers Grove: InterVarsity, 2003).

[5] See W. Wink, *Naming the Powers: The Language of Power in the New Testament* (Philadelphia: Fortress, 1984); *Unmasking the Powers: The Invisible Forces that Determine Human Existence* (Philadelphia: Fortress, 1986); *Engaging the Powers: Discernment and Resistance in a World of Dominion* (Philadelphia: Fortress, 1992); and *The Powers That Be: Theology for a New Millennium* (New York: Doubleday, 1998). For criticisms, see K. Jorgensen, "Spiritual Conflict in Socio-Political Context," in *Deliver Us from Evil: An Uneasy Frontier in Christian Mission*, ed. A. S. Moreau, T. Adeyemo, D. Burnett, B. Myers, and H. Yung (Monrovia: MARC, 2002), 213–30; and S. F. Noll, "Thinking About Angels," in *The Unseen World: Christian Reflections on Angels, Demons and the Heavenly Realm*, ed. A. N. S. Lane (Grand Rapids: Baker, 1996), 1–27.

[6] P. Jenkins, *The Next Christendom: The Coming of Global Christianity* (New York: Oxford University Press, 2002), 98–127. For an account of the integration in African settings of the need to battle disease as part of the ministry of the church, see A. Walls, *The Cross-Cultural Process in Christian History* (Maryknoll: Orbis, 2002), 122–33.

transformation, developing as the Evangelical movement grows in civil stature. Over the past few decades more and more Evangelicals have embraced some form of holism in missions, to the extent that we are at a juncture where the theological foundation for a holistic mission that does not drop evangelism is being laid within Evangelical missiological thinking,[7] and, more recently, in emergent church thinking.[8] One place in which the impact of this increased focus on social transformation has been seen on a pragmatic level was the inflation-adjusted 73.4 percent increase in income for overseas mission from 2001 to 2005 as reported by American agencies whose primary activities were in the areas of relief and development.[9]

We may further add to this the reality that Global South missionaries have been characterized as having a tendency to be more holistic[10] and thus have also been able to avoid the dichotomization that characterizes Western Evangelical missionaries in SIE. Winter is right to raise the concern that Evangelicals adhering to and formulating this newer holistic framework need to ensure that they do not follow the path of reductionism seen after FIE (i.e., holism that lacks evangelism). This will bear close watching over the coming decades.[11]

Of perhaps the greatest significance is Winter's third component: putting before the entire body of Christ visions of both types of transformation that are as big and bold as those of FIE. From the secular world there has been a plethora of visionary thinking along these lines—such as calls to eliminate public debt of Majority

---

[7] E.g., B. Myers, *Walking with the Poor: Principles and Practices of Transformational Development* (Maryknoll: Orbis, 1999); S. Escobar, *Changing Tides: Latin America & World Mission Today* (Maryknoll: Orbis, 2002); Lausanne Committee for World Evangelization, "Lausanne Occasional Paper 33: Holistic Mission," http://www.lausanne.org/documents/2004forum/LOP33_IG4.pdf (2005, accessed October 10, 2007); C. J. H. Wright, *The Mission of God: Unlocking the Bible's Grand Narrative* (Downers Grove: InterVarsity, 2007).

[8] E.g., D. Pagitt and T. Jones, eds., *An Emergent Manifesto of Hope* (Grand Rapids: Baker, 2007).

[9] See A. S. Moreau, "Putting the Survey in Perspective" in *Mission Handbook 2007–2009: U.S. and Canadian Protestant Ministries Overseas*, ed. L. Weber and D. J. Welliver (Wheaton: Evangelism and Missions Information Service, 2007), 43–45.

[10] See Escobar, *Changing Tides*, 19–20, and *The New Global Mission: The Gospel from Everywhere to Everywhere* (Downers Grove: InterVarsity, 2003), 142–54; Jenkins, *The Next Christendom*, and *The New Faces of Christianity: Believing the Bible in the Global South* (New York: Oxford University Press, 2006); and D. Aikman, *Jesus in Beijing: How Christianity Is Transforming China and Changing the Global Balance of Power* (Washington, D.C.: Regnery, 2003).

[11] See D. Hesselgrave, *Paradigms in Conflict: 10 Key Questions in Christian Missions Today* (Grand Rapids: Kregel, 2005), 117–39.

World nations and poverty—but for the reasons Winter mentions, very little (if any) has come from Evangelicals. At least in part this is because Evangelicals have not yet risen to positions of social prominence in ways that enable their voices to be heard, a lingering legacy of SIE. However, should that happen, one of the potential issues that must be faced is that large-scale plans rarely pan out as originally envisioned. For example, W. Easterly asks why it is that the West has given $3.2 trillion dollars in aid over the past 50 years, and yet we still have not successfully been able to get into the hands of children malaria prophylactics costing 12 cents each and able to prevent half of the malaria deaths.[12] Winter notes that malaria costs Africa some 45 million man-years annually.

Such grandiose planning is usually developed by what Easterly calls "planners," people who devise schemes for development that are massively scaled but whose "customer" is the donors rather than the poor in need of aid. He argues for multiple smaller-scale approaches that make a difference, not at the planning level but at the local level if we are truly to see change in our battles against poverty and diseases such as malaria. He calls people who can implement such approaches "searchers" since they focus on the recipient as the ultimate customer (rather than the donor) and ensure not only that the goods are distributed but that they are used properly. Interestingly, at a presentation of his materials to a class at Wheaton College, Easterly mentioned that missionaries seem to get this principle by nature far better than most people. In this sense I agree with Winter on the need for a grander vision, but at the same time I would argue that it would need to take into account the findings of people like Easterly if we are not simply to duplicate the failed efforts at development carried out by the West over the past five decades. The call for such vision may also fit into the American penchant for what Escobar refers to as "managerial missiology" with its inherent constraints.[13]

Further complicating the development of such visionary plans, recent psychological research indicates humans may be hardwired to focus on helping one or two people but this desire to help breaks

---

[12] W. Easterly, *The White Man's Burden: Why the West's Efforts to Aid the Rest Have Done So Much Ill and So Little Good* (New York: The Penguin Press, 2006), 3–4.

[13] Escobar, *Changing Tides*, 18–19.

down when more people—in the exact situation as the first one or two—also need help.[14] In other words we tend to respond more generously with the one who needs help than the 100 who need help. Those who can go beyond this hardwiring and who can think globally tend to be people who can think in multiples of 10 and not get bogged down. Thus, people like former President Jimmy Carter and Bill Gates have engaged in the battle Winter calls Christians to engage in, namely, the eradication of preventable diseases such as malaria. But, as Winter points out, people like Gates lack the theological foundation that will sustain them through the battle, and they certainly do not have the evangelistic framing that is necessary for a truly holistic gospel.

At the same time, there are encouraging signs of broader thinking in Evangelical circles. Missiologists and theologians are taking on a variety of social problems.[15] We also see examples of this broader thinking in cases involving the willingness to partner with non-Christian religions to embark on projects that can profit the entire population of a country.[16]

ADDITIONAL AREAS TO CONSIDER

In the essay, Winter mentions several additional areas that could be considered. Rather than explore those mentioned by him, I am adding five more to his list. In the discussion that follows, I have space only to identify selected issues and to highlight some of the more significant implications each brings for the future of missions.

---

[14] C. Thompson, "Why We Can Count on Geeks to Rescue the Earth," *Wired* 15.9 (September 2007) http://www.wired.com/techbiz/people/magazine/15–09/st_thompson (accessed October 9, 2007).

[15] E.g., on economics, see R. Carroll and M. Daniel, "The Challenge of Economic Globalization for Theology: From Latin America to a Hermeneutics of Responsibility" in *Globalizing Theology: Belief and Practice in an Era of World Christianity*, ed. C. Ott and H. Netland (Grand Rapids: Baker, 2006), 199–212; on the environment, see W. D. Roberts, *Patching God's Garment: Environment and Mission in the 21st Century* (Monrovia: MARC, 1994); and H. Snyder, *Coherence in Christ: The Larger Meaning of Ecology* (New York: General Board of Global Ministries, The United Methodist Church, 2000); on politics, see A. E. Black, D. L. Koopman, and D. K. Ryden, *Of Little Faith: The Politics of George W. Bush's Faith-Based Initiatives* (Washington, D.C.: Georgetown University Press, 2004); on caste, see J. D'souza, *Dalit Freedom Now and Forever: The Epic Struggle for Dalit Emancipation* (Centennial: Dalit Freedom Network, 2004); and on slavery, see the International Justice Mission's work as highlighted in public news documentaries found on the Web site http://www.ijm.org.

[16] E.g., M. L. Daneel (*African Earthkeepers: Wholistic Interfaith Mission* [Maryknoll: Orbis, 2001]) provides a historical account of independent churches and traditional religious practitioners in Zimbabwe engaging together in a "war of the trees"—planting trees as a significant means to battle environmental degradation.

First, the development of even more models for mission will enrich the already existing models. Traditional Western mission agencies will continue to be healthy into the foreseeable future, but their work will be supplemented by people engaging in mission who come from contexts that do not have economic systems that allow traditional faith support to be as viable as it is in the West. Missions from the Global South by necessity will not be limited to the faith missions or even the business-as-missions approaches, though they will use them when possible. Rather, the economic constraints they face will force them to be more creative than Western missionaries have had to be in securing livelihoods while pursuing God's call on their lives.

Second, the entire pace of missions (noted by Winter in the mention of short-term missions) will continue to accelerate just as the pace of life in an increasingly globalized world accelerates. Shows such as *Travel the Road*—this "groundbreaking reality television series that documents the adventurous lives of young missionaries Tim Scott and Will Decker over 18 months, through 25 countries, and across 40,000 miles is a unique look into the world of frontline mission work," http://www.traveltheroad.com—make the appeal of this approach to the next generation even stronger than it already is. Mix in instant updates, Web-based social networking services like FaceBook (http://www.facebook.com) and MySpace (http://www.myspace.com), cheap or free Internet telephony and instant messaging, and the idea of meeting a lifelong friend on a one-week trip to another country is now seen as "normal" for high school students. The reality of immediate global awareness of crises and a shorter span between donor interest and donor fatigue may well combine to tempt Evangelical missionaries and organizations to focus their energies on shorter and shorter projects rather than longer-term strategies.

Third, questions and practices related to finances and partnerships are going to continue to be part of the missions equation. There were more than 1.5 million nonprofit organizations in the USA in 2005 with some 40,000 more added annually,[17] and many of them have Christian purposes as their focus. Thus, the availabil-

---

[17] T. Cohen, "Each 501(c)(3) Is Now," http://www.nptimes.com/May05/npt3.html (2005, accessed October 12, 2007).

ity of funding from foundations that have money to give away has never been greater. On the other hand, neither has the ability to defraud people with scams that channel money into personal pockets rather than holistic mission efforts. Partnerships will continue to be a murky area, with instant global communication and monetary exchange enabling both real-time troubleshooting as well as exacerbating the cultural differences—including goals, aspirations, methods, and communication patterns—of the partners.

Fourth, the Internet as a vehicle for missions will be explored more fully and will be found simultaneously both dangerous and invaluable. Already the fact that anyone can Google any name for information is changing how institutions and people with ongoing work in creative access countries posture themselves. Those working in such areas of the world will need to be even more careful than they are today. The double-bind is that many prospective missionaries in the West do not even consider working with a group or agency that does not have an Internet presence—but that presence needs to be managed by the agencies in a way that does not jeopardize those who are already serving as members in settings where security is a concern. Keeping an accessible public face while not adding risk to existing personnel will present an ever more difficult challenge as the years go by.

Fifth, the ability of humanity to wipe ourselves out of existence will become more important as the decades go by. Current oil concerns will grow and will be supplemented by struggles related to water, waste disposal, environmental degradation, and the like. But even more dangerous is the reality that weapons of mass destruction will no longer be limited to governments or other organizations with large capital and expertise resources. Rather, well-trained and properly equipped individuals will be able to work out their anger or rage—against the West, against materialism, against whatever drives them—in ways that would astonish us today,[18] and this will take on greater and greater priority for mission-related organizations who may well bear the brunt of focused attacks by people who have anti-Christian or anti-missionary agendas.

---

[18] See B. Joy, "Why the Future Doesn't Need Us," http://www.wired.com/wired/archive/8.04/joy.html (2000, accessed October 12, 2007).

CONCLUSION

There can be little doubt that we live in exciting times. God has raised up an army of missionaries that we could hardly have envisioned a century ago. There are new and better understood spiritual, social, and technological resources to draw on in the task of bringing Christ to every people group in the world. Even as persecution of believers in many parts of the world grows, more and more are coming to embrace a relationship with the living Christ. The confluence of dangers and possibilities will make the next 50 years perhaps the most significant yet seen in Christian missions, and Evangelicals from all nations will be at the heart of what happens.

BIBLIOGRAPHY

Aikman, D. *Jesus in Beijing: How Christianity Is Transforming China and Changing the Global Balance of Power.* Washington, D.C.: Regnery Publishing, 2003.

Black, A. E., D. L. Koopman, and D. K. Ryden. *Of Little Faith: The Politics of George W. Bush's Faith-Based Initiatives.* Washington, D.C.: Georgetown University Press, 2004.

Carroll R., M. Daniel. "The Challenge of Economic Globalization for Theology: From Latin America to a Hermeneutics of Responsibility." Pages 199–212 in *Globalizing Theology: Belief and Practice in an Era of World Christianity.* Edited by C. Ott and H. Netland. Grand Rapids: Baker, 2006.

Cohen, T. "Each 501(c)(3) Is Now." http://www.nptimes.com/May05/npt3.html (2005, accessed October 12, 2007).

Daneel, M. L. *African Earthkeepers: Wholistic Interfaith Mission.* Maryknoll: Orbis, 2001.

D'souza, J. *Dalit Freedom Now and Forever: The Epic Struggle for Dalit Emancipation.* Centennial: Dalit Freedom Network, 2004.

Easterly, W. *The White Man's Burden: Why the West's Efforts to Aid the Rest Have Done So Much Ill and So Little Good.* New York: The Penguin Press, 2006.

Escobar, S. *Changing Tides: Latin America & World Mission Today.* Maryknoll: Orbis, 2002.

_____. *The New Global Mission: The Gospel from Everywhere to Everywhere.* Downers Grove: InterVarsity, 2003.

Hesselgrave, D. *Paradigms in Conflict: 10 Key Questions in Christian Missions Today.* Grand Rapids: Kregel, 2005.

Jenkins, P. *The Next Christendom: The Coming of Global Christianity.* New York: Oxford University Press, 2002.

_____. *The New Faces of Christianity: Believing the Bible in the Global South.* New York: Oxford University Press, 2006.

Jorgensen, K. "Spiritual Conflict in Socio-Political Context." Pages 213–30 in *Deliver Us from Evil: An Uneasy Frontier in Christian Mission.* Edited by A. S. Moreau, T. Adeyemo, D. Burnett, B. Myers, and H. Yung. Monrovia: MARC, 2002.

Joy, B. "Why the Future Doesn't Need Us." http://www.wired.com/wired/archive/8.04/joy.html (2000, accessed October 12, 2007).

Lausanne Committee for World Evangelization. "Lausanne Occasional Paper 33: Holistic Mission." http://www.lausanne.org/documents/2004forum/LOP33_IG4.pdf (2005, accessed October 10, 2007).

Moreau, A. S. "Putting the Survey in Perspective." Pages 11–65 in *Mission Handbook 2007–2009: U.S. and Canadian Protestant Ministries Overseas.* Edited by L. Weber and D. J. Welliver. Wheaton: Evangelism and Missions Information Service, 2007.

Myers, B. *Walking with the Poor: Principles and Practices of Transformational Development.* Maryknoll: Orbis, 1999.

Noll, S. F. "Thinking About Angels." Pages 1–27 in *The Unseen World: Christian Reflections on Angels, Demons and the Heavenly Realm.* Edited by A. N. S. Lane. Grand Rapids: Baker, 1996.

Page, S. *Powers of Evil: A Biblical Study of Satan and Demons.* Grand Rapids: Baker, 1995.

Pagitt, D., and T. Jones, eds. *An Emergent Manifesto of Hope.* Grand Rapids: Baker, 2007.

Roberts, W. D. *Patching God's Garment: Environment and Mission in the 21st Century.* Monrovia: MARC, 1994.

Santayana, G. *Life of Reason or the Phases of Human Progress: Reason in Common Sense.* New York: Scribner's, 1905.

Snyder, H. *Coherence in Christ: The Larger Meaning of Ecology.* New York: General Board of Global Ministries, The United Methodist Church, 2000.

Thomas, J. C. "Spiritual Conflict in Illness and Affliction." Pages 37–60 in *Deliver Us from Evil: An Uneasy Frontier in Christian Mission.* Edited by A. S. Moreau, T. Adeyemo, D. Burnett, B. Myers, and H. Yung. Monrovia: MARC, 2002.

Thompson, C. "Why We Can Count on Geeks to Rescue the Earth," *Wired* 15.9 (September 2007). http://www.wired.com/techbiz/people/magazine/15-09/st_thompson (accessed October 9, 2007).

Walls, A. *The Cross-Cultural Process in Christian History.* Maryknoll: Orbis, 2002.

Wink, W. *Engaging the Powers: Discernment and Resistance in a World of Dominion.* Philadelphia: Fortress, 1992.

———*Naming the Powers: The Language of Power in the New Testament.* Philadelphia: Fortress, 1984.

———. *The Powers That Be: Theology for a New Millennium.* New York: Doubleday, 1998.

———. *Unmasking the Powers: The Invisible Forces That Determine Human Existence.* Philadelphia: Fortress, 1986.

Wright, C. J. H. *The Mission of God: Unlocking the Bible's Grand Narrative.* Downers Grove: InterVarsity, 2007.

Wright, N. G. *A Theology of the Dark Side: Putting the Power of Evil in Its Place.* Downers Grove: InterVarsity, 2003.

CHAPTER 16

In Response to "The Future of Evangelicals in Mission"

CHRISTOPHER R. LITTLE

INTRODUCTION

Ralph Winter has entreated the Western evangelical community to recover First-Inheritance Evangelicalism by broadening its missional program to include both personal salvation and social responsibility on a global scale.[1] In doing so, he has added his voice to a grand chorus of respectable evangelical leaders calling for the same. Over 60 years ago, C. F. H. Henry chastised Evangelicals for their lack of societal concern:

> No evangelicalism which ignores the totality of man's condition dares respond in the name of Christianity. Though the modern crisis is not basically political, economic or social—fundamentally it is religious—yet evangelicalism must be armed to declare the implications of its proposed religious solution for the politico-economic and sociological context for modern life. . . .
>
> The battle against evil in all its forms must be pressed unsparingly; we must pursue the enemy, in politics, in economics, in science, in ethics—everywhere, in every field, we must pursue relentlessly.[2]

---

[1] See the essay written by R. Winter, "The Future of Evangelicals in Mission," in the present volume.

[2] C. F. H. Henry, *The Uneasy Conscience of Modern Fundamentalism* (Grand Rapids: Eerdmans, 1947), 84, 86.

In 1982 J. R. W. Stott (who earlier in his career would have differed with Winter[3]) advocated that evangelism and social action should be seen as an equal partnership like "two blades of a pair of scissors."[4] C. Van Engen over a decade ago advanced both narrative and kingdom of God theologies as tools "to bridge the evangelism-social action dichotomy that has plagued evangelical missiology for most of the twentieth century."[5] In 1999, 160 Evangelical leaders from 53 countries met in Brazil and drafted the Iguassu Affirmation, which stressed "the holistic nature of the gospel" in an effort to address political, economic, and environmental concerns of "the human race and the whole of creation."[6]

More recently, S. Escobar elucidated that "mission should consist of service—service both of the spiritual in proclaiming the Word and of the physical in meeting human needs, according to Jesus' model."[7] At the 2004 Forum for World Evangelization in Pattaya, Thailand, C. R. Padilla stressed that "mission is faithful to scripture only to the extent to which it is holistic. In other words, it is faithful when it crosses frontiers (not just geographic but also cultural, racial, economic, social, political, etc.) with the intention of transforming human life in all its dimensions."[8] And in what will probably be recognized for years to come as the most comprehensive and well-argued statement on the holistic missional paradigm, C. Wright states:

> Mission belongs to God—the biblical God. The message of mission is to be drawn from the whole of God's biblical revelation. So we cannot simply relegate the powerful message of events such as the exodus or institutions like the jubilee to a bygone era. They are an integral part of the biblical definition of God's idea of redemption and of God's requirement on his redeemed people. We pay no compliments to the New Testament and the new and urgent mandate of evangelistic mission it entrusts to

---

[3] J. R. W. Stott, *Christian Mission in the Modern World* (Downers Grove: InterVarsity, 1975), 23.

[4] J. R. W. Stott, ed., *Making Christ Known* (Grand Rapids: Eerdmans, 1996), 182.

[5] C. Van Engen, *Mission on the Way: Issues in Mission Theology* (Grand Rapids: Baker, 1996), 66 (cf. pp. 43, 59, 65, 144, 185–86, 261–62).

[6] W. Taylor, ed., *Global Missiology for the 21st Century: The Iguassu Dialogue* (Grand Rapids: Baker, 2000), 18–19.

[7] S. Escobar, *The New Global Mission: The Gospel from Everywhere to Everyone* (Downers Grove: InterVarsity, 2003), 154.

[8] C. R. Padilla, "Holistic Mission," in *A New Vision, A New Heart, A Renewed Call*, ed. D. Claydon (Pasadena: William Carey Library, 2005), 1:220.

us in the light of Christ by relegating the Old Testament and the foundations for mission that it had already laid and that Jesus emphatically endorsed. Whole Christian mission is built on the whole Christian Bible.[9]

YESTERDAY'S SOLUTION IS TODAY'S PROBLEM

Of course, these writers are attempting to overcome Fundamentalism's disdain for the social gospel that Evangelicalism has inherited to one degree or another.[10] But as the end of the first decade of the twenty-first century approaches, it is fairly obvious that they have won the debate. Evangelicalism can no longer be characterized by a one-sided concern for humanity's spiritual welfare. How is such an assertion sustainable? In 2001, agencies reporting evangelism or discipleship as their primary activity accounted for 58.7 percent of the total amount spent on overseas ministries, whereas relief and development was only 35.1 percent.[11] In 2005, the figures were 47.5 percent for evangelism or discipleship and 46.1 percent for relief and development.[12] In addition, the increase in income from 2001 to 2005 for relief and development was 73.4 percent while for evangelism or discipleship it was only 2.7 percent.[13] Assuming the continuation of this trend, one can be fairly certain that the missions community in the USA is presently spending more on alleviating human suffering than on addressing the eternal destiny of the lost. In fact, this has already happened in Canada. In 2005, agencies reporting evangelism or discipleship as their primary activity comprised only 24.9 percent of the total amount spent on overseas ministries, but for relief and development it was a surprising 73.6 percent.[14] As such,

---

[9] C. Wright, *The Mission of God: Unlocking the Bible's Grand Narrative* (Downers Grove: InterVarsity, 2006), 306.

[10] See the informative article by J. Carpenter ("The Fundamentalist Leaven and the Rise of an Evangelical United Front," *The Evangelical Tradition in America*, ed. L. Sweet [Macon: Mercy University Press, 1984], 257ff) that recounts the role Fundamentalists played in launching the National Association of Evangelicals. Also, it must be noted that, although Fundamentalism placed social ministries in a secondary category, it nevertheless persisted in humanitarian efforts (cf. J. Patterson, "The Loss of a Protestant Missionary Consensus: Foreign Missions and the Fundamentalist-Modernist Conflict," in *Earthen Vessels: American Evangelicals and Foreign Missions, 1880–1980*, ed. J. Carpenter and W. Shenk [Grand Rapids: Eerdmans, 1990], 81–82).

[11] D. Welliver and M. Northcutt, *Mission Handbook: U. S. and Canadian Protestant Ministries Overseas 2004–2006* (Wheaton: Evangelical and Missions Information Service, 2004), 26.

[12] L. Weber and D. Welliver, *Mission Handbook: U. S. and Canadian Protestant Ministries Overseas 2007–2009* (Wheaton: Evangelical and Missions Information Service, 2007), 44.

[13] Ibid., 45.

[14] Ibid., 63.

those who believe the Canadian missionary movement is being "marginalized" cannot be far wrong.[15]

The same predicament is also facing the church in Europe. J. A. Kirk, who reconsiders "the most pressing problems facing the Church in mission," states:

> Mission, which in some circles used to be almost identified with evangelism, is now almost completely disassociated from it. It is now aligned, more or less, with service to the community and ethical pronouncements and action in the political sphere, referred to as its prophetic ministry. Such a limited understanding of mission appears to take its cue partly from the surrounding culture. . . . However, one suspects that for some Christians the basic cause of hesitancy about evangelism is due to uncertainty about the truth of the message of Jesus Christ in the light of so many competing claims to truth.[16]

His solution to the problem is that "the time has surely come, specifically in the post-Christian environment of Europe, to argue forcefully again that the church is . . . by definition, evangelistic."[17] If this is the case for post-Christian Europe, then in light of the above data it must certainly be the case for North America also as it turns postmodern.

FROM KINGDOM TO THE GLORY

Winter points out that "kingdom" was apparently a bad word in Second-Inheritance Evangelicalism.[18] Yet it is not the word itself but the meaning attached to it that matters. Some twenty-first-century Evangelicals are now promoting the idea that the kingdom of God is evinced through the philanthropic efforts of secularists. For instance, J. Rowell asserts that the generous donations of people like Warren Buffett demonstrate the kingdom's impact on society "even when conversions have not yet occurred."[19] This scenario sounds dangerously reminiscent of what transpired in the World Council of Churches last century when, under the

---

[15] Ibid., 73.

[16] J. A. Kirk, *Mission Under Scrutiny: Confronting Contemporary Challenges* (Minneapolis: Fortress, 2006), xi, 47.

[17] Ibid., 47.

[18] Winter, 167.

[19] J. Rowell, *To Give or Not to Give? Rethinking Despondency, Restoring Generosity, and Redefining Sustainability* (Tyrone: Authentic Publishing, 2006), 246; see J. Engel and W. Dyrness, *Changing the Mind of Missions* (Downers Grove: InterVarsity, 2000), 79–80.

influence of J. C. Hoekendijk, the world was seen as the locus of God's kingdom activity independent of the church.[20] This line of reasoning eventually led to elevating "humanization" as the goal of mission at the Uppsala Assembly in 1968. Evangelicals at the time took issue with this emphasis and countered with the Frankfurt Declaration.[21] Thus, history appears to be repeating itself as "evangelicals have already begun to tread a path similar to that followed by conciliar ecumenists in the past."[22] Indeed, in "their desire to develop a holistic understanding of mission, Evangelicals probably need to heed S. Neill's warning: 'when everything is mission, nothing is mission.'"[23]

If the Evangelical community is to maneuver successfully around potential potholes in mission, it will need to incorporate the following truisms when reflecting on the kingdom of God. Instead of assuming that the kingdom is "the dominant motif"[24] of Scripture and "the hub around which all of mission work revolves,"[25] it is imperative to recognize that the Bible presents many unifying or centering themes. In reality, divine revelation has no single center of gravity as scholars readily admit.[26] But even if scholars could agree on the main theme of the Bible, it would not be the kingdom of God. A. Köstenberger offers the following two criteria for accepting an integrating motif in the New Testament as valid: (1) the motif must be been found "in all the major NT corpora, the Synoptics as well as John, Paul as well as the General Epistles"; and (2) the motif must be "a shared, foundational belief of Jesus

---

[20] J. Hoekendijk, "The Church in Missionary Thinking," *International Review of Missions* 41(1952): 332–35; see T. Yates, *Christian Mission in the Twentieth Century* (New York: Cambridge University Press, 1996), 163–64.

[21] P. Beyerhaus, *Missions: Which Way? Humanization or Redemption* (Grand Rapids: Zondervan, 1991), 107–20ff.

[22] D. Hesselgrave, *Paradigms in Conflict: 10 Key Questions in Christian Missions Today* (Grand Rapids: Kregel, 2005), 330.

[23] See the essay written by C. Van Engen, "'Mission' Defined and Described," in the present volume, 7; see S. Neill, *Creative Tension* (New York: Doubleday, 1959), 81. A clear example of what Neill was referring to is given by Escobar (pp. 149–50, 153–43) when he refers to mission being accomplished within the context of the church. This contradicts the conventional understanding of mission in which the belief-unbelief divide is crossed; see L. Newbigin, *One Body, One Gospel, One World: The Christian Mission Today* (London: Wm. Carling, 1958), 29.

[24] A. Glasser, "Biblical Theology of Mission," in *Evangelical Dictionary of World Missions*, ed. A. S. Moreau (Grand Rapids: Baker, 2000), 127.

[25] J. Verkuyl, *Contemporary Missiology: An Introduction* (Grand Rapids: Eerdmans, 1978), 203.

[26] See C. Blomberg, "The Unity and Diversity of Scripture," in *New Dictionary of Biblical Theology*, ed. T. D. Alexander et al. (Downers Grove: InterVarsity, 2000), 66; and P. House, "Biblical Theology and the Wholeness of Scripture," in ed. S. Hafemann, *Biblical Theology: Retrospect & Prospect*, 276.

and the early church."[27] The kingdom of God falls short on both counts. It is weakly represented in John's Gospel (only mentioned in three verses: 3:3,5; 18:36), and the proclamation of the early Christians

> shifts in emphasis from the kingdom to the Messiah, and consequently it is not so much a repetition of what he proclaimed as rather a proclamation of him. . . . With the shift away from the emphasis on the kingdom of God there comes an increased emphasis on the experience of salvation and eternal life.[28]

Moreover, although the church is derivative of the kingdom, the church is prerequisite to the kingdom in human experience. This thought comes directly from Jesus: "Unless someone is born again, he cannot see the kingdom of God" (John 3:3). As such, one cannot have kingdom without church since "the coming of the kingdom realizes itself in the conversion of sinners."[29] In other words, the "kingdom consists of those who respond to the message in repentance and faith, and thereby come into the sphere of God's salvation and life."[30] And the apostle Paul clearly indicated that God's reign in the life of his people entails "righteousness, peace, and joy in the Holy Spirit" (Rom 14:17).

Furthermore, the realization of the kingdom in this world is beyond the control of the church. Even proponents of Liberation Theology such as J. M. Bonino warn against any "utopian function" of eschatology when he says that "the objections against expressions like 'building' the Kingdom are legitimate protests against naïve optimism or at times justified protection of the primacy of divine initiative."[31] Of course, the kingdom is "the undying and infallible hope of the Christian and a reality that works already in many manifest and latent ways in the Community of Christ, but

---

[27] A. Köstenberger, "Diversity and Unity in the New Testament," in Hafemann, *Biblical Theology*, 154.

[28] I. H. Marshall, *New Testament Theology* (Downers Grove: InterVarsity, 2004), 205. D. Horrell (*An Introduction to the Study of Paul* [New York: Continuum, 2000], 10) adds that "there is a clear difference at least in language and terminology between Jesus' announcement of the kingdom of God and Paul's gospel, focused on the death and resurrection of Christ. The phrases 'son of man' and 'kingdom of God,' for example, occur frequently in the Synoptic Gospels on the lips of Jesus but rarely appear in the epistles ('son of man' never in the NT epistles; 'kingdom of God' only eight times in the Pauline epistles"; see Hesselgrave, *Paradigms in Conflict*, 347–48).

[29] J. H. Bavinck, *An Introduction to the Science of Missions* (Phillipsburg: P&R, 1960), 155.

[30] Marshall, *New Testament Theology*, 80.

[31] J. M. Bonino, *Doing Theology in a Revolutionary Situation* (Philadelphia: Fortress, 1975), 142, 151.

it can never be the direct object and achievement of our labours, because it is the hand of the Father."[32] Thus, "to promise that Christianity will dispel economic misery and social disturbance is to invite inevitable disillusionment, because economic misery and social disturbance are caused and cured by many factors entirely outside the control of the Church or missions."[33] Accordingly, "Christians . . . should be wary of making over-ambitious claims for particular manifestations of [the kingdom's] presence."[34] This is especially true when it comes to placing paradisiacal expectations on the prayer "Your kingdom come."[35]

Finally, there are legitimate alternatives to the kingdom of God as integrating ideas that should be pursued in mission theology.[36] One such alternative articulated by J. Stamoolis from within the Eastern Orthodox tradition is "to acknowledge, promote, and participate in the glory of God."[37] Evangelicals have recently started to take this doxological motif seriously while reflecting upon the missional task of the church in the world.[38] In doing so, they are moving forward by returning to the past. G. Voetius—who has been credited with formulating "the first comprehensive Protestant theology of mission"—rightly asserts that the "final and ultimate goal of missions . . . is the glorification and manifestation of divine grace. . . . God is not only the first cause but also the ultimate goal of missions. . . . Church planting as well as conversion reaches its final goal in the exaltation of God's name."[39] This theocentric approach holds great promise for counteracting the present drift toward horizontalization in mission.

---

[32] H. Kraemer, *The Christian Mission in a Non-Christian World* (New York: Harper & Brothers, 1947), 48.

[33] Ibid., 60.

[34] Kirk, *Mission under Scrutiny,* 93–94.

[35] See Winter, 190.

[36] Van Engen, *Mission on the Way,* 20.

[37] J. Stamoolis, *Eastern Orthodox Mission Theology Today* (Eugene: Wipf and Stock, 2001), 52.

[38] See J. Piper, *Let the Nations Be Glad! The Supremacy of God in Missions,* 2nd ed. (Grand Rapids: Baker, 2003), 20–38ff; G. Van Rheenen, "Changing Motivations for Missions: From 'Fear of Hell' to the 'Glory of God,'" in *The Changing Face of World Missions: Engaging Contemporary Issues and Trends,* ed. M. Pocock et al. (Grand Rapids: Baker, 2005), 173–76ff; and C. Little, *Mission in the Way of Paul: Biblical Mission for the Church in the Twenty-First Century* (New York: Peter Lang, 2005), 47–73ff.

[39] J. Jongeneel, "The Missiology of Gisbertus Voetius: The First Comprehensive Protestant Theology of Missions," *CTJ* 26 (April 1991): 70, 68.

DOXOPHANY IN MISSION THEOLOGY

In answering the question, "What is the meaning of creation and history?" E. Stauffer says, "The revelation of God's glory, or doxophany." He continues: "What is it to be a creature? To glorify God, to share in doxology. Every creative act calls something into existence for the glorifying of God and every act of divine self-revelation is meant to recall the creature to this glorification."[40] The following diagram is an attempt to outline how this mission of the triune God to glorify Himself has been disclosed in Scripture.

Several things need to be emphasized in relation to this diagram. First, God reveals His glory to receive glory, honor, worship, and devotion from all creation.[41] Second, Jesus "was sent to reveal and accomplish the *gloria dei.*" As such, His life "is an acted doxology (Matt 4:1ff. [with John 17:4])."[42]

Third, "the divine doxophany in the advent of Christ calls the Church into being [whereby] the original destiny of mankind comes to realization in the historical function of the Church, i.e. in the service rendered by *ecclesia christi* to the *gloria dei.*"[43] This service necessitates "a people of God engaged in declaring God's mighty acts so that those as yet not a people might glorify God by becoming 'God's own people.'"[44] Fourth, God's kingdom is penultimate to God's glory,[45] that is, *basileia*-centric mission is ultimately eclipsed by *doxa*-centric mission. Consequently, human needs must remain subordinate to the glorification of God because if "the pursuit of *God's* glory is not ordered above the pursuit of *man's* good . . . *man* will not be served and *God* will not be duly honored."[46] Fifth, the means of mission by way of word and deed (Matt 5:16; Rom 15:8–11) should conduce to the goal of mission,

---

[40] E. Stauffer, *New Testament Theology* (New York: MacMillan, 1955), 228–29. J. Edwards (*The Works of Jonathan Edwards* [Peabody: Hendrickson, 1998], 1:119) came to a similar conclusion: "The great end of God's works, which is so variously expressed in Scripture, is indeed but ONE; and this one end is most properly and comprehensively called, THE GLORY OF GOD."

[41] S. Hawthorne, "The Story of His Glory," in *Perspectives on the World Christian Movement: A Reader*, 3rd ed., ed. R. Winter and S. Hawthorne (Pasadena: William Carey Library, 1999), 37.

[42] Stauffer, *New Testament Theology*, 28.

[43] Ibid., 229.

[44] E. Martens, "The People of God," in *Central Themes in Biblical Theology: Mapping Unity in Diversity*, ed. S. Hafemann and P. House (Grand Rapids: Baker, 2007), 250; see D. Bosch, *Transforming Mission: Paradigm Shifts in Theology of Mission* (Maryknoll: Orbis, 1991), 168.

[45] See Jongeneel, "The Missiology of Gisbertus Voetius," 77.

[46] Piper, *Let the Nations Be Glad!*, 18.

GLORIFICATION OF THE HOLY TRINITY
(John 8:54; 13:31–32; 16:14–15; 17:1,4–5)

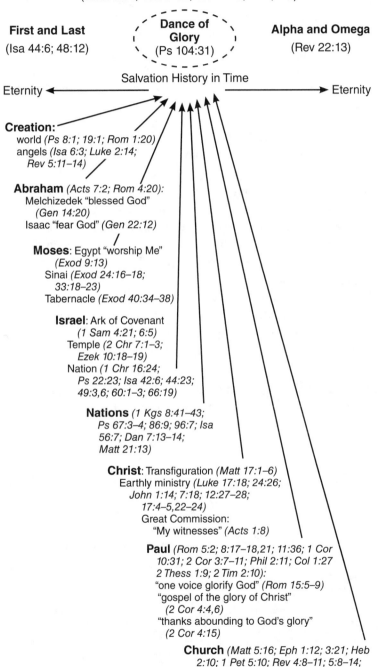

First and Last

(Isa 44:6; 48:12)

Dance of Glory

(Ps 104:31)

Alpha and Omega

(Rev 22:13)

Salvation History in Time

Eternity ←——————————————————————→ Eternity

Creation:
world *(Ps 8:1; 19:1; Rom 1:20)*
angels *(Isa 6:3; Luke 2:14;*
Rev 5:11–14)

Abraham *(Acts 7:2; Rom 4:20):*
Melchizedek "blessed God"
(Gen 14:20)
Isaac "fear God" *(Gen 22:12)*

Moses: Egypt "worship Me"
(Exod 9:13)
Sinai *(Exod 24:16–18;*
33:18–23)
Tabernacle *(Exod 40:34–38)*

Israel: Ark of Covenant
(1 Sam 4:21; 6:5)
Temple *(2 Chr 7:1–3;*
Ezek 10:18–19)
Nation *(1 Chr 16:24;*
Ps 22:23; Isa 42:6; 44:23;
49:3,6; 60:1–3; 66:19)

Nations *(1 Kgs 8:41–43;*
Ps 67:3–4; 86:9; 96:7; Isa
56:7; Dan 7:13–14;
Matt 21:13)

Christ: Transfiguration *(Matt 17:1–6)*
Earthly ministry *(Luke 17:18; 24:26;*
John 1:14; 7:18; 12:27–28;
17:4–5,22–24)
Great Commission:
"My witnesses" *(Acts 1:8)*

Paul *(Rom 5:2; 8:17–18,21; 11:36; 1 Cor*
10:31; 2 Cor 3:7–11; Phil 2:11; Col 1:27
2 Thess 1:9; 2 Tim 2:10):
"one voice glorify God" *(Rom 15:5–9)*
"gospel of the glory of Christ"
(2 Cor 4:4,6)
"thanks abounding to God's glory"
(2 Cor 4:15)

Church *(Matt 5:16; Eph 1:12; 3:21; Heb*
2:10; 1 Pet 5:10; Rev 4:8–11; 5:8–14;
7:9–12; 14:6–7; 15:2–4; 19:1; 21:23)

which is "the giving of thanks to abound to the glory of God" (2 Cor 4:15).[47] In saying this, however, one must be ever aware that there is no guarantee of success in employing these means in contributing to the enduring *gloria dei* since even though the crowds "glorified God" in response to what Jesus did (Matt 9:8; 15:31; Luke 7:16), at the end of His life there were only a handful of fearful disciples (John 20:19).[48]

SCIENCE AS A MISSIONARY METHOD

The missions movement from the West has been described as "one of the greatest secularizing agencies" of the past several centuries.[49] This predicament resulted from proclaiming a gospel of "Christian enlightenment,"[50] which among other things confidently affirmed "that every problem and puzzle could be solved."[51] It is difficult not to conclude that when Winter suggests mission should recruit science as a method to "destroy all forms of evil, both human and microbiological,"[52] he is compounding the problem.

The epistemological foundation of science is positivism, which presumes "that scientists, by means of instruments and senses, can gain an accurate, objective knowledge of reality."[53] However, science "is built on the cultural assumptions of the West and is deeply influenced by social and psychological processes."[54] Moreover, because "theories taken as fact today are replaced by others tomorrow. . . . We can no longer equate scientific knowledge about reality with reality itself. The old assumption that scientific theories have a one-to-one correspondence with reality has

---

[47] See Bavinck, *An Introduction to the Science of Missions,* 155; Beyerhaus, *Missions: Which Way?,* 114; Marshall, *New Testament Theology,* 432; and A. Yannoulatos, "The Purpose and Motive of Mission," *International Review of Mission* 54(1965): 287.

[48] Yet "no guarantee" does not imply that doxological mission is ultimately thwarted (see Rev 7:9–12).

[49] J. Bonk, *Missions and Money: Affluence as Western Missionary Problem . . . Revisited,* revised and expanded ed. (Maryknoll: Orbis, 2006), 342; cf. P. Hiebert, *Anthropological Reflections on Missiological Issues* (Grand Rapids: Baker, 1994), 197.

[50] R. Allen, *The Spontaneous Expansion of the Church* (Grand Rapids: Eerdmans, 1962), 84.

[51] Bosch, *Transforming Mission,* 342.

[52] Winter, 190; cf. pp. 168–70.

[53] P. Hiebert, *Missiological Implications of Epistemological Shifts: Affirming Truth in a Modern/Postmodern World* (Harrisburg: Trinity Press International, 1999), 11. In relation to what has transpired historically when Christianity became too closely aligned with science, Hiebert states: "Positivism with its notion of progress gave rise to theologies that equated the Kingdom of God with the utopia being created by science and Christian morality, a utopia that will wipe out famine, oppression, and war and will restore the world to a pristine society. In so doing, the center of theology moved from God and his activities to humans and their efforts" (pp. 21–22).

[54] Hiebert, *Anthropological Reflections,* 21.

been shattered."[55] Ultimately, then, science is "a Western mind game"[56] that vainly attempts to reduce "all areas of human experience . . . to empirical verifiable categories."[57] "This reductionism not only distorts reality but . . . produces 'fantasies of omnipotence,'" which regrettably contradicts the mission strategy inherent in "the vulnerability of the cross."[58]

There are additional dilemmas with Winter's proposal. He expects the church to do that which Christ Himself was unable to do during His earthly sojourn, namely, the complete annihilation of "the works of the devil" (1 John 3:8). Indeed, Jesus was sent for this purpose, but it is only at the "recapitulation"[59] when He hands over the kingdom to the Father (1 Cor 15:24) that the power of death will be abolished (1 Cor 15:26). In the meantime, creation is under a curse whereby Satan is able to inflict God's image bearers with disaster, disease, and death (see Gen 2:17; 3:14–19ff; Job 1:12–19; 2:6–8; Matt 12:22; Mark 6:13; Luke 8:2; 9:42; 13:11; Rom 8:20; Heb 2:14).[60] Consequently, "we also groan . . . , eagerly waiting for adoption, the redemption of our bodies" (Rom 8:23).[61] Also, the idea of "a faith that works"[62] needs to be considered canonically.[63] James connects this concept to Christian conduct within the church (Jas 2:1–26) and Peter to those outside the church: "Conduct yourselves honorably among the Gentiles, so that in a case where they speak against you as those who do evil, they may, by observing your good works, [cf. Matt 5:16] glorify God in a day of visitation" (1 Pet 2:12; see 3:8–17ff). On this

---

[55] Ibid.

[56] Hiebert, *Missiological Implications*, 31.

[57] W. Shenk, "Mission Strategies," in *Toward the 21st Century in Christian Mission*, ed. J. Phillips and R. Coote (Grand Rapids: Eerdmans, 1993), 219.

[58] Ibid., 220, 230.

[59] Yannoulatos, *The Purpose and Motive of Mission*, 285; see Eph 1:10.

[60] However, not all incidents of disease recorded in Scripture are attributable to the devil (Matt 8:14–15; 9:35; John 9:1–4), and in some cases it is a consequence of God's judgment (1 Cor 11:29–30; Rev 2:22–23).

[61] In relation to this, Winter disparages Evangelicals who had an "otherworldly focus" (p. 165). Yet Scripture commands God's people to "seek what is above, where the Messiah is, seated at the right hand of God. Set your minds on what is above, not on what is on the earth" (Col 3:1–2; see John 14:2–3; 2 Cor 5:1–2; Phil 3:20; Heb 11:16; 2 Pet 3:13). In addition, it appears Winter believes that by addressing evil, impediments to grasping God's "mysterious purposes" will be surmounted (p. 188). Yet Job never knew the reason for his tribulations (Job 40:1–5; 42:1–6), and people today are no different—there are definite limits to human knowledge of divine prerogative (see Deut 29:29; Rom 11:33).

[62] Winter, 188.

[63] Hesselgrave warns, "Unless conservatives dialogue canonically, both theological and missiological dialogues are as apt to compound confusion as they are to dispel it" (p. 352).

subject A. Harnack documents that the difference in "moral life" among Christians was the reason that Christianity initially proved so attractive to pagans.[64] Furthermore, the belief that the eradication of disease through the scientific method will lead to widespread conversions to Christ amounts to a denial of history—it hasn't happened in the past, so one wonders why it would happen today. If scientists, Christian or otherwise, discover a cure for malaria or AIDS tomorrow, the average person will simply chalk it up to the abilities of humans to overcome their own challenges, and in doing so, they will glory in themselves rather than in God. And finally, science is not a closed system cut off from the spirit world. Just as Satan is able to deceive and manipulate the sorcerer to his own ends, he is able to do so with the scientist. Thus, while science relentlessly seeks for physical cures to physical abnormalities, the unseen cause may in some cases be spiritual (see Matt 9:2–7; Luke 13:10–13; 2 Cor 12:7; Jas 5:15).

KEEPING THE MAIN THING THE MAIN THING

But in the end Winter arrives at the right place in that, while correctly affirming that mission includes both word and deed, he maintains word must take "priority."[65] In doing so, he has aligned himself with the Lausanne's Grand Rapids Report on Evangelism and Social Responsibility: "The supreme and ultimate need of all humankind is the saving grace of Jesus Christ, and that therefore a person's eternal, spiritual salvation is of greater importance than his or her temporal and material well-being (cf. II Cor. 4:16–18)."[66] Accordingly, although evangelism may not necessarily assume a temporal priority, it remains the logical one.[67]

This priority is clearly detected in the ministry of Jesus. As W. Larkin Jr. points out in relation to Jesus' declaration regarding his messianic mission:

Of the four infinitives from Isaiah that show the purpose of the

---

[64] A Harnack, *The Expansion of Christianity in the First Three Centuries* (Eugene: Wipf and Stock, 1998), 1:460.

[65] Winter, 168. A. Fernando hesitates to adopt the "language of priority" ("Getting Back on Course," *Christianity Today* 51 [October 2007]: 43). Yet given the "tendency among some evangelicals to downplay verbal proclamation," he acknowledges that "if talk of priority will help the church to a fresh commitment [to evangelism], then so be it" (p. 45).

[66] Stott, *Making Christ Known*, 183.

[67] Ibid. See S. Moreau, G. Corwin, and G. McGee, *Introducing World Missions: A Biblical, Historical, and Practical Survey* (Grand Rapids: Baker, 2004), 88–89.

Spirit's anointing and sending of Jesus, three involve preaching. The poor are evangelized (*euangelizomai*); the prisoners have release and the blind have recovery of sight proclaimed (*kērussō*) to them; the year of the Lord's favor, the Jubilee year, is proclaimed (*kērussō*).[68] The other purpose is to send the oppressed away in freedom. Luke, then, regards the primary activity of Jesus' ministry as preaching. Other tasks are present, such as Jesus' healing and exorcism ministry or his sacrificial death and mighty resurrection, but these either validate or become the content of the gospel message.[69]

Having gleaned this strategy from their master, the disciples follow suit. In the wake of the resurrection, their

> primary role is that of witnesses (Luke 24:48; Acts 1:8). Their task is one of proclamation (Mark 16:15; Luke 24:47) and teaching (Matt. 28:19–20). . . . They are to proclaim "repentance for forgiveness of sins" (Luke 24:47), for they are to be witnesses of Jesus' death and resurrection (Luke 24:26).[70]

The same holds true for Paul: "Within the scope of his missionary commission [the first task] was primary evangelism. Paul's ambition was to go where the gospel had not yet been preached (Rom. 15:20–21). His strategy focused on preaching and evangelizing Jews as well as Gentile[s]."[71] Therefore, if the "Spirit-inspired missionary acts of Jesus, Paul and the apostles, as well as their Spirit-inspired reflection on their practice, are authoritative for us, in a way in which no other post-apostolic missionary practice or reflection is,"[72] then the church concerned about fidelity to

---

[68] L. Legrand (*Mission in the Bible: Unity and Plurality* [Maryknoll: Orbis, 1990], 60) comments that "the verb *kērussein* becomes the standard designation for Jesus' basic activity (9 times in Matthew, 14 in Mark, 9 in Luke)."

[69] W. Larkin Jr., "Mission in Luke," in *Mission in the New Testament: An Evangelical Approach*, ed. W. Larkin Jr. and J. Williams (Maryknoll: Orbis, 1998), 158. This is taken as paradigmatic for holistic missioners (see Engel and Dyrness, *Changing the Mind of Missions,* 23; Padilla, "Holistic Mission," 222).

[70] J. Harvey, "Mission in Jesus' Teaching," in *Mission in the New Testament: An Evangelical Approach*, ed. W. Larkin Jr. and J. Williams (Maryknoll: Orbis, 1998), 47.

[71] A Köstenberger and P. O'Brien, *Salvation to the Ends of the Earth: A Biblical Theology of Mission* (Downers Grove: InterVarsity, 2001), 258; see E. Schnabel, *Early Christian Mission: Paul and the Early Church* (Grand Rapids: InterVarsity), 2:1548.

[72] Escobar, *The New Global Mission,* 22; see Wright, *The Mission of God,* 129. Consequently, mission theologians should not be taking their lead from either First- or Second-Inheritance Evangelicalism but from biblical models of mission that inform and guide twenty-first-century missional practice.

God's mission can do no other than to preserve this evangelistic priority.[73]

Advocates of any missional paradigm in which no priorities can be assumed or in which proclamation is downplayed[74] must deem Jesus and the apostles an embarrassment. At any particular time Jesus could have directed His energies toward dismantling the unjust Roman tax system. Paul also could have approached any one of the temples of Aphrodite throughout the Roman Empire in an attempt to rescue prostitutes. However, "Jesus never attempted to attack or change the social and economic structures of Galilean or Judean society,"[75] and Paul

> never directly engaged in any such work nor endeavoured to direct the Christian churches of his foundation in the doing of them. He could not have done so. Social activity of this kind was a fruit of the Spirit and it could not be expected to appear until the apostles had done their work and had ministered the Spirit.[76]

Both Jesus and His followers operated in this fashion by discerning the fact—which some are obscuring today[77]—that for the human heart to implement both the vertical and horizontal dimensions of the Great Commandment (Matt 22:37–39), it must first be regenerated by way of the Great Commission (Matt 28:19–20).[78] Indeed, "the very fact of Christian social responsibility presupposes socially responsible Christians, and it can only be by evangelism and discipling that they have become such."[79] Consequently, the "evangelical task primarily is the preaching of the Gospel, in the interest of individual regeneration by the supernatural grace of

---

[73] See Kraemer, *The Christian Mission,* 295.

[74] E.g., Padilla, "Holistic Mission," 226–27; Kirk, *Mission Under Scrutiny,* 49; Wright, 61, 317–23ff.

[75] Schnabel, *Early Christian Mission,* 1,577.

[76] R. Allen, *The Ministry of the Spirit: Selected Writings of Roland Allen* (London: World Dominion Press, 1960), 104–5.

[77] E.g., Wright, *The Mission of God,* 304; S. Strauss, "A Single Priority or Two Commands to Be Obeyed?" *Occasional Bulletin* 20(3): 1.

[78] This is precisely what M. Russell ("A Brief Apology for Holistic Mission: My Response to 'The Universal Priority of Proclamation' by Kurt Nelson," *Occasional Bulletin* 20[3]: 3) overlooks when suggesting that loving "God and neighbor" be adopted as the guiding principle in mission. Lost people cannot properly implement such things until they have first been redeemed, which thereby necessitates the priority of the Great Commission. In addition, there is no greater demonstration of love than explaining the message of reconciliation to God through Christ to the lost because whatever else they may be facing, this remains their greatest need.

[79] Stott, *Making Christ Known,* 183.

God, in such a way that divine redemption can be recognized as the best solution of our problems, individual and social."[80] And if societal transformation is not forthcoming as a result of pursuing proclamation as a priority, the problem is not with this priority but with a circumvention of the discipling process itself.[81]

CONCLUSION

In a world where the church "has to struggle for the purity of her missionary work"[82] and in which many good endeavors can be undertaken at the expense of the best, the church has no right to recreate mission in its own image. Rather, the church must remind itself that issues of "ultimacy" imply "primacy."[83] C. S. Lewis wisely observes that "there are a good many things which would not be worth bothering about if I were going to live only seventy years, but which I had better bother about very seriously if I am going to live forever."[84] Yes, hell is eternally worse than any temporal disease (see Matt 25:46; Heb 10:31; Rev 20:11–15), and the only entity that God has placed in the world to address this subject for the sake of the world is the church. Oprah can build schools; Madonna can sponsor orphanages; and Bill Gates can promote global health, but only the church is entrusted with the apostolic role of gospel proclamation whereby people are brought to the foot of the cross to "glorify God for His mercy" (Rom 15:9). "All other motives and purposes may, according to circumstances, be of greater and less secondary importance and value, but if they take the place of this primary motive and purpose, mission . . . must in the long run die from its lack of valid foundation."[85] Therefore, as Christians living

> in the twenty-first century [who] have not seen the crucified and risen Messiah, but . . . have believed the teaching of the apostles . . . [it] is our task to hear, understand and proclaim

---

[80] Henry, *The Uneasy Conscience,* 88.

[81] See Wright, *The Mission of God,* 321.

[82] J. Van Den Berg, *Constrained by Jesus' Love: An Inquiry into the Motives of the Missionary Awakening in Great Britain in the Period Between 1698 and 1815* (Rotterdam: University of Rotterdam, 1956), 212.

[83] Wright, *The Mission of God,* 316–19ff. But Wright never comes around to making this connection, even though he recognizes "the nonultimacy of death" (p. 439).

[84] C. S. Lewis, *Mere Christianity* (New York: MacMillan, 1952), 59; see Luke 12:4–5.

[85] Kraemer, *The Christian Mission,* 293.

their witness. We do not proclaim our own experience . . . rather, we proclaim the word of the first witnesses.[86]

They could have done no better, and neither can those who desire to follow in their footsteps.

BIBLIOGRAPHY

Allen, R. *The Ministry of the Spirit: Selected Writings of Roland Allen*. London: World Dominion Press, 1960.

———. *The Spontaneous Expansion of the Church*. Grand Rapids: Eerdmans, 1962.

Bavinck, J. H. *An Introduction to the Science of Missions*. Phillipsburg: P&R, 1960.

Beyerhaus, P. *Missions: Which Way? Humanization or Redemption*. Grand Rapids: Zondervan, 1971.

Blomberg, C. "The Unity and Diversity of Scripture." Pages 64–72 in *New Dictionary of Biblical Theology*. Edited by T. D. Alexander et al. Downers Grove: InterVarsity, 2000.

Bonino, J. M. *Doing Theology in a Revolutionary Situation*. Philadelphia: Fortress, 1975.

Bonk, J. *Missions and Money: Affluence as Western Missionary Problem . . . Revisited*. Revised and expanded ed. Maryknoll: Orbis, 2006.

Bosch, D. *Transforming Mission: Paradigm Shifts in Theology of Mission*. Maryknoll: Orbis, 1991.

Carpenter, J. "The Fundamentalist Leaven and the Rise of an Evangelical United Front." Pages 257–88 in *The Evangelical Tradition in America*. Edited by L. Sweet. Macon: Mercer University Press, 1984.

Edwards, J. *The Works of Jonathan Edwards*. Vol. 1. Peabody: Hendrickson, 1998.

Engel, J. and W. Dyrness. *Changing the Mind of Missions*. Downers Grove: InterVarsity, 2000.

Escobar, S. *The New Global Mission: The Gospel from Everywhere to Everyone*. Downers Grove: InterVarsity, 2003.

Fernando, A. "Getting Back on Course." *Christianity Today* 51 (October 2007): 40–45.

---

[86] Schnabel, *Early Christian Mission,* 1580.

Glasser, A. "Biblical Theology of Mission." Pages 127–31 in *Evangelical Dictionary of World Missions*. Edited by A. S. Moreau. Grand Rapids: Baker, 2000.

Harnack, A. *The Expansion of Christianity in the First Three Centuries*. Vol. 1. Eugene: Wipf and Stock, 1998.

Harvey, J. "Mission in Jesus' Teaching." Pages 30–49 in *Mission in the New Testament: An Evangelical Approach*. Edited by W. Larkin Jr. and J. Williams. Maryknoll: Orbis, 1998.

Hawthorne, S. "The Story of His Glory." Pages 34–48 in *Perspectives on the World Christian Movement: A Reader*. 3rd ed. Edited by R. Winter and S. Hawthorne. Pasadena: William Carey Library, 1999.

Henry, C. F. H. *The Uneasy Conscience of Modern Fundamentalism*. Grand Rapids: Eerdmans, 1947.

Hesselgrave, D. *Paradigms in Conflict: 10 Key Questions in Christian Missions Today*. Grand Rapids: Kregel, 2005.

Hiebert, P. *Anthropological Reflections on Missiological Issues*. Grand Rapids: Baker, 1994.

———. *Missiological Implications of Epistemological Shifts: Affirming Truth in a Modern/Postmodern World*. Harrisburg: Trinity Press International, 1999.

Hoekendijk, J. "The Church in Missionary Thinking." *International Review of Missions* 41 (1952): 324–36.

Horrell, D. *An Introduction to the Study of Paul*. New York: Continuum, 2000.

House, P. "Biblical Theology and the Wholeness of Scripture." Pages 267–79 in *Biblical Theology: Retrospect & Prospect*. Edited by S. Hafemann. Downers Grove: InterVarsity, 2002.

Jongeneel, J. "The Missiology of Gisbertus Voetius: The First Comprehensive Protestant Theology of Missions." *Calvin Theological Journal* 26 (April 1991): 47–79.

Kirk, J. A. *Mission Under Scrutiny: Confronting Contemporary Challenges*. Minneapolis: Fortress, 2006.

Köstenberger, A. "Diversity and Unity in the New Testament."
    Pages 144–58 in *Biblical Theology: Retrospect &*
    Prospect. Edited by S. Hafemann. Downers Grove:
    InterVarsity, 2002.

Köstenberger, A. and P. O'Brien. *Salvation to the Ends of the*
    Earth: A Biblical Theology of Mission. Downers Grove:
    InterVarsity, 2001.

Kraemer, H. *The Christian Mission in a Non-Christian World*.
    New York: Harper & Brothers, 1947.

Larkin, W., Jr. "Mission in Luke." Pages 152–69 in *Mission in*
    the New Testament: An Evangelical Approach. Edited by
    W. Larkin Jr. and J. Williams. Maryknoll: Orbis, 1998.

Legrand, L. *Mission in the Bible: Unity and Plurality*.
    Maryknoll: Orbis, 1990.

Lewis, C. S. *Mere Christianity*. New York: MacMillan, 1952.

Little, C. *Mission in the Way of Paul: Biblical Mission for the*
    Church in the Twenty-First Century. New York: Peter
    Lang, 2005.

Marshall, I. H. *New Testament Theology*. Downers Grove:
    InterVarsity, 2004.

Martens, E. "The People of God." Pages 225–53 in *Central*
    Themes in Biblical Theology: Mapping Unity in
    Diversity. Edited by S. Hafemann and P. House. Grand
    Rapids: Baker, 2007.

Moreau, S., G. Corwin, and G. McGee. *Introducing World*
    Missions: A Biblical, Historical, and Practical Survey.
    Grand Rapids: Baker, 2004.

Neill, S. *Creative Tension*. New York: Doubleday, 1959.

Newbigin, L. *One Body, One Gospel, One World: The*
    Christian Mission Today. London: Wm. Carling and Co.
    Ltd., 1958.

Padilla, C. R. "Holistic Mission." Pages 216–31 in *A New*
    Vision, A New Heart, A Renewed Call. Vol. 1. Edited by
    D. Claydon. Pasadena: William Carey Library, 2005.

Patterson, J. "The Loss of a Protestant Missionary Consensus: Foreign Missions and the Fundamentalist-Modernist Conflict." Pages 73–91 in *Earthen Vessels: American Evangelicals and Foreign Missions, 1880–1980*. Edited by J. Carpenter and W. Shenk. Grand Rapids: Eerdmans, 1990.

Piper, J. *Let the Nations Be Glad! The Supremacy of God in Missions*. 2nd ed. Grand Rapids: Baker, 2003.

Rowell, J. *To Give or Not to Give? Rethinking Dependency, Restoring Generosity, and Redefining Sustainability*. Tyrone: Authentic Publishing, 2006.

Russell, M. "A Brief Apology for Holistic Mission: My Response to 'The Universal Priority of Proclamation' by Kurt Nelson." *Occasional Bulletin* 20(3): 3–4.

Schnabel, E. *Early Christian Mission: Paul and the Early Church*. Vol. 2. Downers Grove: InterVarsity, 2004.

Shenk, W. "Mission Strategies." Pages 218–34 in *Toward the 21st Century in Christian Mission*. Edited by J. Phillips and R. Coote. Grand Rapids: Eerdmans, 1993.

Stamoolis, J. *Eastern Orthodox Mission Theology Today*. Eugene: Wipf and Stock, 2001.

Stauffer, E. *New Testament Theology*. New York: MacMillan, 1955.

Stott, J. *Christian Mission in the Modern World*. Downers Grove: InterVarsity, 1975.

———, ed. *Making Christ Known*. Grand Rapids: Eerdmans, 1996.

Strauss, S. "A Single Priority or Two Commands to Be Obeyed?" *Occasional Bulletin* 20.3 (2007):1–6.

Taylor, W., ed. *Global Missiology for the 21st Century: The Iguassu Dialogue*. Grand Rapids, Baker, 2000.

Van Den Berg, J. *Constrained by Jesus' Love: An Inquiry into the Motives of the Missionary Awakening in Great Britain in the Period Between 1698 and 1815*. Rotterdam: University of Rotterdam, 1956.

Van Engen, C. *Mission on the Way: Issues in Mission Theology*. Grand Rapids: Baker, 1996.

Van Rheenen, G. "Changing Motivations for Missions: From 'Fear of Hell' to the 'Glory of God.'" Pages 161–81 in *The Changing Face of World Missions: Engaging Contemporary Issues and Trends*. Edited by M. Pocock et al. Grand Rapids: Baker, 2005.

Verkuyl, J. *Contemporary Missiology: An Introduction*. Grand Rapids: Eerdmans, 1978.

Weber, L. and D. Welliver. *Mission Handbook: U.S. and Canadian Protestant Ministries Overseas 2007–2009*. Wheaton: Evangelical and Missions Information Service, 2007.

Welliver, D. and M. Northcutt. *Mission Handbook: U.S. and Canadian Protestant Ministries Overseas 2004–2006*. Wheaton: Evangelical and Missions Information Service, 2004.

Wright, C. *The Mission of God: Unlocking the Bible's Grand Narrative*. Downers Grove: InterVarsity, 2006.

Yannoulatos, A. "The Purpose and Motive of Mission." *International Review of Mission* 54 (1965): 281–97.

Yates, T. *Christian Mission in the Twentieth Century*. New York: Cambridge University Press, 1996.

CHAPTER 17

The Missing Key to the Future of Evangelical Mission

MIKE BARNETT

INTRODUCTION

Ralph Winter challenges us to think outside the box as we contemplate the future of Evangelicals in mission. He stimulates our minds, stirs our hearts, and occasionally causes us to squirm in our seats as he exhorts us to get busy with the remaining tasks of God's mission. We wouldn't expect less from this renowned trailblazer of twentieth-century mission frontiers.

In this brief response I highlight key points in light of responses by Scott Moreau and Christopher Little. I affirm some and challenge others. In addition, I suggest a missing key to the future of evangelical mission.

CRITICAL QUESTIONS

Historical Interpretations. Moreau refers to Winter's chapter as "looking backward while going forward." But as we look backward, we must be careful to see the past clearly. As a student of church history, I marvel at Winter's sweeping statements on the demise of Christians in First-Inheritance Evangelicalism (FIE) and his dismissal of those in Second-Inheritance Evangelicalism (SIE).

Winter suggests the second great "reduction" of Evangelicalism resulted because of deficiencies in these two groups.

> Many leading families of FIE influence gradually slipped in both faith and political standing. At the same time, Moody and others impacted millions of noncollege Americans who, even after conversion, were almost completely isolated from both civic leadership and college education.
>
> This new Evangelicalism-of-the-masses, characteristic of SIE, significantly boosted church attendance in the USA and created 157 Bible Institutes. However, it had little stake in politics or social action and tended to suspect the smaller number of continuing, socially upscale college-educated evangelicals from the FIE as being "liberal" (which by then they often were). (p. 165)

Winter attempts to explain (or blame) this second reduction on the demise of old-school Evangelicals and the lack of relevance of new-school Evangelicals.

Such a simple characterization of the two branches of Evangelicals over a period of decades is unproven at best and misleading at worst. Can we really conclude that the social fabric of our country was hardly influenced by the masses? Were we truly held culturally captive by a few secular, elite, highly educated, liberal activists for the past 130 years? Is it possible that the twentieth-century boom in church growth and private Christian education in America had little impact on life in the public square throughout two great wars, the depression, the civil rights movement, the sixties revolution, the tragedies of the seventies, the Reagan years, the dot-com phenomenon, post-9/11, and the age of globalization? Winter may argue that the theology of the uneducated working-class masses was defective, but surely their influence was not. Likewise, his solution—to develop a holistic theology—may not be the foundational solution he envisions. My point is that *the history is simply not so simple*. Winter himself comments that the story of SIE is complicated. Thus, we must take care not to over-simplify the past,[1] lest our solutions for the future be naïve and less effective.

---

[1] Winter is a master of simplifying history, but sometimes he overstates or understates to the detriment of his argument—e.g., his statements that the two awakenings "led to" the revolutionary and civil wars (p. 164).

Intuition. Winter speaks of the "keen intuition of socially sensitive missionaries" (p. 179) as a factor in maintaining a sense of social responsibility in their practice of missions. He credits this *theologyless* (my word) intuition to the worldview of FIE. It seems to me that this mysterious-sounding impulse, this intuition, is in fact the leadership of the Holy Spirit in the lives of Christ followers. It is the same intuition that resides in SIE missionaries to this day. And I doubt it was theologyless. True, the grand "civilizing" endeavors of the "The Great Century"[2] transformed societies, and Winter rightly indicts secular historians for overlooking this fact. But social transformation through the lives and work of missionaries did not stop with FIE. Even after the nineteenth century, missions, missionaries, their agencies, and churches established hospitals, schools, orphanages, farms, and community development centers. Most of these institutions of social change were nationalized in the late twentieth century, and the role of the missionary transitioned to a facilitator of such endeavors. But the impact of SIE and postmodern missionaries continues. God's Spirit still leads.

The Donor Myth. I currently work as a strategy consultant with four different mission organizations, and I agree with Winter that donors are becoming more strategic in their giving. Little should be pleased to hear that they want to see kingdom results. But this increased sense of stewardship does not reflect some kind of antiholistic reductionism. The statistics that all three authors cite regarding increased giving to relief and development organizations are evidence that donors do have an understanding (or intuition?) of the place of social ministry in mission. But today's donors want kingdom results. They expect these results to flow from a variety of platforms that minister to the needs of people. We must not confuse donor concern for strategic results with an aversion to creative and socially engaged ministries.

The Relief and Development Myth. Likewise I cannot agree (especially with Little) that increased relief and development efforts signal the end of evangelism and church planting. Southern Baptists gave approximately $17 million for tsunami relief and

---

[2] This is Latourette's term for the early modern missions movement—the late eighteenth through the early twentieth centuries (see K. S. Latourette, *A History of the Expansion of Christianity*, vols. IV-V [New York: Harper & Brothers, 1941]).

development after the December 2004 Indian Ocean earthquake. These funds were used strategically to assist victims and build relational bridges for future projects and kingdom work. These funds were also "over and above" gifts given by church members who trusted their denomination to use them in a way that honors God. This is simply one example of the worldwide aid and development industry that continues to grow.

I am not discouraged by the proliferation of Christian non-government organizations (NGO) around the world. It reflects a variety of social dynamics: transfer of wealth, opening of previously closed societies, increased global awareness, shifts of influence to the majority world, and so on. Though we absolutely need the prophetic voice of someone like Little to keep us focused on the priority of proclamation, I question his conclusion that "one can be fairly certain that the missions community in the USA is presently spending more on alleviating human suffering than on addressing the eternal destiny of the lost" (p. 203). Relief and development is a capital intensive venture. Discipling is a human resource intensive venture. We may be spending more dollars on "relief and development" by name, but we cannot discount the kingdom returns on such investments, especially if the NGO workers have that same intuition. As this book acknowledges, God takes the initiative in the world for His mission. Lately He is doing it through relief and community development projects.

WORD OR DEED?

The question of the priority of word or deed simply will not go away. Little, one of my colleagues, has been in the middle of this fray.[3] The topic relates to the church from its beginnings. It was surely an issue in Acts 6 when Stephen and his coworkers were

---

[3] This issue resurfaced in recent years among North American missiologists. D. Hesselgrave's book (*Paradigms in Conflict: 10 Key Questions in Christian Missions Today* [Grand Rapids: Kregel, 2005]) may have been the catalyst. I required my doctor of ministry class members to write a publishable essay in response to one of Hesselgrave's chapters. One of them, K. Nelson of East-West Ministries, responded to chap. 4 on "Holism and Prioritism." His essay was published ("The Universal Priority of Proclamation") in the *Occasional Bulletin* (20.1, pp. 3–6), and shortly afterward the bulletin dedicated an entire issue (20.3, pp. 3–6) to the topic with Nelson responding to critiques of his article by S. Strauss and M. Russell. Since then the April 2008 issue of Winter's *International Journal of Frontier Missiology* (*IJFM*) focused on "Word and Deed: A Century of Polarization?" It included a foundational chapter by C. Little with responses from several world-class missiologists. (By the way, upon request, Nelson wrote an excellent response to Little as well, but for some reason *IJFM* decided not to include his article.)

appointed. Throughout the history of the church, radical Christ followers like Francis of Assisi, Count Nicholas von Zinzendorf, John Wesley, William Carey, William Wilberforce, William Booth and Catherine Booth, Martin Luther King Jr.,[4] and even former President Jimmy Carter stepped up for the sake of social transformation. Yet those same disciples of Christ, including Stephen, also had a strong voice for the gospel.

Which comes first: word or deed, proclamation or service, evangelism or social ministry? Winter offers a three-phase summary. First we are to be "peopling the kingdom" or "gaining a new relationship with God for as many humans as possible." Next, we will see new believers glorify God through their good works. Finally, we must "organize" our good deeds for deliberate discovery and exposition of God's glory and concern for global poverty and disease (p. 173).

It seems Winter concurs (or concedes) with Little that our priority must always be proclamation. At least he believes this is what we should do first. Or does he? Later he paradoxically notes that though we believe works follow faith, so "in our outreach to unbelievers *those very works displaying God's glory better come first*" (p. 181, emphasis his). Perhaps the biblical tension protects us from abuses of either extreme. I prefer not to think of proclamation as the first thing in a sequence followed by deeds. I understand proclamation as our main and ultimate thing. Thus, it is our priority. Do we first proclaim and then serve? Maybe, maybe not. It depends on the situation, the relationship, the leadership of God's Spirit in the life of the witness and the sought one. But regardless of how and when we serve, we have not fulfilled the Great Commission unless and until we proclaim. Woe unto Evangelicals if our next "inheritance" subjugates the priority of proclamation. History teaches us that such a movement would be short lived.

Phase two is a result of how we proclaim. I affirm Winter's emphasis on teaching to obey (p. 187). We corrupt Jesus' command to disciple when we reduce it to simply teaching truth. Instead, we must teach people to follow truth—to obey all He commanded (Matt 28:18–20). We do this through relationships

---

[4] Writing on King's impact on the social fabric of twentieth-century America, F. Rutledge ("When God Disturbs the Peace," *Christianity Today* [June 2008]: 30–31) poses the question "Is our gospel too small?" and then suggests an answer: "Our gospel may be small because we fail to believe that God animates many social movements."

and community. Herein lies the relational opportunity to serve. The command to disciple includes baptizing. This is a result of proclaiming the good news of the Father, Son, and Holy Spirit. This begins the life transformation that connects us with the Holy Spirit who empowers us to obey. When we obey, we do good deeds and that in turn glorifies God. This is the "doxological" mission that Little writes about and Winter endorses.[5]

The third phase is about mission strategy. This is the bottom line of Winter's chapter. We must develop a strategy for mission that proactively seeks to defeat evil on a global scale. We must plan to eradicate disease and overcome poverty worldwide. When we do this, God's reputation will be defended, and He will no longer be blamed for "all such unaddressed evil" (p. 188) in the world.

I like the sounds of this priority of word that results in deed that glorifies God and delivers the world from evil. I appreciate Winter's challenging call for big action on a global scale. Why shouldn't the church be concerned and engaged in social transformation? May it be so . . . but not without the ultimate and eternal spiritual transformation that encompasses God's mission.

WINTER'S PROPOSITION

Winter's stated goal is to open a conversation about what missionaries, mission agencies, and missions scholars should do next. He asserts that we need a both/and, word/deed theology. He believes the mission movement, more than church movements or the secular world, *holds the key* to open this strategy door of mission. He declares war on the evils of the world. He takes on disease, poverty, oppression, and suffering on a global scale. He charges agencies to internationalize intuition-driven strategies of local missionaries (p. 187). This is not a new idea for Winter. I've heard him on several occasions advocate for this next level of missions. I've listened to his plea for a missionary-led cure for cancer and a call for eradication of malaria and other chronic diseases. I commend him for his vision and call for action. He consistently submits that missionaries are the future soldiers of this war. And here is where I see a problem.

---

[5] See D. Howell, *Servants of the Servant: A Biblical Theology of Leadership* (Eugene: Wipf and Stock, 2003), 298–300.

THE WRONG KEY?

For Winter, the mission is accomplished through missionaries, mission agencies, and missions scholars. He wants a bold new plan for changing the world. He calls for "empowering evangelism" (p. 182) that combines word and deed. He insists on a more intentional, broader theology (p. 187) to replace proactively the historical "theological intuition of loving missionaries" (p. 179) and to tackle the bigger global problems of the world. He "yearn[s] to see evangelical missions be able to give more direct, credible credit to Jesus Christ" for social transformation (p. 186). He charges mission agencies to co-opt the local intuitions of their missionaries and implement national strategies and international campaigns for broader implementation (p. 187). For Winter, the key lies with the parachurch. I respectfully submit, that for God, the key is *the church*.

I am reminded of the "two structures" argument that prevails in Winter's missiology. For decades he and others have made the case for the prominent and independent role of the parachurch (sodality) in the mission strategy of God.[6] Is this where we get off track with God and His mission? It seems to me that Scripture clearly prescribes that since the resurrection of Christ, God works *through the church* (modality) to accomplish His mission of discipling all nations. The role of the missionary is to equip the saints who do the work (Eph 4:10–12), and through that work of the church the entire universe recognizes the reality and wisdom of God (Eph 3:10). This is why the New Testament (after the four Gospels) centers on the work of the Holy Spirit to reproduce the church "all over the world" (Col 1:6). This is God's secret, His mystery—the fact that He works through gathered believers among all peoples, not just Israel.

Do we need missionaries, mission agencies, and missions scholars. Absolutely! But are they *the key*? Their role is to preach the gospel among those who have yet to hear and to equip them to plant and grow reproducing Great Commission churches. Therein lies the key: Great Commission churches—churches that disciple Christ followers and connect them with the truth and the Spirit

---

[6] R. D. Winter, *Perspectives on the World Christian Movement* (Pasadena: William Carey Library, 1999), 129, 220–30.

of God in a way that grows that understanding, that intuition of God's mission. *The key is the churches.*

Biblically and historically speaking, missionaries follow merchants, the ordinary believers. That is what happened in Acts 2. Pilgrims and merchants on pilgrimage in Jerusalem heard the gospel in their own tongues and returned home with good news to tell. This explains how Paul wrote letters to churches he never visited (Romans and Colossians). Who planted those churches? Ordinary followers of Jesus Christ who had an extraordinary story to proclaim. Roman missionaries followed their soldiers, and Nestorian missionaries followed their merchants through the silk roads. Jesuit missionaries came to the new world with the discoverers. Around the world today, doctors, educators, businesspeople, agriculturalists, soldiers, athletes, and immigrants carry the gospel to those who have yet to hear it. God uses them to change entire societies. This is the plan of God since His promise to Abraham (Gen 12:2–3). This is the key to the future of Evangelicals in mission.

Moreau touches on this dynamic when he turns to W. Easterly's critique of Western efforts to aid the rest of the world. His analysis is interesting. The problem seems to be one of alignment. "Planners" devise appropriately "grandiose" and "massively scaled" schemes, but they seldom succeed because they focus on donors instead of local "searchers" or implementers. Was Easterly reading God's mission manual here? In fact, aren't the searchers the key to the strategy of God's mission? From biblical times and throughout history, God has worked through ordinary individual followers (searchers) of Christ more than exceptional or famous benefactors of the gospel. God speaks through Christ followers who are connected to, released by, and serving on behalf of local churches.

Nothing new here. As the war in Iraq so tragically illustrated, societies are seldom transformed by international campaigns of "shock and awe" at the highest levels. Social, cultural, and individual change happens from the grass roots of communities—in local, relational, familial, tribal, face-to-face, and one-on-one settings. This is how God designed mankind. Moreau also refers to secular research that "indicates humans may be hardwired to focus on helping one or two people" instead of whole communities (p. 194). Exactly. This is how God wired us. This is how He chose to bless all peoples—through one man, Abraham, and his descendants, both physical and spiritual (Gen 12:2–3). This is how Jesus modeled and commanded us to reach the nations—baptizing them and teaching them to obey, one group of 12 at a time, *through the church.*

I applaud Winter's call for a faith that works, but I think he is using the wrong key to open the mission door to the kingdom.

THE RIGHT KEYS?

Does the church's responsibility let the missionaries, mission agencies, and mission scholars off the hook? Never. They also have a critical role to play in the mission of God. I like Moreau's five "additional areas to consider" (p. 195). I offer the following general suggestions in addition to his.

Missionaries. Missionaries must always stay connected to a local church. This means more than simply maintaining church membership. It means, regardless of how long or remote your field assignment, making sure the church knows that they provide more than financial support for you. Ensure that your accountability flows through the church. If you ever lose that individual relational connection with the local church, you lose your witness. Many missionaries have done so.

Mission Agencies. Eliminate the sense that you are competing with the local church, whether it is a sending or receiving church. Dispel the thought that you are the expert. Abolish the "them/us" syndrome. If you cannot get your organizational mind wrapped around traditional, organic, and/or emerging forms of sending churches, then (to quote a Hiebert principle of crossing culture) recognize that it's your problem, not theirs, and find a solution. Agencies that figured this out in the 1990s are thriving today.

Missions Scholars. Professors, please stick to the basics. Don't let tuition-drivenness push you away from the basics of biblical witness, evangelism, discipling, church planting, and reproduction from Jerusalem to the ends of the earth. Do not assume that your students have the basics. And always model what you teach.

CONCLUSION

The good news is that Winter's prediction of a recovery of FIE's word/deed approach is already upon us. I share Moreau's cautious optimism. The 20-somethings I teach do not disappoint me. They understand the mission of God far better than my 20-somethings generation did. They have that intuition for proclamation that includes social transformation. They want to introduce others to Christ. They want to make a difference. They are willing to go anywhere at any time. Above all, they want to do it together and for Jesus.

This is a book on God's mission, His initiative in the world. It reminds us that God is the actor. He is the implementer. Only God will conquer evil on a universal scale, and He has clearly revealed that He will do it *through Jesus Christ and His body, the church.* Meanwhile, we must be diligent to disciple all peoples by baptizing and teaching them to obey all He commanded. We must release and train missionaries to be effective equippers of those who represent the church, and we must support our mission agencies and sharpen our mission strategies for future impact on individuals, communities, and the whole world. We must affirm our missions scholars to equip the equippers for God's mission. We must pray that His name be hallowed and His kingdom come. Looking backward while going forward—this is the future of Evangelicals in mission.

BIBLIOGRAPHY

Hesselgrave, David J. *Paradigms in Conflict: 10 Key Questions in Christian Missions Today.* Grand Rapids: Kregel, 2005.

Howell, Don. *Servants of the Servant: A Biblical Theology of Leadership.* Eugene, OR: Wipf & Stock, 2003.

Latourette, Kenneth Scott. *A History of the Expansion of Christianity,* vols. IV–V. New York: Harper & Brothers, 1941.

Nelson, Kurt. "The Universal Priority of Proclamation." *Occasional Bulletin,* vol. 20, no.1, September 2007.

Rutledge, Fleming. "When God Disturbs the Peace." Christianity Today, June 2008: 30–31.

Winter, Ralph D. *Perspectives on the World Christian Movement.* Pasadena: William Carey Library, 1999.

———, ed. "Word and Deed: A Century of Polarization?" *International Journal of Frontier Missiology* (IJFM), vol. 25, no. 2, April–June 2008.

CHAPTER 18

In Response to Ralph Winter's "The Future of Evangelicals in Mission"

J. MARK TERRY

INTRODUCTION

There seems to be a disconnect between the title of Ralph Winter's essay, "The Future of Evangelicals in Mission," and the essay itself. Those who read the essay expect Winter's prognostications about the future of Evangelical missions. What they discover is an essay on the history of Evangelicalism and an apologetic for what the future of missions *should* be. Winter only briefly mentions a few future trends in missions and does not expand on his short list. Though the essay does not provide what the title promises, it does help the reader understand the historical and theological basis for holistic missions.

WINTER'S APPEAL FOR HOLISTIC MISSIONS

In his essay Winter rehearses the history of the Evangelical movement, especially the impact of the First and Second Great Awakenings, which he labels First-Inheritance Evangelicalism (FIE). Winter argues, and correctly so, that both Awakenings birthed both evangelistic and social ministries on the part of Evangelicals.

The First Great Awakening (1720–1740) bore more fruit in

social ministry than is generally recognized. Following in the steps of the Pietists, the leaders of the First Great Awakening established schools, colleges, and orphanages. For example, W. Tennent's "Log College" eventually became Princeton University and Seminary. G. Whitefield established seven orphanages and labored mightily to raise money for their support.[1]

The Second Great Awakening (1800–1830) also bore much social fruit. This Awakening not only prompted the establishment of schools and colleges; it also led Evangelicals to participate in a number of social movements, especially the Abolition Movement and the Temperance Movement. Evangelicals engaged in these social movements while they also churched the Western frontier and established religious organizations like the American Sunday School Union, the American Tract Society, and the American Bible Society. Winter recounts these efforts and applauds them. In this he follows in the scholarly steps of T. L. Smith, whose *Revivalism and Social Reform* put to rest the idea that the revivalists were so heavenly minded they could do no earthly good.

Winter also reminds his readers that the foreign missionaries of the nineteenth and early twentieth centuries demonstrated a holistic approach to missions. Though they did not go out intending to embrace missiological holism, Winter asserts that the pioneer missionaries intuitively understood the need for a holistic approach. The early missionaries preached the gospel, but they also started schools, hospitals, leprosariums, orphanages, and agricultural stations—all with the intent of winning the lost to Christ and ministering to their social and physical needs. Some of the institutions were established as means of converting the local people, while the missionaries established other institutions because of the Christian compassion they felt for the suffering they encountered.

Before World War II foreign mission boards generally employed a balanced approach to work overseas. They certainly evangelized and planted churches, but they also founded schools and hospitals. In fact, D. McGavran complained that there were too many humanitarian institutions and not nearly enough church planters.[2] After World War II evangelical entrepreneurs such as

---

[1] J. M. Terry, *Evangelism: A Concise History* (Nashville: B&H, 1994), 122–24.
[2] D. A. McGavran, *The Bridges of God* (New York: Friendship Press, 1955), 50–53.

Bill Bright and Bob Pierce established many parachurch organizations. These organizations tended to emphasize evangelism, like Campus Crusade for Christ, or human needs ministry, like World Vision. One could categorize the new organizations as Great Commission agencies (make disciples) and Great Commandment agencies (help your needy neighbors). Of course, this is the essential nature of parachurch organizations; they tend to focus narrowly on one ministry. Agencies that emphasize social ministry seem often to neglect evangelism, and the reverse could be said of organizations that stress evangelism.

In his essay Winter decries the separation of evangelism from social ministry that has characterized Evangelical missions in the past 60 years. He appeals to Evangelicals to return to their historical roots. Winter's thesis that Evangelical missions has been holistic in the distant past is historically sound.

Winter's thesis is also sound biblically. A careful reading of the Gospel accounts reveals that Jesus came preaching *and* healing. Jesus fed the multitudes, exorcised demons, and brought the dead to life. In Luke 4:18–19 Jesus shared His job description, as it were. He declared the recipients of His ministries were the poor, the brokenhearted, the captives, the blind, and the oppressed. Matthew 9:36 teaches us that Jesus had *compassion* for the multitudes He met in Galilee because of their great needs. In the Great Commission Jesus exhorted His disciples to teach their converts "everything." This teaching aspect of the Great Commission is often forgotten and neglected by Evangelicals in their zeal to "make disciples of all nations."

The apostle Paul also mentioned the social obligations of Christians: "For we are His creation—created in Christ Jesus for good works, which God prepared ahead of time so that we should walk in them" (Eph 2:10). What makes this verse so fascinating is that it is found in the same pericope with vv. 8–9, one of the great soteriological passages in the New Testament. This passage reminds us that salvation is not an end in itself, but rather believers are saved from sin and set apart for "good works," which include both holy living and holistic service to others (see Jas 2:14–16).

Winter's thesis is also theologically sound. Chris Little's excellent response leads the reader through a survey of the relevant theological literature, so we need not duplicate that. Suffice it to say that Little's response shows that Evangelicals have written a lot on this topic. While the Fundamentalists of the early twentieth century may have dichotomized evangelism and social ministry, this has not been true of Evangelicals, at least not since the Lausanne Congress in 1974. The Lausanne Covenant's statement on Christian Social Responsibility states in part:

> Here too we express penitence both for our neglect and for having sometimes regarded evangelism and social concern as mutually exclusive. Although reconciliation with other people is not reconciliation with God, nor is social action evangelism, nor is political liberation salvation, nevertheless, we affirm that sociopolitical involvement are both part of our Christian duty. . . . The salvation we claim should be transforming us in the totality of our personal and social responsibilities. Faith without works is dead.[3]

R. Sider's *One-Sided Christianity*[4] reminded Evangelicals of the need for a balanced, or holistic, ministry. Christian love demonstrated through social ministry and deeds of kindness and mercy influence the lost to inquire about the Savior who inspires the service. Similarly, the truly caring Christian does not fail to address humankind's greatest need—reconciliation with almighty God. This is where the liberation theologians fell short. They helped us understand the corporate nature of sin and God's special concern for the poor, valid theses to be sure, but they neglected humanity's spiritual dilemma. If the Fundamentalists neglected the bodies of the poor, the liberation theologians neglected their souls. The dichotomy between evangelism and social ministry is a false one. In fact the two emphases can combine to produce a ministry that is true to the Scriptures and effective. One hand truly does wash the other.

We can certainly agree with Winter's desire for a more fulsome theology of the atonement. Evangelicals have typically emphasized the substitutionary atonement of Christ. There is no need to abandon that position, but the *Christus Victor* theory of

---

[3] J. R. W. Stott, ed., *Making Christ Known: Historic Documents from the Lausanne Movement, 1974–1989* (Grand Rapids: Eerdmans, 1996), 24.

[4] R. J. Sider, *One-Sided Christianity* (Grand Rapids: Zondervan, 1993).

the atonement, articulated by G. Aulen,[5] expands our understanding of Christ's work on the cross. Not only did Christ die in our place; He also triumphed over Satan and the forces of evil. In so doing, Christ defeated sin, sickness, suffering, and sorrow in the age to come.

Little ends his response to Winter with a section on *primacy.* Can we say that evangelism or social ministry is primary? Little correctly concludes that evangelism must be primary because evangelism addresses humanity's eternal destiny, while social ministry addresses temporal needs. Stating this does not denigrate social ministry, but it does highlight the ultimate question: Where will you spend eternity?

Scott Moreau assesses Winter's thesis from a missiological perspective. He affirms Winter's desire to see a more holistic approach and lists some personal predictions: that technology will become more and more important and that financial constraints will force missions agencies to adopt new models and approaches. Moreau is surely correct on both counts.

To conclude this first section, we can affirm Winter's thesis. For historical, biblical, and theological reasons, Winter's thesis is well made. Evangelicals should embrace a holistic approach to missions. Still, that was not the assigned title. What might have Winter discussed in his essay?

FUTURE TRENDS IN EVANGELICAL MISSIONS

The following are trends in Evangelical missions that Winter might have emphasized. Some trends are evident now and will continue. Other trends are just emerging.

Globalization

Globalization is hard to define. It means different things in different contexts. For example, there is the globalization of media, and there is economic globalization as well. One can travel all over the world and see Shell Oil Company signs and buy Coca Cola. Viewers in Asia can watch Cable News Network and ESPN. In missions, globalization means that instead of the North evangelizing the South or the West evangelizing the East, now there

---

[5] G. Aulen, *Christus Victor* (London: SPCK, 2010).

are no clear distinctions between sending and receiving nations. American missionaries still serve in the Philippines, while Filipinos serve as missionaries in Thailand. An Indian professor may teach missions in Great Britain, while a British professor teaches in Bangalore, India. The body of Christ has truly become global, and thankfully so.

Urbanization

The world's population is increasingly urban. P. Johnstone says, "The twenty-first century will be an urban world, just as the previous 20 centuries of Christianity have been a rural world."[6] As of August 2007 more than 50 percent of the world's people live in urban centers. In China alone there are 80 cities with a population of one million or more.[7] Most of the success stories in Christian missions have been in rural areas, primarily among village people. In the twenty-first century, Evangelical missiologists will struggle to develop effective strategies to reach the world's cities.

Pentecostal-Charismatic Churches

P. Brierley's helpful book *Future Church* notes the phenomenal growth of the pentecostal-charismatic churches around the world.[8] They grew from 12 million members in 1960 to an estimated 150 million in 2010. Much of this growth will be recorded in indigenous churches and denominations in the Majority World that have no formal connection with North American denominations. Why are they growing so rapidly? One reason is surely their style of worship; it appeals to cultures that enjoy a lively, participative style of worship. Second, their emphasis on healing and deliverance ministries meets the needs of people who are too poor to afford expensive medical care, even if it is available. Third, their flexible approach to leadership allows capable people to rise to leadership, regardless of their formal education. It may well be that, should the Lord tarry, the twenty-first century will be characterized as the pentecostal-charismatic century in Protestant missions.

---

[6] P. Johnstone, *The Church Is Bigger Than You Think* (Ross-Shire: Great Britain: Christian Focus Books, 1998), 241.
[7] See the United Nations report posted on www.unfpa.org.
[8] P. Brierley, *Future Church* (London: Monarch Books, 1998).

Orality

Late in the twentieth century, missiologists came to under-stand that 60 percent of the people in the world are oral learn-ers. This means they are illiterate or semiliterate and absorb and disseminate information through oral means. This has prompted major changes for many missions agencies. Up until 1985 most missionaries emphasized literacy-based evangelism. They distrib-uted gospel tracts, gave away copies of John's Gospel, and en-couraged people to join evangelistic home Bible study groups. These methods are all appropriate if the population is literate, but the methods missed the majority of the world's population, espe-cially in the 10–40 Window. The development of Chronological Bible Story Telling in the 1980s by New Tribes Mission has made it possible to reach oral learners more effectively than ever before. Now people can be evangelized, discipled, and trained in church leadership—all by means of biblical stories, dramas, and songs.

Christianity in China

When the communist government of China expelled the mis-sionaries in 1950, there were approximately 3 million Christians in China. By 2000 there were (perhaps) as many as 100 million. That number continues to increase rapidly. As the number of Christians grows and China prospers economically, the church in China will exercise more influence in the twenty-first century. Now several house church networks in China have committed themselves to the "Back to Jerusalem Movement." This is a project to send 100,000 Chinese missionaries to evangelize the countries between China and Jerusalem. Some missionaries have already been deployed, and others are still receiving training. This project promises to be one of the most interesting developments in missions in the new century.

Missions Research

One characteristic of contemporary missions is an emphasis on research. This trend will continue and significantly increase in the coming years. Missions research involves several aspects. One is people group research. Organizations like the Joshua Project list and categorize people groups as reached and unreached, and so on. Beyond that, many organizations do ethnographic studies on people groups to discover their worldview and cultural characteristics. Other studies are done to ascertain the progress of Christianity within a people group or geographical area. For example, one missions administrator, John Sapp, asked me to facilitate a research study on the number of churches and Christians in Kenya. He said, "If you believe the reports, everyone in Kenya has been saved three times." Computer databases and global positioning system (GPS) devices have made research and mapping more efficient and also made it easier to access information.

Short-Term Missions

Short-term missions really began as a program for youth groups in Evangelical churches. Operation Mobilization (OM) and Youth with a Mission (YWAM) pioneered this in the 1960s. Today many Christians from North America, Korea, Singapore, Australia, and New Zealand have participated in short-term mission trips. Most of these trips last about two weeks. R. Wuthnow of Princeton University discovered that 1.5 million Christians from the United States make a missions trip overseas each year.[9] Another positive development is that many families are now embarking on mission trips so that their children can experience life on the mission field.

Where do all these groups go? R. Priest and J. Priest note that only 13 percent of short-term missionaries go to a country within the 10–40 Window. Usually, the short-term teams go to a country where they can work with an existing church. They also favor nations that are easier to enter and cost less to visit, especially those in the Caribbean, Central America, and South America. This fact demonstrates the interest churches have in direct participation in missions rather than fulfilling strategies formulated by mission agencies. Many missions agencies would certainly make 10–40 Window destinations a higher priority for volunteers.[10]

Still, there is no doubt that short-term missions is here to stay. In fact, this trend will grow in the coming years. Churches and

---

[9] Cited in R. J. Priest and J. P. Priest, "They see everything, and understand nothing: Short-Term Mission and Service Learning," *Missiology: An International Review* 36 (January 2008), 54.
[10] Ibid.

missions agencies realize that young adults in North America will only support missions if they feel a personal connection with the missionaries. The best way to achieve this is through short-term missions, especially mission trips.

Postmodernity

It is difficult to define *postmodernity* because it insists that everything is relative. In fact, the basic premise of postmodernity is "there are no absolutes." Essentially, postmodernity is a reaction against the individualism, rationalism, and scientific positivism of modernity.

Missiologists recognize that within a particular culture some segments of society might be premodern, while others are modern or postmodern. Postmodernity has affected missions through young missionaries. Many of them have received an education steeped in postmodernity. On the mission field their postmodern worldview manifests itself as distrust of authority and disdain for the history and traditions of their mission agency.

Postmodernity presents Evangelical missions with dangers and opportunities. C. Van Engen has listed some dangers in postmodernism: (1) valuelessness and atomization of persons, (2) relativism in the fields of theology and ethics, (3) rejection of referential use of language, and (4) rejection of purpose and progress in history. In short, postmodernism, at least in its extreme forms, would reject the exclusivity of Christ, the inerrancy of Scripture, and the progress of history toward the kingdom of God.[11]

In spite of its drawbacks, Van Engen suggests that postmodernity may provide opportunities for missionaries. First, it helps missionaries see that missions in the twenty-first century will be "global and local, rather than national and denominational." This is evident in the increasing number of megachurches that are doing missions directly instead of working through missions agencies. Second, postmodernist Christians hold that the gospel is holistic. The Lord means for the gospel to affect all of life and all relationships. Third, postmodernism affirms that the church is truly the body of Christ, not a "gathering of isolated, autonomous

---

[11] C. Van Engen, "Postmodernism," in *Evangelical Dictionary of World Missions* (Grand Rapids: Baker, 2000), 773.

individuals." Fourth, postmodernism emphasizes the spiritual realm, including angels, demons, and spiritual forces.[12]

Missions to Youth

When one mentions youth missions, most North Americans think of a church youth group going on a summer missions trip. Here we refer to missions efforts directed at young people throughout the world. In some countries more than 50 percent of the population consists of youth, while in others the number is approaching 75 percent. Naturally, this is especially true of nations with high birthrates. Surprisingly, though, few missions agencies have specifically targeted youth. This is puzzling because research has shown that young people are consistently more open to the gospel than adults. Many agencies work with university students, but few direct their ministry to young people outside the universities. Some have suggested there is a global youth culture that transcends national boundaries. These young people are unified by communication media and technology. They can be reached through creative means. In fact, some missionaries have established Internet cafes in order to reach urban youth.

Unreached People Groups (UPGs)

The concept of Unreached People Groups (UPGs) is not new to Evangelical missions, and neither is an emphasis on reaching these groups. For the last 20 years, discussions about contemporary missions have often started with the 10–40 Window and its UPGs. Though Evangelicals have discussed UPGs for 20 years, more than 6,000 UPGs remain. Evangelicals will not abandon these people groups who lack a viable, indigenous church. Evangelical missionaries will continue to focus on the UPGs in the coming decades. This fact has an important implication.

Persecution

As missionaries continue to penetrate UPGs, persecution will increase—persecution of both international missionaries and local believers. Most of the UPGs are located in areas where political and religious gatekeepers seek to hinder mission work in every

---

[12] Ibid.

way possible. So, when the gospel enters, the gatekeepers will try to stamp it out just like a grass fire. Satan does not surrender ground easily or cheaply, and the spiritual warfare in these places will be fierce. Casualties are inevitable. Missionaries and national believers alike will suffer physically, emotionally, and spiritually.

Networking and Partnerships

Thirty years ago most Evangelical missions agencies operated independently of one another. They did cooperate by joining umbrella organizations like the Evangelical Foreign Missions Association (now The Mission Exchange) or the Interdenominational Foreign Missions Association (now CrossGlobalLink) and in funding mutually beneficial projects such as schools for missionaries' children, but generally each mission agency did its own thing. Today the scene is radically different. Since 1990 mission boards have worked together much more closely. One example of this is the partnership agreement made by 23 missions agencies when Mongolia opened its doors to missions. The missions organizations met together and divided up the responsibilities involved in evangelizing the Mongolian people. This agreement was different from the old comity agreements that were so common in 1900. Those comity agreements assigned responsibility for evangelization geographically, while the newer partnership agreements assign responsibility functionally—that is, the agreement specifies that this agency will handle the broadcasting ministry, while that one will undertake Bible translation work. This interagency communication and networking demonstrates good stewardship of resources and aids the progress of missions.

Business as Missions

In the latter years of the twentieth century, business assumed an important role in Evangelical missions. Business as missions took three forms. First, some Western missionaries went out as *tent makers*. This term comes from the practice of the apostle Paul who was a tent maker by trade and often supported himself and his missionary colleagues by making tents. In modern missions a tent maker is a missionary with a profession or skill who practices that profession in another culture in order to do missions work. A second type of business as mission is the use of business as a *platform*. A platform is a means of obtaining a visa in order to live in another country. Because many nations no longer grant traditional missionary visas, missionaries use creative access to gain entry into closed countries. Often these are business platforms, like opening a travel agency, operating a restaurant, or establishing an import-export business. Third, some Christian entrepreneurs have founded businesses in the Majority World in order to bless the people economically and win a hearing for the gospel. This third type especially will increase in the current century.[13]

Missionary Teams

In the late twentieth century most Evangelical missions agencies adopted a team approach. Now most missionaries serve on teams. Many of these teams are multinational and multiethnic, and that raises issues of cultural adjustment. The advantages of missionary teams are synergy, companionship, continuity, and varied spiritual gifts. This trend in missions is likely to continue, even though many teams have struggled with adjustment and cohesiveness. With more experience in teaming and more preparatory training for working in teams, the situation will improve.

Internationalization

As the majority of Christians has shifted from the northern hemisphere to the southern hemisphere, the number of Majority World missionaries has increased. While the Majority World missionaries do not yet constitute a majority of foreign missionaries, they will before 2050. This is a healthy trend in church history. The challenge for the Majority World churches will be to provide improved financial support and member care for their growing missionary forces.[14]

Technology and Mass Media

Modern technology has made missionaries more efficient and effective. The use of computers has made it possible to cut in half the time required to translate the Bible. E-mail makes it possible

---

[13] See M. Barnett and T. Steffen's *Business as Mission* (Pasadena: William Carey Library, 2006).

[14] M. Jaffarian, "Are There More Non-Western Missionaries than Western Missionaries?" *International Bulletin of Missionary Research* (July 2004), 131.

for missions administrators to stay in close touch with their missionaries. Web sites make it possible to disseminate information about missions to supporters, students, and researchers as never before. Satellite television enables missionary broadcasters to beam gospel programs to selected areas and people groups. Missionaries in remote areas can use cellular telephones that relay signals via satellites. These improvements would surely boggle the mind of pioneer missionaries who had to wait for months for a letter to arrive. Future missionaries will discover ways to use the Internet to evangelize people in restricted access countries, disciple them, and equip them for leadership.

Member Care

Member care refers to "nurture and development of missionary personnel."[15] It deals with many aspects of missionary life, including selection of personnel, prefield training, field adjustment, personal and family crises, children's education, resignation, and retirement. Missionary administrators seldom spoke of member care 30 years ago, but those days are over. Member care is a major aspect of modern missions for two reasons. The younger missionaries demand it, and the younger missionaries need it. The younger missionaries demand member care because they are more family oriented and less job oriented. They are not willing to sacrifice their families for the work as did previous generations of missionaries. The younger missionaries need member care because so many of them come from dysfunctional family backgrounds. They bring this emotional baggage with them to the field and often require counseling.[16]

CONCLUSION

Ralph Winter is right to promote a more balanced, holistic approach to Evangelical missions. Scott Moreau correctly wonders if Evangelical missions can do this on the scale that Winter envisions. The efforts of Rick and Kay Warren and Saddleback Church to address the needs of AIDS victims in southern Africa may give

---

[15] K. O'Donnell, "To the Ends of the Earth, To the End of the Age," in *Doing Member Care Well*, ed. K. O'Donnell (Pasadena: William Carey Library, 2002), 4.

[16] K. Baker, "Boomers, Busters, and Missions: Things Are Different Now," in www.tentmakernet.com (accessed December 12, 2008).

some indication as that ministry develops. Without a doubt, by midcentury the evangelical missionaries doing missions will be predominantly missionaries from the Majority World. This internationalization of the missionary force will make it look like the multitude that will gather around God's throne (Rev 7:9). That verse gives us hope for the kingdom of God and for the ultimate success of missions.

BIBLIOGRAPHY

Aulen, Gustav. *Cristus Victor.* London: Society for the Propagation of Christian Knowledge, 1937.

Baker, Ken. "Boomers, Busters, and Missions: Things Are Different Now," in www.tentmakernet.com (accessed on 12 December 2008).

Barnett, Mike, and Tom Steffen. *Business as Mission.* Pasadena: William Carey Library, 2006.

Brierley, Peter. *Future Church.* London: Monarch Books, 1998.

Johnstone, Patrick. *The Church Is Bigger Than You Think.* Ross-shire, Great Britain: Christian Focus Books, 1998.

McGavran, Donald A. *The Bridges of God.* New York: Friendship Press, 1955.

Priest, Robert J., and Joseph Priest. "The See Everything and Understand Nothing." *Missiology: An International Review* 36 (January 2008).

Stott, John R. W. *Making Christ Known.* Grand Rapids: Eerdmans, 1996.

Terry, John Mark. *Evangelism: A Concise History.* Nashville: B&H, 1994.

Van Engen, Charles. "Postmodernism," in *Evangelical Dictionary of World Missions.* Grand Rapids: Baker, 2000.

CHAPTER 19

Responding to "The Future of Evangelicals in Mission"

ED STETZER

Even if you don't agree with him, the late Ralph Winter was an intriguing writer. He has made enormous contributions to missiology. Most of these contributions have come, like his chapter in this book, with great intuitive sweeps of energetic thought that may or may not be on target. As Mark Terry has pointed out in his response, a disconnect exists between the title of Winter's essay and what he actually wrote. This is because we, the editors, gave him the title and then changed the title. The rest is all Ralph as he largely went his own direction.

EVALUATING WINTER'S ESSAY

What shall we make of this? We asked him to write on the subject of the future of missions because we sincerely wanted to know where he thinks missions is heading. He sincerely responded with an essay that expresses a great hope for *where* the future of missions may go. However, in writing what he chose to write, he dismissed a number of wonderful insights that I wish he had thoroughly developed. I'll come back to these.

In writing what he did, he remained true to himself and in passionate consonance with his recent thought. By writing what he wrote, he also drew from his respondents the type of analysis that we were hoping to give when we assigned him this task. His essay is creative to the max, including another Winter-like construct to match his "sodality structure vs. modality structure" insight from the past. I mean, of course, the concept of First-Inheritance Evangelicalism (FIE) and Second-Inheritance Evangelicalism (SIE). With this essay, will Winter have an impact in the future on how present-day Evangelicals connect themselves to Wilberforce and the others of the Clapham Sect? Probably. Will his simplifications of SIE history grab the imaginations of younger readers in a way that will fix their thinking for the next generation of missiology? Barnett hopes not since *the history is simply not so simple.*"

But Winter's telling of history—especially his choice of illustrations like referencing the nature of Oberlin College and its connection to Harriet Beecher Stowe—will cause me to dip into my own history library to learn more. Will his projection of where Evangelical missiology *should* go resonate with Evangelical readers, causing the missiological community to turn and tack into the wind against the general understanding of Evangelical missiologists today? I doubt it. But it *is* provocative. And through his provocation, others that we've asked to respond to him have populated the predicted future with many other projections that are worthy of as much examination as Winter's.

Of course, reading the future is the task of fortune tellers and science-fiction writers. One of my friends, who is a science-fiction writer, has told me that science fiction is really "a spreadsheet of possibilities"—that is, if you feed a projection of the future into a particular event, especially a culture-altering event like 9/11, what will the outcome be? Change the nature of the event and you change the projected future. In that sense, perhaps, we asked Winter to write a spreadsheet of the future, and he infused a wild hope for changing the world's future—the way Wilberforce and his cohorts changed the legality of slavery. Maybe Winter was longing for that *particular* change to continue, citing the millions that remain in slavery to this day. His prediction is that the SIE folk will become more like the FIE folk, especially in flexing political and economic muscle to change this temporal world in good but temporal ways. My response is: I hope not.

After all, didn't the SIE people withdraw support from the FIE group in part *because* the latter was taking this step away from direct evangelism? Didn't the withdrawal of fundamentalists from the liberals occur *because* liberals had rejected the inerrancy of Scripture in an attempt to close the gap with the Darwinistic discoveries of the science of the day? Didn't the Evangelicals of the last generation recoil from the World Council of Churches because they sought to replace evangelism with a *missio Dei*/kingdom of God approach that ignored evangelism and disenfranchised the church? In some ways Winter's essay is déjà vu all over again. I'm relatively certain Winter didn't intend that, but that appears to be the net effect of his writing.

Christopher Little notices this and worries aloud about it. He reminds us of the "when everything is mission, nothing is mission" truism. He reminds us that we cannot have the kingdom of God without the church. Certainly, Winter does seem to address many of his ideas to deep-pocket, donor types rather than the modestly paid missiological scholars gathered around this table. A missing connection seems to emerge here, or rather too much of a connection, between believers and unbelievers in the task of bringing in the kingdom.

More importantly, Little wonders about the kingdom concept being the central motif of Scripture. What about the glory of God motif? Little fears that Winter's emphasis on science is compounding the problem rather than helping it. Furthermore, in one of his more memorable statements, Little counters Winter with "hell is worse than temporal disease." As evangelical Christians, that's what we've always said, isn't it? Does bending our collective efforts to answer the prayer "Your will be done on earth" distract us from our responsibility to eternity?

Barnett has similar problems with Winter (and with Little). In addition to questioning Winter's history, Barnett, as a historian, speaks to what he calls "the donor myth"—the suggestion that donors ignore the social action responsibilities in favor of Evangelical results. They are more holistic than that, Barnett contends, citing his own experience as a strategy consultant with four different mission agencies. He also addresses the "relief/development myth"— the myth that as money for relief goes up evangelism efforts go down. It's not that simple. Relief is capital intensive—taking more dollars—while discipleship is resource/labor intensive, requiring less money but more people. According to Barnett, dollars may not be the best way to evaluate true investment.

Barnett brings us back to that 1973 innovation of Winter: the modality/sodality structures.[1] He argues that Winter has identified the wrong structure as the key to future missions. It will not be in the parachurch sodalities as Winter suggests. The key to the future will be the modality—the church. God, the Creator and Implementer, will conquer evil through Jesus Christ and the church (Rev 19:11–21). Barnett urges missionaries, mission agencies, and mission scholars to focus on the basics and to *model* what they teach.

EVALUATING WINTER'S PREDICTIONS

Both Little and Barnett laud Winter for being interesting and provocative. The other two reviewers did, too, but they tend to ignore Winter's final prediction in order to focus more on what he jettisoned. What were these insights? Here's the first example: "There is the shrinking of the globe and the tendency of local churches in the West to have a more direct hand in what happens at a distance. The urgent value of veteran mission agencies will tend to be overlooked" (p. 176).

Now this is intriguing and provocative. Yes, local churches in the West are tending to learn more, probe more, and perhaps require more of missionaries than they once did. The mission agencies, viewed as the "middle man," will be shunted for more direct, wholesale mission information and experience. What will result from this trend? Think in sci-fi terms—how will this change alter the spreadsheet of the future? Do mission agencies need to adapt in order to fill a different role? Is this a *positive* trend, or is it *negative*? And if it *is* the future, how do we all prepare for it? Some surmise that these projections will be the outcome: "The massive trend to send out young and old for two weeks will continue to drain money from more serious mission, adding helpful educa-

---

[1] Ralph Winter, an author and scholar of the history of Christian missions, addressed the All-Asia Mission Consultation in Seoul Korea in 1973 and outlined two "redemptive structures" that God's purposes have produced in every generation. These two structures he calls "modality" and "sodality." See http://www.mustardseedorder.com/cm/community/19.

tion to the local sending churches but very little direct or indirect contribution to missions" (pp. 176–77).

Decidedly, short-term mission trips will continue, despite the suggestions from some quarters that they result in "Christian tourism" more than missions. Winter identifies his opinion of the practice with his word term—"*drain* money." This is a question of God's economy: What is the best expenditure of God's money? Allowing the professionally trained missionaries to make the best application of it for nationals or spending it on enjoyable, albeit educational, travel for laypersons? If this did not have a direct impact on missions giving, the question might need more focused attention. But we should ask these questions, Is there a saturation point where field missionaries find their energies sapped from engaging locals by having to serve as guides for laypersons from home? Has this saturation point been reached? If the trend continues, what will the missionary task look like? One might conclude that the nature of church planting movements in the Two-Thirds World will radically transform the role and tasks of missionaries in the future.

Here's another issue from Winter:

> An unexpected but growing trend is that of what is called "insider movements," which requires us in the West to recognize modern parallels between (1) the much disputed decision of the Jerusalem Council in Acts to allow Greek culture to become another "earthen vessel" for the gospel, and (2) the decision of millions of Chinese, Hindus, and Africans who have already chosen to follow Christ within their own cultural traditions without identifying with formal, Western Christianity. This new appearance of biblical faith is already a phenomenon as large or larger than formal Christianity in those three continents. (p. 177)

Here Winter delivers a glancing reference to the contextualization questions that have concerned us in the first two sections of this book. And his offhanded comments will come as a surprise to some earnest Evangelicals, who are much more concerned with ensuring that the gospel is conveyed to the foreign fields in its received—and heavily impacted by Greek philosophy and culture—form. Now this is a subject for a sci-fi writer.

What happens in the future if Western Christianity is set aside by a new Eastern Christianity, as different from ours as the Eastern Orthodox perspectives have always been to the West? If the Lord tarries, what would the world of 100 years from now look like? Is this a *problem* we need to nip in the bud—as the Judaizers believed they needed to do with Paul's preaching? Or is it simply evidence that the Holy Spirit is ready to bypass Christian organizations that spend too much time talking and not enough time doing? That could certainly be said about the unmet challenges found in the megalopolis populations around the world. The special challenge of cities will continue to be studied.

Yes, what about the mushrooming cities that are daily changing the population figures, such as Bombay, Sao Paulo, Shanghai, Delhi, Karachi, Jakarta, Tokyo, New York, and many more? How will we address these megalopolises, especially since we Westerners have not really figured out how to reach our own urban settings? In the West some are trying to place a growing emphasis on reaching these urban population centers, but historically much of the success and focus of Western Christianity has been on reaching the suburbs, towns, boroughs, and villages. The human need, suffering, and lack of Jesus in the megalopolitan cities is exponential and overwhelming. The complexity, population density, and resource challenges of making a significant impact among megalopolis millions have often bewildered the westernized church. But the challenge remains—what does such a possibility summon from us? Another aspect of this challenge relates to whether the literate West can adapt to a world that is largely nonliterate. The challenge of nonliterate masses will continue to grow.

The oral nature of the world's mushrooming population has been addressed by missiologists, but we have not really come to understand what YouTube and similar Internet innovations are going to mean to missions. The news media really hasn't either, but you can sense their uncertainty. M. McLuhan, a relic of the late 1960s, knew nothing of the coming Internet, but he did project the "retribalization of Man"—a time when the written colonial languages of English and French would fade in importance. We shall see. In the meantime, a younger generation of Christians is likely to be trying all manner of ways to make missionary contact through the Web. What will be the result—especially if, as Mark Terry suggests, a worldwide youth culture is emerging? It will be a culture that understands, all too well, the world's problems.

Here's Winter's next issue: "The need to do something about poverty, human slavery, and the eradication of disease (much exacerbated by globalization) will increasingly occupy everyone but more specifically emboldened and wealthy evangelicals" (p. 177).

Here we are again, back to the issue of how to balance social justice and evangelism. Church history has proven the dangers of being unbalanced. We must not drift toward an unbalanced paradigm of either being radicals of social justice or being verbal flamethrowers. As Jesus was full of grace and truth, healing and confronting, meeting real needs and calling for repentance, so we must strive to be the people of God who are both ministers of grace and communicators of truth. We must be the hands, feet, and voice of Jesus Christ in a largely destitute world.

At this point we have addressed some insights surrounding Winter and some niceties. Scott Moreau and J. Mark Terry said nice things about Winter's essay but then departed from it, listing their own prognostications. Since no one knows how things will turn out, and since this was our original hope for Winter's essay, I have commented on their ideas. Moreau, after worrying about "managerial missiology" (which relates to Winter's first idea above), went on to list five future mission trends that we might consider:

SCOTT MOREAU'S PREDICTIONS

More and more non-Western mission agencies will emerge. While this may be a shock still to the folks in Western churches, this is nothing new to missiologists. It *is*, however, to be applauded, encouraged, and supported. These non-Westerners will address many population segments that we could never reach effectively.

The pace of missions, like everything else, will accelerate. This will be due to instant updates from the mission field—the kind of thing we've talked about already with the instant communication of the Internet. This may be ruggedly challenging, but it *will* happen. Therefore, we need to prepare our responses to it.

Finances and partnerships will grow increasingly diverse. This is part of the first two and will be difficult for Westerners to tolerate, given our propensity for being in charge. This may run head-on into the trend of managerial missiology coming from less trained (in contextualization anyway), Western megachurches.

The Internet will be a vital vehicle of missions. We've touched on that and will touch it again.

The ability of humanity to wipe us out will continue to grow. This is not a cheerful thought, but the tightening resources of the world and the wider distribution of weapons of mass destruction make this the "doomsday" projection of our future scenarios. Since secular sci-fi constantly reviews these ideas, perhaps we can step around them for a while. We do need to recognize that the clock is ticking on world evangelization.

MARK TERRY'S PREDICTIONS

Mark Terry doubled Moreau's output and then some, but some overlap was comforting in the sense that as multiple respondents add to the list, we get the sense that we're not overlooking anything. The ideas that Terry added are:

Pentecostal-Charismatic Churches. It is becoming clearer each year that Pentecostalism is the form of Christianity that will attract the majority of the world. Perhaps Evangelicals, who are not Pentecostal, need to consider how they will relate with these groups in the years ahead, specifically at the point of partnerships.

Christianity in China. Actually, Winter did approach this idea, but it's worth repeating. God's Spirit is at work beyond the direct touch of Western Evangelicals. Perhaps we need to give some direct conversation to how we can partner together more effectively in order to reach the largest country in the world. Many are doing so already, but China is a big place.

Member Care. An increased need to see members ministered to in ways that go beyond the current interaction will develop. Here we've brushed the edge of that holistic social concern, Winter addresses, but now we're including the impact of Christian upon Christian. This need will continue to grow, and it should. It comes directly from the New Testament.

Unreached People Groups. This is a focus already well under way on the part of Evangelical missions, but it must not be overlooked. We need to keep this as a future focus until there are NO unreached people groups left upon this planet. This is well within the reach of the combined body of Christ in this generation—if we keep at it.

Missions to Youth. This is a great insight, worthy of plenty of group strategizing. It involves an understanding of youth culture, as if it is a cross-cultural encounter that requires contextualization. It involves continuing to pursue technological expertise. It involves opening leadership to missionary types who are younger but far more skilled with this mode of contact. And this, of course, leads into Terry's *other* future trend.

Postmodernism. How do we address it? How do we reach it? How do we perceive it? The varieties of postmodernism make understanding and addressing it a daunting challenge. Still, it is essential that Evangelicals exegete the postmodern culture and communicate the gospel to postmodernists contextually, just as they seek to do in premodern cultures.

Would the church of the first century recognize the postmodern church? Yes, because our Scripture is the same as that of old. Yes, as long as we maintain absolute adherence to those Scriptures, we've done our best, in our turn, to preserve the faith once delivered. If I've seen any overarching theme through all of these essays, it is this: we must draw a line of communication from the revealed, inspired, infallible, inerrant Scriptures of the Old and New Testaments to a world that has never heard them.

CONCLUSION

All of the rest of our issues relate to the task of communicating the gospel to the world, which we can only do in partnership with, and under the guidance of, the Holy Spirit. We will not arrive at an agreed-upon definition of missions, but this is a good description of what missionaries have always done—or tried to do. We may not agree completely regarding theology, on interpretations of that Living Word. Given the history of the church, I can say that I'm pretty sure we won't. We may trace our way into the future with trepidation born of the uncertainty of coming events. We can only suppose what's coming, and try to prepare for anything. But we must never let go of that line that stretches from the inspired writers of the Bible to us—nor should we fail to pass it along to others, along with the joy it brings. In this, may we all be faithful—to the glory of God!

CHAPTER 20

CONCLUSION: A Scientific Postscript—Grist for the Missiological Mills of the Future

DAVID J. HESSELGRAVE

INTRODUCTION

One Sunday afternoon the Danish philosopher Soren Kierkegaard was seated in his usual chair in an outdoor café in Frederiksberg Garden. While smoking a cigar, he began to muse about his life to that point. Here he was in process of becoming an old man (Kierkegaard died at the age of 42), having greatly enjoyed his indolence and having accomplished nothing lasting. All the while those about him had benefited mankind by making life easier—some by building railways and steamboats, others by perfecting the telegraph, and still others by writing "short recitals of everything worth knowing." After lighting a second cigar, a thought flashed into his mind: "You must do something, but inasmuch as with your limited capacities it will be impossible to make anything easier than it has become, you must with the same humanitarian enthusiasm as the others, undertake to make something harder!"

Kierkegaard mused that there must come a time when things will combine so as to make everything people want to be so easy that the only want left will be to make things more difficult. Since it had become so easy for Danes to become Christians and not Jews or Muslims—and to become Lutheran Christians and not

Catholic Christians for that matter—Kierkegaard decided that his indolence had forced on him the only task that remained: namely, to make everything, including becoming a Christian, just as difficult as possible.

In *A Concluding Unscientific Postscript* Kierkegaard forwards this task (his "mission"?) by advancing, in the words of V. Ferm, an "exposition of the subjectivity of truth, the subjective nature of Christianity and a fundamental tenet of existentialism: the subjectivity of a (passionate) experience." Ferm also indicates that "postscript" in the title suggests the author's unfulfilled desire to terminate his work with this writing, and the word "unscientific" gives expression to his view that the ethical-religious sphere has nothing at all to do with scientific objectivity.[1]

I must demur. The ethical-religious sphere has everything to do with scientific objectivity—well, *almost* everything! Throughout the preceding pages of this book, we have been scaling missiological heights and breathing the rarified air of contemporary missions thinking, guided all the while by some of our most outstanding Evangelical mission theorists. My coeditor has provided us with invaluable insights as to the significance of their offerings. Now it remains for me to help guide our descent back down to a firm foundation where we Evangelicals endeavor both to better understand and to carry out our God-given mission as Christians. I find this to be a most difficult task because, for me at least, it has everything to do with scientific objectivity when *science* is understood as knowledge that grows out of study as well as experience. Admittedly, we cannot get away from our personal experiences. Nor would we. Our experiences are an important part of who we are, how we think, and what we do. They help to *form* us. But we are not confined to them. We are *informed* by study—by what we learn from others, by what we learn about our world, and, most importantly, by that which God has revealed to us.

Thus, I begin with the life experiences of two missionaries/missiologists—D. A. McGavran and myself. I do so because the observations and recommendations that will follow are best understood against the background of their pilgrimages, as I explain later.

---

[1] V. Ferm, ed., *Classics of Protestantism* (New York: Philosophical Library, 1959), 324.

MY SPIRITUAL AND MISSIOLOGICAL JOURNEY

No human being is simply the product of his or her life experience. But, on the other hand, in part all of us think as we do and act as we do as a result of our background and experience. That may be especially true in my case because of my varied ancestry, education, and ministry experience.

A Lighter Hold on Subjectivism, Existentialism, and Experientialism

My paternal grandparents were prominent universalists. My grandfather was enamored with Swami Vivekananda whom he met at the first World Parliament of Religions held in Chicago in 1893. My maternal grandparents were members of a liberal Methodist church. So were my parents until the time of their conversion to Christ when I was a small child. Their conversion led to my own at the tender age of eight.

The church of my formative years was fundamentalist. Our pastors were undereducated even by the standards of that time, but they were godly and spiritual men from whom I learned much. However, our church joined the Assemblies of God denomination during my early teens. As often happens in such situations, the church's sudden entrance into Pentecostalism was attended by spiritual experiences of the more extreme variety. Both truth and spirituality were tested by receiving (sometimes contradictory) messages directly from God and by spiritual experiences that allowed (sometimes inadvisedly) for leadership positions in the church. When it came time to decide where to take my seminary training, I elected to follow the lead of my older brother by enrolling in the seminary of, and ministering in fellowship with, the Evangelical Free Church of America. The EFCA had roots in pietism but neither disparaged nor depended on spiritual experiences as such. As can be inferred from the name, the EFCA was opposed to the kind of dead orthodoxy that characterized the State Lutheranism against which Kierkegaard reacted. But more of that part of the story is yet to come. First, I must pause to recount my experience as a philosophy major at the University of Minnesota.

My introduction to existentialism occurred in the 1940s when my adviser and one of my most absorbing classroom teachers was the premier Kierkegaardian scholar, Paul Holmer. Holmer titillated his students with stories of childhood confessions of sinfulness exacted by his overzealous preachers and his conversion from some of the strictures of the Covenant Church of that time to a more embracing Lutheranism. He also entertained his students by such ploys as playfully but inelegantly diagnosing a local evangelical philosopher's weakness as being "diarrhea of the mouth" and by accusing a fellow-faculty logical positivist of "getting religion" once a week on Sunday while attending a Unitarian church nearby. After the passage of a few years, Holmer was appointed dean of Yale Divinity School. Our paths did not cross for many years until, during his retirement and my tenure as professor of missions at Trinity Evangelical Divinity School, he visited us and delivered a lecture to our student body. At that juncture, and perhaps as a function of his infirmities and the aging processes, he appeared to be much less sure of himself than he was at a younger age. Nevertheless, we reminisced briefly, and I thanked him for introducing me to the redoubtable Dane, Soren Kierkegaard, among other Scandinavian philosophers. In spite of deep differences in philosophy and theology, I could do so and do it sincerely. It was Professor Holmer, after all, who had first pointed me to Abraham's raised, knife-bearing hand in Kierkegaard's *Either/ Or* and warned easygoing evangelical students as to the spiritual danger of discovering a ram in the thicket before feeling the pain of a believing father's heart. Holmer had warned us of the dangers of a facile acquiescence to propositional Christianity devoid of the kind of passionate faith that Kierkegaard decried in his *A Concluding Unscientific Postscript.* And he, along with the rest of those world-class philosophy faculty members at the University of Minnesota during that era, demonstrated that, left to their own devices, proponents of various forms of philosophy were capable of canceling one another out without the aid of us Evangelicals!

It was a great experience, but in the end it did seem that the study of philosophy was rather impractical. In graduate school I changed my major to my undergraduate minor—communication.

A Firm Embrace of Objectivism, Revelation, and Intelligibility

In the 1940s the seminary of the Evangelical Free Church was small. It had its weaknesses, but its strength lay in a spiritual and knowledgeable faculty. My professor of Bible and theology, Carl R. Steelberg, was one of the most knowledgeable Bible scholars I had ever met. Moreover, despite my youthfulness, he demonstrated confidence in me by recommending me as teacher of a large Sunday school class of professionals in a church on Chicago's far south side. Then, as if to help make sure that I would not besmirch his reputation, he pointed me to scintillating ideas growing out of the biblical text and also out of W. M. Smith's *Peloubet's Notes.* As a result, and despite my immaturity and natural limitations, the response of the class was most exhilarating. In short, my seminary experience awakened in me a profound appreciation for biblical revelation and for the importance of communicating its changeless message as opposed to the ever-changing machinations of mortal men.

It is not unusual for Evangelical seminaries these days to offer 25 or so courses in missions. Despite Trinity's deep commitment to missions, my seminary regimen in the 1940s included but one required course in missions—the only missions course offered! It is not surprising then, that missionary service itself, though designed to assist in the launching of the new Evangelical Free Church of Japan, also constituted yet another phase of my education. Immediately upon our arrival in Japan in 1950, we were faced not only with the anticipated but poorly prepared for challenges of Shintoism, Buddhism, and other Eastern faiths and thought patterns but also with the eviscerating effects of universalism, higher criticism, and the social gospel in Japanese Christian institutions and churches. We found that as early as the 1880s these and other suborthodox and heterodox ways of thinking had impacted the Christian movement with the result that churches had largely capitulated to Shinto nationalism during World War II. In fact, pressured by the government, prominent Protestant prelates had formed the Nihon Kirisuto Kyodan (the United Church of Christ in Japan) at the behest of the government and had dutifully reported its formation to the Sun Goddess at Ise in order to invoke her blessing! Subsequently, those Christians who had refused to compromise—largely holiness people—paid a tremendous price for insubordination. It was my good fortune to have the assistance of two of them in evangelism and in organizing several of our early Free Church churches.

But there is more that is important to this part of my story. Evangelicals were not the only ones to respond to opportunities in the new Japan of postwar years. Liberal and especially neoorthodox missionaries and theologians were there as well. During my first term in the Tokyo area, lecture series by E. Brunner and other neoorthodox notables were featured in various universities. During my second term in Kyoto, we were visited by the likes of C. Hartshorne, N. Ferre, and P. Tillich.

I remember well attending one of Tillich's lectures in the University of Kyoto. Tillich chided fundamentalists and Evangelicals for believing that the Bible is literally true. He even took aim at his colleague R. Bultmann, reporting that "one day I addressed Professor Bultmann and said, 'You make a great mistake when you speak of demythologizing the Bible. It's the myths that have most meaning. They are precisely what we need!'" He then proceeded to talk about the creation account, the story of Christ, and so on, and sought to show how, understood as symbols and myths, their meanings were both significant and much the same as those of the Kojiki, Sutras, and other sacred texts. Kyoto University President Matsushita was a universalist. He was there. So was his daughter. She had been a member of my weekly Bible class, but after that lecture I never saw her again throughout the entire last five years of my second term.

There is much more to tell, of course. Stories of pastors and students confronting Western philosophy troubled by such questions as the promise of symbolic logic, the possibility of miracles, and the potential of existentialism. Stories of many who decided to follow Jesus only to turn back when their crosses became too heavy for them. But also stories of promising young men like Andrew Furuyama who dreamed of becoming an ambassador for his country but instead became a nationally and internationally known ambassador for Jesus Christ. Stories of great women like Mrs. Moriue who, as a Christian in a community characterized by Shinto nationalism and an all-pervasive Buddhism, nevertheless was honored as "woman of the year" in her city of 60,000 people. Stories of established professionals like Hiroshi Sakakida, who placed his prestige as a Kyoto University professor and specialist in diabetic medicine on the line as an open and humble witness for the Lord Jesus. Stories of wonderful churches such as the Free Church in Urawa City with a ministry that has resulted in the sending out of numerous missionaries and the planting of nine or 10 daughter churches. Japan was and is a remarkable mission field. For me, its challenges and its Christians constituted, and still constitute, a unique school of missionary training.

After completing my dissertation ("A Propaganda Profile of Soka Gakkai Buddhism") and other requirements for a doctorate at the University of Minnesota in 1965, I received an invitation from Trinity Evangelical Divinity School to serve as professor of world mission and evangelism and chairman of the department. The Free Church had undertaken the task of greatly enlarging the school in an effort to reinforce conservative doctrine in general and the authority and inerrancy of the autographs of Scripture especially. Myself excepted, faculty invitees had established reputations in their respective fields and came from various Christian institutions: theologians C. F. H. Henry and R. Culver; apologists J. W. Montgomery and N. Geisler; Old Testament scholars G. Archer, T. McComiskey, and W. Kaiser; New Testament specialists W. Smith, W. Liefeld, and R. Longenecker; and, within a year or two of my arrival, mission and evangelism notables such as J. H. Kane, P. Little, and A. Johnston. It was a great team, and I was blessed beyond measure in being able to learn from all of them.

THE PILGRIMAGE OF DONALD ANDERSON MCGAVRAN

At the end of the day, however, Fuller's Donald McGavran made one of the largest contributions and provided some of the greatest encouragements to my missiological understanding. He arrived in Minneapolis for a lecture series on the day I was moving to Trinity, so I phoned him to introduce myself, welcome him to the Twin Cities, and explain my situation. Always the consummate gentleman, he not only thanked me but gave me an open invitation to visit Fuller's School of Mission as his guest in order to acquaint myself with its faculty, students, and library holdings. That was in 1965. Two or three years later I took advantage of his kind invitation and then reciprocated by inviting him to TEDS as guest lecturer.

As a mission strategist, D. McGavran was certainly one of the premier missiologists of the twentieth century. Originally he went to India with the Disciples of Christ as an educational missionary, believing (as he once told me) that "education was the only door through which Indians could become Christians." After becoming acquainted with Methodist Bishop Waskom Pickett and his studies on "mass movements" in India, McGavran's thinking was revolutionized. He became a student of, and then one of the world's leading authorities on, the growth of the church around the world. He led missions to the realization that people come to faith in Christ and become members of his church not only or even primarily as individuals but as members of clans, castes, and classes of society—as parts of what he called "homogeneous units." For this changed understanding and its implications for church growth he is almost universally recognized. But there was to be still another change in his thinking that, while less recognized and understood, in the final analysis may yet prove to be just as important or even more so.

McGavran was no stranger to criticism. Early on, McGavran's church growth school of thought was often criticized by Evangelicals as being based more on the social sciences than on sacred Scripture, and also on the basis that his well-known *Bridges of God*[2] and other dealings with the biblical text were more eisegetical than exegetical. Much later S. Escobar categorized McGavran's church growth missiology as being "managerial."[3] But it was not his evangelical but his ecumenical colleagues who, in the late 1960s, meted out one of the most devastating rebuffs of McGavran's long and illustrious career.

The theme chosen for the Assembly of the World Council of Churches to be held in Uppsala in 1968 was "Behold I Make All Things New," a theme designed to highlight what God is doing in the world and to call upon the church to join Him in the doing of it. Over long months McGavran prodded Assembly organizers

---

[2] D. A. McGavran, *The Bridges of God: A Study in the Strategy of Missions* (New York: Friendship, 1955).

[3] S. Escobar, "Evangelical Theology in Latin America: The Development of a Missiological Christology," *Missiology: An International Review* XIX.3 (July 1991): 328.

and leaders to give consideration to his question, "What of the Two Billion?"—a reference to over two billion people in the world who, it was reckoned, had not yet heard the gospel of Christ. At Uppsala, however, leaders largely ignored both McGavran and his probing question. In fact, they augmented the Assembly theme with the slogan "Let the world set the agenda" and invited a pop singer, Pete Seege, to sing the popular song "Pie in the Sky When You Die." McGavran certainly was not the only one who was deeply disturbed and decried this mockery of the Christian gospel, but he was certainly one of them.[4]

Long before Uppsala, while still in India, McGavran had changed his mind as to the nature of conversion and, indeed, mission itself. By the 1970s and 80s his thinking underwent still other changes that, as far as McGavran himself was concerned, were most significant. That is made clear by the unequivocal manner in which he expressed himself in three writings.[5]

A Refined Commitment to a "High View of Scripture"

There was little in McGavran's extensive formal education to encourage a "high view of Scripture" and much to discourage it. Even after establishing his School of Church Growth, McGavran was justly criticized for neglecting the biblical text. Later on in the 1970s, however, he spoke forcefully concerning the importance of the "infallibility," "verbal inspiration," and "unparalleled reliability" of the Bible. He insisted that its words are the words of men but also the words of God and that its understandings are not limited by the understandings of the ancient times in which they were written. He wrote:

> Intelligent discussion of cultures and Christianity must be accompanied by a clear statement of whether or not the speakers believe in the inspiration and authority of the Scriptures. *But more must be said than this. Most Christians claim to believe in the inspiration and authority of the Bible, but they believe it in different ways. Consequently, their clear statement must also*

---

[4] W. J. Petersen and R. Petersen, *100 Christian Books That Changed the Century* (Grand Rapids: Baker [Fleming Revell], 2000), 110.

[5] See *The Clash Between Christianity and Culture* (Washington, DC: Canon, 1974); "Missions Face a Lion" (1988), a manuscript in the possession of this author, a version of which was published in *Missiology: An International Review* 17.3 (July 1, 1989): 335–56; and several personal letters addressed to this author (1988).

describe the way in which they believe in the Bible. Their doc-
trines of revelation and inspiration must be stated before their
pronouncements can be evaluated.[6]

A Restricted View of the Nature of Biblical Mission

From the time of his later ministry in India, McGavran's commitment was to "Great Commission mission"—to "finding, feeding and folding lost sheep." Suborthodox theology is the enemy of this kind of mission, but it is not its only enemy. A view of mission that is too broad is also its enemy. If the former is characterized as "a low view of Scripture and a high view of culture" in *The Clash Between Christianity and Culture,* the latter is described and denied in his monograph "Missions Face a Lion." In that monograph McGavran reconstructed the history of missions in the modern era (especially that of the twentieth century) as developing in two different streams or groups of missionaries with two different understandings of Christian mission:

> The first group of missionaries held that mission is discipling men and women and segment of society after segment of society, people after people, caste after caste. The second group of Christians held that mission is helping men and women of all religions and all segments of society to live better lives. Mission is famine relief, mission is development of communities, mission is doing good works by medicine, education, agriculture, and the like. . . .
>
> The difference between these two understandings of the missionary task was clear. The first held that justice and racial equality are excellent goals, desired by God, and that the best way to get them is to lead large numbers of people in every nation to become practicing Christians filled with the Holy Spirit and directed by the Bible. The second held that mission is helping men and women of every religion, particularly Christians, to act more justly in their daily lives and to be more brotherly to the Africans, Asians, Europeans, and Americans in the midst of them.
>
> In short, is mission primarily evangelism, or is it primarily all efforts to improve human existence?[7]

After participating in mission endeavors for the larger part of

---

[6] McGavran, *The Clash Between Christianity and Culture*, 52 (emphasis added).
[7] "Missions Face a Lion," 5 (manuscript).

the "Great Century in Christian Mission," McGavran's answer to that question was unequivocal and unambiguous: "evangelism."

A Renewed Commitment to the Indispensable Linkage Between Sound Theology and Authentic/Missiology

Ultimately, McGavran became convinced that the only theology that will sustain Great Commission mission is a theology that takes seriously biblical teachings having to do with the lostness of mankind, the uniqueness of Christ, the necessity of conversion, the "perfecting" of the saints, and the establishment of churches that are truly Christian. With that in mind, and in order to enable Evangelical missiologists to discuss Christian mission without digressing into topics necessitated by lack of agreement on cardinal Christian doctrines, one of McGavran's final legacies to Christian missions was to urge and support the formation of what he chose to call a "society of *Christian* missiology." He wrote to me as follows:

> I want to lay before you, David, a very important item. . . . I think that the evangelical professors of missions need to establish a nationwide organization called openly and courageously "The American Society of Christian Missiology."
>
> You see what has happened is that, when the present American Society of Missiology was formed, it took in—against my advice—both Roman Catholic missiologists and conciliar missiologists. Thus, The American Society of Missiology seems to say that missiology is everything done outside the four walls of the church. The net result is that the heart of all missiology, which is the discipling of segment after segment of the world's population, has been gravely neglected.[8]

Without necessarily agreeing with McGavran *en toto*, certain Evangelical leaders did agree with the proposition that biblical mission/missiology is best advanced by the kind of consultation and cooperation that is based on a clearly delineated statement of the cardinal doctrines of the Christian faith. The Evangelical Missiological Society was the result, and it may never have come into being without McGavran's urging and support.

---

[8] Personal letter to the author (April 7, 1988).

THREE KEYS TO RESOLVING THE DILEMMA FACING TWENTY-FIRST-CENTURY EVANGELICAL MISSIONS/MISSIOLOGY

Finding one's way around in contemporary missiology is like trying to get through a maze. Most doors lead into rooms that provide no door of escape other than the door of entry. The challenge now facing the Evangelical movement is to find a way out before the movement is permanently disabled. But by this time some of my readers will have grown weary of biography. They will say, "If the task at hand is to aid evangelical mission leaders and missiologists in going forward in view of the plethora of notions that have surfaced in this book, for example, why not get straightway to that task? Why beat around the bush like this? If you have a solution to the dilemma—or at least some reasonable suggestions for its resolution—why not inform us and be done with it?"

These are legitimate questions and they deserve honest answers. I do indeed have some suggestions that may be helpful, which I intend to state and apply in the pages that follow. But before doing so, allow me to explain the reasons for proceeding as I have. First, I would remind readers that subjective elements are important to the thinking of all of us. If, as is universally acknowledged, "every man is his own historian," it follows that every person is his or her own missiologist. Second, certain aspects of the preceding biographical information are available only by my telling them. McGavran's larger story is readily available, but not those that accrue to my conversations and correspondence with him that date to the late years of McGavran's life. Nor have I related my own story in this connection heretofore. Third, it is remarkable that two life experiences that have such diverse theological and ecclesiastical starting points—and progress through such decidedly different associations and influences—could arrive at the same destination and result in the formation of such singular importance as that of the Evangelical Missiological Society. Though I should not lay claim to more than Scripture affirms, it does seem to me that all of this was more than purely accidental.

So I proceed to a way of dealing with the challenge before us. It consists of employing three important "keys" that, to me at least, are at once both obvious and singularly important to the future of evangelical missions/missiology.

The First Key: Differentiate Between
Missiology as Science and Task

The first key is to *distinguish between missions/missiology as a broad-based social science discipline and missions/missiology as a narrower and distinctly Christian endeavor.* I remember well the discussion that led to the organization of the American Society of Missiology. Those who initiated and led the effort made abundantly clear that their primary goal was to lend credibility and visibility to missiology as a social science discipline by encouraging scholarship, promoting research and writing, and representing mission studies in the academy. At the time I was among the majority who approved of the idea. But, due I believe to his previous experiences in theologically and ecclesiastically inclusive organizations such as the proposed ASM, McGavran was cool to the idea. As time passed, he felt vindicated in his opposition and came to the place where he advocated the formation of a society of *"Christian* missiology" as indicated above. That, it seemed to some of us, would be unnecessarily confrontational and would put the new society in a bad light from the beginning. Accordingly, the older Association of Evangelical Professors of Mission was reorganized into the Evangelical Missiological Society in which all mission specialists, not just teachers, were welcomed. The meaning and importance of the label "evangelical" was made clear by requiring that every member confess agreement with the Statement of Faith of either the IFMA or the EFMA. That satisfied McGavran's primary concern, which was to provide a forum in which, for example, participants could discuss ways of reaching the lost without having to discuss whether people were actually lost apart from Christ and ways of presenting the uniqueness of Christ cross-culturally without having to address the question of whether He is the only Savior!

Missiologists are certainly justified—even obligated—to organize so as to maintain high standards and achieve right goals in academia. At the same time those missiologists whose primary commitment is to advance biblical mission are certainly justified, even obligated, to organize themselves so as to accomplish that goal by means of careful study, concerted advocacy, and active participation. Both kinds of organization are necessary, but to distinguish each in terms of these goals and appropriate *modus operandi* is of the essence.

It is easier, however, to deal with this distinction organizationally than to deal with it conceptually. After all, whether a discipline of study or a mandated enterprise, and whether truly Christian or not, missions/missiology is indeed a science (and an art as well). J. H. Bavinck's missions book includes both secular and religious content.[9] Therefore, in effect, I make a further distinction here: I distinguish between content that emanates from secular study and that which emanates from biblical revelation and theology. Though ultimately judged on the basis of divine revelation in Scripture, the veracity of those ideas and conclusions stemming from historical, anthropological, communicational, statistical, geographical, and other secular sources can and should first be evaluated by standards appropriate to those sciences.

The Second Key: Recognize Scripture as the Standard of Measurement

The second key is *to recognize Scripture as the objective and final standard by which all questions and proposals having to do with missionary faith and practice are to be measured.* The quintessential problem of liberal arts education is that, by its very nature, liberalism pursues truth without possessing a final standard by which truth is to be measured. "Always learning and never able to arrive at a knowledge of the truth" (2 Tim 3:7 ESV) is the way the apostle Paul described truth-seeking as a purely human enterprise. Defined and described theologically as the science of *Christian* mission, however, missiology is not in that position. When the Interdenominational Foreign Missions Association (now Cross-Global Link) was organized after World War I in 1917, the member missions affirmed and declared "their belief in and defense of the historic Christian faith" in the following words: "We believe that the Bible, consisting of Old and New Testaments only, is verbally inspired by the Holy Spirit, is inerrant in the original manuscripts, and is the infallible and authoritative Word of God."[10]

---

[9] J. H. Bavinck, *An Introduction to the Science of Missions*, trans. D. H. Freeman (Grand Rapids: Baker, 1969).

[10] E. L. Frizen Jr., *75 Years of IFMA: 1917–1992* (Pasadena: William Carey Library, 1992), 435.

When the National Association of Evangelicals, the Evangelical Foreign Missions Association, and the Evangelical Theological Society were organized shortly after World War II, they adopted the same position vis-à-vis the Bible. (So did mission representatives who signed the Lausanne Covenant, but this came about later in 1974.) In part, this was done to distinguish the Evangelical movement from the positions taken by neoorthodox and liberal theologians. But it also served as a compass for Evangelicalism as understood early on. But it was not long until the words *inerrant* and *infallible* were divorced in such a way as to provide for the latter without confessing to the former.[11] In view of this I am not completely satisfied with McGavran's depiction of his position as being a "high view of Scripture," but I am happy with his notion that missiologists do well to preface their works with a declaration, not alone of their belief in the authority of the Bible but also of the *kind* of authority they ascribe to the biblical text! To avoid doing so is not unlike a group of lawyers discussing constitutional law apart from a consideration of differences as to the authority and nature of the constitution itself.

The Third Key: Harness the Potential of Discussion and Dialogue

The third key is *to engage in Evangelical dialogue concerning mission proposals and problems in venues provided by the church and its missions.* When faced with issues having to do with the relationship between the gospel and culture in the 1970s, invitees to a Lausanne-sponsored gathering in Willowbank, Bermuda (1978), engaged in a dialogue that helped to set parameters for subsequent discussions. Several years later in 1982, 50 leaders met in a consultation in Grand Rapids to discuss the relationship between mission as evangelism and mission as including social responsibility—an issue that had emerged as especially significant after Lausanne 1974. Regional and annual conferences of the Evangelical Missiological Society have often featured discussions and dialogues on subjects as diverse as power encounter and prayer walking, the education of missionary children, and mission as business. And

---

[11] See D. A. Hubbard, *What We Evangelicals Believe* (Pasadena: Fuller Theological Seminary, 1979), 18.

when Ralph Winter first introduced his new "kingdom mission" interpretation of the Great Commission, he and his colleagues invited Evangelical specialists in education, medicine, and other sciences as well as missiology to Techny, Illinois, in order to review his proposal and provide feedback.

This third key will not be without its detractors for a variety of reasons. For one thing, Evangelical mission leaders like to think in terms of the "two structures" (church and missions) as being spiritually linked but also independent of each other. This third key is based on the notion that Christ is *building* His church and that He is *using* missionary organizations and schools in the building of it. Thankfully, missions engage in church planting and as a practical matter they do "have churches." But from a deeper theological point of view, churches have missions; missions do not have churches.

Another implication of this understanding is that mission leaders and missiologists have a solemn obligation to be faithful to the church in its various expressions—the witness of the apostolic church of the first century, the great creeds of the church down through history, and the counsel and determinations of the contemporary church—when it comes to any and all important deliberations. Insofar as possible, important missionary enclaves should be assembled by doctrinally sound and duly constituted churches and then missions entities, not just by individuals or self-appointed organizers. And normally they should include representatives of the larger church—Bible scholars, theologians, philosophers, and apologists for example—not just missionaries and missiologists. Interdisciplinary dialogue is not only nice; it will be more and more necessary in the days ahead.

Yet another implication of this understanding is that the temptation to forego serious dialogue in the interest of fellowship, love, and unity must be resisted and overcome. Those illustrious planners of the great missionary conference at Edinburgh in 1910 ruled theological discussions out of order (even discussions having to do with the nature of mission) as well as discussions having to do with the conversion of Catholics. They did so in order to enhance spiritual fellowship and promote Christian unity. But they made a colossal error. And over ensuing years, the Ecumenical Movement, to which the 1910 conference gave rise, paid a tremendous price for following the Edinburgh precedent.[12] In Scripture, *dialogismos* does involve the distinct possibility of disputation and argument but always to the end that truth might prevail. It is axiomatic that all of us err in thought, in word, and in deed. God is well served when the errors of *any* individual or group are revealed and corrected. Biblically, there is no disconnect between unity and truth or between love and truth. The unity for which Christ prayed was a unity *in* truth modeled after that of the holy Trinity (John 17:21). True love rejoices in the truth (1 Cor 13:8). Unless truth is the goal, love is not the motivation. *A better biblical case can be made for being a watchman standing on the wall than can be made for being an observer sitting on the fence.*

CHARLES VAN ENGEN: "'MISSION' DEFINED AND DESCRIBED"

Now we turn to the specific proposals of Charles Van Engen, Paul Hiebert, and Ralph Winter, and to the issues raised by their respective respondents and coeditor Ed Stetzer. As indicated above and exemplified in the present volume, Evangelical missiology is both blessed and burdened with a host of proposals—blessed because some of them are biblical and helpful, burdened because some of them are questionable and even deleterious. As author of this concluding chapter, I do not propose to make anything like a determination as to which is which. Though my opinion will be evident to the reader, my primary purpose is to provide grist for the mills of Evangelical missiologists in the future—to overview the writings of my colleagues and point to some issues that may prove to be defining issues for Evangelical missions/missiology in this twenty-first century.

Van Engen's View of the Nature of Christian Mission

Nothing could be more obvious than the fact that the entire future of Evangelical missions/missiology rests upon a correct determination of the nature of Christian mission itself. No topic could be more critical than the topic assigned to Van Engen:

---

[12] See D. J. Hesselgrave, "Will We Correct the Edinburgh Error? Future Mission in Historical Perspective," *Southwestern Journal of Theology* 49.2 (Spring 2007): 121–49.

"'Mission' Defined and Described." And he has responded by providing a marvelous overview of the ways in which "mission" has been understood by various segments of the church and its missions down through history. From a missiological perspective, his chapter alone is worth the price of this book. It is appropriate that all four respondents are most appreciative of his essay, as is Stetzer. At the same time Keith Eitel cautions that some kinds of creativity that have gone into past and especially present proposals are altogether too expansive and may in the future, as has often been the case in the past, divert us from accomplishing the main task of mission—which is to proclaim the gospel and win people to Christ. Enoch Wan, on the other hand, expresses concern that Van Engen's treatment might be reductionistic in that it does not fully explore the significance of *missio Dei*, especially as *missio Dei* reflects the "interactive pattern of the triune God." Wan offers an extensive list of resources that feature the "richness" of the trinitarian understanding of mission—a list that is invaluable to missiologists but too overwhelming for laypersons to contemplate reading. Darrell Guder, while generally commendatory, thinks that Van Engen's desire for a "cohesive, consistent, focused, theologically deep, missiologically broad, and contextually appropriate evangelical missiology" for the twenty-first century would be greatly enhanced by giving attention to Karl Barth's view of mission as expressed in the last full volume of his *Church Dogmatics*. Guder assures missiologists that it is indeed a daunting task to read and grapple with this latter work, but he adds "that difficulty is appropriate to the task that we face as Christendom disintegrates, which is to rediscover that mission is truly the mother of theology." Not without reason Andreas Köstenberger seeks to ground, define, and describe mission in the biblical text. His "12 theses," while falling well short of Martin Luther's numerical precedent, are substantively and objectively of similar importance in refocusing the discussion on the Lord Jesus Himself and what He and His personally appointed missionaries said and did about their (and our) mission in the world. Finally, Ed Stetzer is approving or disapproving of what Van Engen and his respondents have written largely on the basis of whether their conclusions are sufficiently informed sociologically and praxeologically to be equal to the challenges of the future.

But how do the "three keys" bear upon this particular discussion? In answer to that question, I choose to begin where Van Engen's discussion concludes, namely, with his answer to Gloria and the other members of her Global Outreach Task Force.

Unlocking Van Engen's Understanding of Mission

1. Differentiating Between Missiology as Science and Task. First, Gloria's church is to be commended for appointing the task force, and Gloria and her task force are to be commended for undertaking the job of defining mission and suggesting ways of carrying it out. Van Engen himself is to be commended for suggesting that the members of the task force should think, share, and work together to write their own definition of *mission* and use that definition to promote mission understanding and involvement in their church. But I am not as comfortable with his suggestion that, if the task of examining and determining the biblical meaning of mission becomes overly arduous and time-consuming, the task force consider adopting Van Engen's own carefully crafted definition (taking over 40 years!)—even with the caution that he does not claim finality for it.

Only 10 years ago Ralph Winter expressed more confidence in laity than in the experts when it comes to defining and describing Christian mission. He wrote:

> *The future of the world hinges on what we make of this word "mission."* Yet at this moment it is almost universally misunderstood—in both liberal and conservative circles. About the only people who still think of mission as having to do with preaching the gospel where Christ is not named, with being a testimony to the very last tribe and nation and tongue on this earth, are the often confused people in the pew. In this matter their instincts outshine those of many eminent [theologians] and ecclesiastical statesmen.[13]

Winter wrote this to promote the idea that biblical mission had to do first of all with world evangelization—with providing

---

[13] R. D. Winter, "The Meaning of 'Mission': Understanding This Term Is Crucial to Completion of the Missionary Task," *Mission Frontiers Bulletin* 20.33–34 (March-April 1998):15.

a church for every people and the gospel for every person! It was written before Winter himself had a change of mind and began to promote his "kingdom mission"—his "radically new interpretation of the Lord's Prayer and the Great Commission" that even many missiologists find confusing. Perhaps Winter was right earlier on. But I deal with his new proposal later on in this chapter. At this junction I simply draw attention to his observation that the instincts of those in the pew may actually outshine those of many eminent theologians and ecclesiastical statesmen—and also those of many missiologists!

It is right that members of the task force are made aware of the fact that Van Engen's definition reflects not only 40 years of reflection on the biblical text but also 40 years of reflection on a great variety of missiological subjects. They should also be made aware of what the discipline of missiology entails: "The conscious, intentional, ongoing reflection on the doing of mission. It includes theory(ies) of mission, the study and teaching of mission, as well as the research, writing, and publication of works regarding mission."[14] In effect, a thousand judgments as to the validity and importance of biblical studies—but also historical, sociological, cultural, communicational, and other studies—have gone into Van Engen's definition. To adopt it actually entails concurrence with the preponderance of Van Engen's judgments in those cases. That may be a responsibility that, in the final analysis, neither the task force nor Van Engen himself would want to assume.

2. Recognizing Scripture as the Standard of Measurement. Van Engen could have augmented his first suggestion by pointing to some of the most critical Bible passages having to do with Christian mission and providing some basic aids to Bible study and the interpretation of the biblical text. That would accord with the Reformation principle having to do with the authority, perspicuity, and intelligibility of Scripture. Is it not with that principle— and the affirmations of Evangelicals as indicated above—with which we have to do here? I think so. The Second Key comes into play here because in defining mission we are dealing with considerations of theology and faith. The question that presents itself is

---

[14] H. A. Neely, "Missiology," in *Evangelical Dictionary of World Missions*, gen. ed. S. Moreau (Grand Rapids: Baker, 2000), 633.

clear: Is Van Engen's particular brand of "evangelical missiology" biblically based, theologically sound, and evangelically acceptable? Guder and Stetzer are enthusiastic not only in endorsing but in going beyond it. Eitel and Köstenberger are united in questioning it. Wan is approving but thinks it needs refinement.

It is appropriate to examine this a little more closely. Wan, Guder, and Stetzer all seem to be desirous of discovering and elaborating an Evangelical missiology that can be described as "cohesive, consistent, focused, theologically deep, missiologically broad, contextually appropriate, and praxeologically effective." That's a pretty tall order, but Guder claims to have found it in the theology/missiology of K. Barth. A quick look at that claim is in order.

As for theological *depth*, there can be no doubt that Barth's theology is "deep." His *Church Dogmatics* alone totals some six million words and comprises 13 volumes! Over time his theology developed into deep reflection on what he considered the strengths and weaknesses of the theologies/philosophies of liberals such as Hermann, Feuerbach, and Schleiermacher; the dialectic and crisis theologies of the Blumhardts and Kierkegaard; and still more. In the end, however, his theology was not so much an examination of truth as it was "a conversation, a process, an active struggle, an act of guidance."[15] As far as Evangelicals are concerned with Barth and his conclusions, three questions become immediate and appropriate. First, exactly how is missiological depth to be defined and determined? Second, is there any way of dealing with Barth's epistemology and theology/missiology without revisiting his neoorthodox approach to the inspiration and authority of Scripture? Third, does theology rightly flow out of mission, or is the converse true?

As for missiological *broadness*, we might want to consider B. McLaren's interpretation of the missional church as put forward by Guder and others. Citing Guder, McLaren says that the term refers to "attempts to find a generous third way beyond the conservative and liberal versions of Christianity so dominant in the Western world." He also states that "rather than seeing missiology

---

[15] M. Parsons, "Karl Barth," in *New 20th Century Encyclopedia of Religious Knowledge*, gen. ed. J. D. Douglas (Grand Rapids: Baker, 1991), 64.

as a study within theology, theology is actually a discipline within Christian mission."[16] For McLaren at least, the outcome is apparent in the fact that the first descriptor McLaren uses to describe his own position is "missional." This is elaborated in the subtitle (or byline) of his book: "Why I am a missional + evangelical + post-protestant + liberal/conservative + mystical/poetic + biblical + charismatic/contemplative + fundamentalistic/Calvinist + anabaptist/anglican + methodist + catholic + green + incarnational + depressed-yet-hopeful + emergent + unfinished Christian." I will leave it to others to decide the validity of all of this. Whatever else it is, it is certainly "missiologically *broad.*"

When it comes to cohesiveness, consistency, depth, broadness, and so on, readers do well to look at K. Eitel's recent article and the recent book by A. Köstenberger and P. O'Brien.[17] Such reading might well convince inquirers into these matters that, in the end, these qualities must be measured first of all by the veracity of divine revelation and only secondarily by the astuteness of theologians and missiologists.

3. Harnessing the Potential of Discussion and Dialogue. Two avenues are open to Evangelicals when it comes to resolving the problem of the nature of mission. One is intentionally to ignore the problem and hope that it will resolve itself or simply go away. The other is intentionally to deal with the problem and its various manifestations in an orderly and reasonable manner and to do so in recognition of the fact that, though discussants may not agree, continuing discussion in the light of Scripture is certainly more hopeful for the future than the alternative.

The first avenue has already been traveled. It is a road to nowhere. Those noble organizers of the World Missionary Conference held in Edinburgh in 1910 decided to take the easy way out by simply assuming that theological and ecclesiastical issues— including the nature of mission and the conduct of mission in Catholic lands—could be avoided in the interests of promoting fellowship and advancing missions in other ways. Supported by various historians of missions, I have termed that decision the

---

[16] B. D. McLaren, *A Generous Orthodoxy* (Grand Rapids: Zondervan, 2004), 105.

[17] K. E. Eitel, "Evangelical Agnosticism: Crafting a Different Gospel," *Southwestern Journal of Theology* 49.2 (Spring 2007): 150–67; A. J. Köstenberger and Peter O'Brien, *Salvation to the Ends of the Earth: A Biblical Theology of Mission* (Downers Grove: InterVarsity, 2001).

"Edinburgh error" and pointed out that, over the years, it allowed for a variety of contradictory definitions of the Christian mission such as:

"The mission is church."
"The church is mission."
"Everything the church does is mission."
"Everything the church is sent to do is mission."
"The mission is to build the kingdom and establish *shalom*."
"Let the world set the [mission] agenda."
"Humanization is mission."
"Our mission is *missio Dei,* the mission of God"
"Our mission is to complete Christ's mission on earth."[18]

Evangelicals do well to correct the Edinburgh error. As an alternative, Evangelical leaders should choose to travel the road of discussion and debate even though it may well prove to be more difficult. To make dialogue more significant, EMS and other groups should invite theologians, philosophers, and Bible scholars to join them in new explorations of the relationship between theology, apologetics, and missiology in charting a path for future mission.

By way of conclusion, my observation is that, left to their own devices, Evangelical mission thinkers and practitioners tend to become overly creative and unduly adventurous. Intentionally, but often unintentionally, missionary activism and pragmatism tend to impinge on Evangelical theology. Two cases in point may serve to illustrate. Both occurred shortly after the founding of the EMS. In the one case, an impeccably dressed and impressive stranger appeared at a meeting of the EMS in Wheaton. After the opening session, he introduced himself to me as an officer in the missions section of the Church of Jesus Christ of Latter Day Saints in Salt Lake City. He explained that he had been sent with two purposes in mind: first, to invite me to come to Salt Lake as their guest in order to tour their facilities and become familiar with their missions personnel and program; second, to inquire as to the possibility of membership in the recently formed EMS. In answer to that

---

[18] D. J. Hesselgrave, *Paradigms in Conflict: 10 Key Questions in Missions Today* (Grand Rapids, Kregel, 2005), 329.

question, I explained that anyone of moral rectitude who can in good faith sign our doctrinal statement would be most welcome. I hoped to see him again, but he vanished from the scene as quickly as he had appeared.

The second case in point occurred in a meeting of the members of the AD 2000 Movement held about the same time in Colorado Springs. Requirements for membership in the Movement had become an issue with the admittance of certain non-Evangelical Protestant and Catholic prelates. A paper had been circulated in which it was proposed that representatives of any denomination or group with a "vision for world evangelization" be welcomed to join. However, though considerable discussion occurred in out-of-the-way places and times, the question was never broached in a formal way for a reason that became obvious to all. The church that was perhaps as qualified as any on the basis of "a vision for world evangelization" was the Church of Jesus Christ of Latter Day Saints. While some few were enthusiastic about that particular possibility, even their enthusiasm cooled significantly when it was pointed out that consistency and courtesy dictated that Jehovah's Witnesses be welcomed on the same basis. At that the idea was dropped and, to my knowledge, was never brought up again.

The lesson of this bit of missions history seems clear: biblical theology is logically and practically prior to mission vision and missiological exploration. So much for theological depth and missiological breadth. Considerations of contextual appropriateness and "praxeological effectiveness" will fit nicely into discussions to follow.

PAUL G. HIEBERT: "THE GOSPEL IN HUMAN CONTEXTS"

Before proceeding, we must adjust our thinking somewhat. Charles Van Engen is still very much alive and, by the grace of God, will yet be alive for many years and well able both to defend and to adjust his missiology as the case may be. Paul Hiebert and Ralph Winter have now "finished their course." They are no longer among us either to defend or to change the missiological systems they have bequeathed to us. It is up to us and others who follow them to make the most of their unique and invaluable legacies while at the same time recognizing that their missiologies, like those of all the rest of us, must ultimately be judged on the basis of Scripture.

Thoughts on Hiebert's Transformational Approach to Mission Theory and Practice

As Darrell Whiteman points out, Hiebert had impeccable credentials as a missiologist. Brought up in India as part of a knowledgeable missionary family, he became essentially bicultural. His formal training in the social sciences and theology was of the highest order. Forty years of studying, researching, and writing allowed him to hone his craft and expand his thinking. Hiebert was a professor of anthropology and author of a standard text on the subject. He was recruited from the university to join the faculty of Fuller Theological Seminary, later to move to Trinity Evangelical Divinity School at which institution he made his later contributions. In that context I came to know him as both an astute scholar and a humble servant of God.

Nothing I might say here could greatly add to, or detract from, the missiological legacy of my late colleague and friend, Paul Hiebert. His legacy has been secure for long years and is made even more secure by this essay—one of his final writings—and those of his respondents and my coeditor. Postmodern critical realist epistemology, a Peircian semiotic that leads beyond dynamic equivalence to double translations, missional theology as bridge-building between Scripture and humans, metatheologizing, critical contextualization, the Church as hermeneutical community, transformational missiology and theology—these and a variety of insightful ideas are not only or primarily theoretical products of a brilliant mind; they are also practical suggestions emanating from a deep desire to advance the cause of Christian missions. Hiebert both broadens and deepens missiology by insisting that missionaries go beyond and beneath the particulars of culture in order to deal with underlying predilections and axiologies and, where necessary, endeavor to transform them in ways consonant with the kingdom of God. It's an awesome challenge. Little wonder that Michael Pocock concludes that future discussions of contextualization issues will almost always be impacted by Hiebert's thinking. Or that, coming from a direction that contrasts greatly with that of Hiebert, Norman Geisler nevertheless prefaces his points of disagreement with 10 areas of agreement that are basic to an evangelical theology of mission. Or that Avery Willis Jr. chooses to begin his remarks where Hiebert ends and, despite differences, proposes nine "steps toward the contextualization of truth" that still reflect Hiebert's basic thinking, if not his nomenclature.

Unlocking Hiebert's Transformational Missiology

1. Differentiating Between Missiology as Science and Task. Overall it seems to me that Hiebert's missiology must be considered to be among the most comprehensive and cohesive anthropologically informed missiological systems conceived during my 60 years of involvement on the field and in the academy. Perhaps that is to be expected, but it seems to me to be characterized by a knowledge of anthropology and culture that at times overshadows the theological commitment that Hiebert both professed and possessed. Hiebert entertained a distinct tentativeness as to the objectivity and value of historic and contemporary theologies, especially systematic theologies. His "critical realist epistemology" made a clear distinction between revelation and theology. The former is God given and therefore reflects reality as it is. The latter is humanly conceived and therefore reflects reality only to a degree. Theological statements are always partial and limited by one's perspective. They reflect the biases of the individuals by whom—and the cultures in which—they were and are constructed and therefore must be tested dialogically in the contexts of local churches. Even then they remain as theology and are not to be equated with revelation.

Now few theologians with whom I am acquainted would take issue with the distinction that Hiebert makes here. But some would take issue with what they perceive as a diminishing of the importance of theology nonetheless. I think, for example, of C. F. H. Henry who, recognizing how deeply Empiricism and Existentialism have penetrated Evangelicalism during the past century, exhorts us to restore deductive theology to a place of importance and even primacy. Recognizing that God's Spirit uses truth as a means of persuasion and confers personal assurance as a gift, Henry insists that the roles of presuppositional theology, rational consistency, and the biblical canon are all essential if we are to avoid fideism and mere theological probability.[19]

As for "fideism and mere theological probability," it is of considerable interest that, though Hiebert himself is understandably reticent to criticize L. Newbigin, another of his Trinity colleagues, H. Netland, does so and at that very point. While expressing appreciation for Newbigin's larger work, Netland takes issue with Newbigin's fideistic idea that "there is no platform from which one can claim to have an 'objective' view which supercedes all the 'subjective' faith-commitments of the world's faiths."[20] Netland says that if, as in Newbigin's view, a Christian does no more than claim priority for God's self-revelation in Jesus without giving rational reasons for doing so, then that Christian forfeits the right to reject other faiths as false and in the process opens himself or herself up to the charge of self-refutation. To put it in Netland's own words, "The mere thesis of fideism appeals to rationality norms, such as the principle of non-contradiction, which logically cannot be merely faith postulates."[21] The implications of this truth for missions and missiology are enormous. We will return to some of these implications in a moment, but I mention it here because, though Hiebert justly commends Newbigin in his essay, he himself neither exposes nor—I am confident—espouses it.

2. Recognizing Scripture as the Standard of Measurement. Like McGavran, Hiebert was not given to emphasizing or explaining his precise understanding of inspiration and the authority of the Bible. Unlike McGavran, he did not seem to think that discussions such as this one required explication of the *kind* of authority inherent in the biblical text. Nevertheless, that Hiebert was a firm believer in inerrancy and the full authority of Scripture was evidenced by his acceptance of his appointment to the Trinity faculty because appointment entailed agreement with a confessional statement, the first item of which affirms the inerrancy of the autographs of the biblical text. Hiebert's "double translations" approach to the translation of Scripture also evidences this commitment. According to

---

[19] C. F. H. Henry, *Toward a Recovery of Christian Belief: The Rutherford Lectures* (Wheaton: Crossway, 1990), xi.

[20] H. A. Netland (*Dissonant Voices: Religious Pluralism and the Question of Truth* [Grand Rapids: Eerdmans, 1991], 181) quoted L. Newbigin, *The Open Secret* (Grand Rapids: Eerdmans, 1979), 190.

[21] Netland, 182.

Hiebert, Peircian semiotics takes us beyond dynamic equivalence to double translations in which translators seek to preserve the forms of Scripture (often by means of footnotes and parenthetical clarifications) while also communicating biblical ideas accurately. This is in accord with the approach taken in some of our best contemporary Bible translations such as the English Standard Version and the Holman Christian Standard Bible, both of which are used in this monograph. The editors of the latter, for example, introduce their work with the following paragraph:

> The Bible is God's revelation to man. It is the only book that gives us accurate information about God, man's need, and God's provision for that need. It provides us with guidance for life and tells us how to receive eternal life. The Bible can do these things because it is God's inspired Word, *inerrant in the original manuscripts.*[22]

Again, the editors of the English Standard Version contrast dynamic equivalence translation philosophy with their own when they contrast their philosophy with that of certain other versions:

> In contrast to the ESV, some Bible versions have followed a "thought-for-thought" rather than a "word-for-word" translation philosophy, emphasizing "dynamic equivalence" rather than the "essentially literal" meaning of the original. A "thought-for-thought" translation is of necessity more inclined to reflect the interpretive opinions of the translator and the influences of contemporary culture.[23]

I emphasize this because I am persuaded that this view of Scripture is behind not only Hiebert's "double translation" theory but also his transformational and critical contextualization methodologies and, indeed, the whole of his missiology. This undoubtedly contributes to the distinction that he makes between divine revelation and (human) theologies. Only the former is objective and absolute. At best, all else is something less than that. All else is judged by it.

3. Harnessing the Potential of Discussion and Dialogue. Our discussion has brought us to the response of still another former

---

[22] Holman Christian Standard Bible, 2004 (emphasis added), ix.
[23] English Standard Version, 2002, vii–viii.

Trinity colleague, N. Geisler. He finds 10 areas of agreement with Hiebert, but he also lists seven areas of disagreement. I dare say that some of these disagreements could be overcome without too much difficulty if a face-to-face conversation were possible. But one disagreement that would remain is reflected in Stetzer's rejection of Geisler's resort to Aristotelian logic, which Stetzer deems to be essentially "Western" and culture bound. Many will be tempted to agree with Stetzer at this point. The disagreement here is important and not merely academic. Theologically it is related to *imago Dei* doctrine. Epistemologically it bears mightily on a cross-cultural Christian apologetic.

Clearly, this should be a matter for interdisciplinary dialogue and discussion. Some students of culture themselves would disagree with Hiebert—at least partially. As early as 50 years ago, E. Perry, F. H. Smith, and E. R. Hughes developed a trinary understanding of cultural epistemology based on a study of Indian and Chinese thinking on the one hand and the thinking of Western cultures on the other. They found differences in cultural thinking to be more a matter of priority than of kind. According to them, all peoples think in three ways—conceptual postulationally, concrete relationally and psychically intuitionally. The difference between cultures is not one of kind but of the assignment of differing priorities to each of the three ways of thinking. Westerners assign priority to "conceptual/postulational thinking"; Chinese (and, I would add, most tribals as well) give priority to "concrete relational/ pictorial thinking"; and Indians prioritize "psychical/intuitional thinking" considering it to be the highest form of knowing.[24]

To the extent that Perry, Smith, and Hughes are correct: Western rational thinking is not simply Western; it is also Chinese and Indian, though not to the same degree. This understanding is in accordance with that of those Christian scholars who believe that, however identified, Western thinking ("logic") is not unique to Western culture. Divine revelation supports it as being intrinsic

---

[24] E. Perry, *The Gospel in Dispute* (Garden City: Doubleday, 1958), 99–106; see D. J. Hesselgrave, *Communicating Christ Cross-Culturally: An Introduction to Missionary Communication*, 2nd ed. (Grand Rapids: Zondervan, 1991), 303; and Hesselgrave, "Revelation and Reason in Cross-Cultural Apologetics and Missiology," *Journal of the International Society of Christian Apologetics* 2.1 (Winter 2009): 5–22.

to the *imago Dei*. The God of the Bible is the "God of reason" as well as the God of revelation. That is why C. Henry says that

> the Protestant Reformers are to be applauded for their under-standing of the existence of God, the world and other selves as being prephilosophical. Building on their understanding, we must now insist on axioms that underlie the core beliefs of Christianity and we must also insist on the role of logical consistency as a negative test of truth.[25]

As I say, in accord with Geisler and many others (including Ralph Winter, as will be evident below), I believe that apologetics will be of increasing importance to future mission. With that in mind I conclude this discussion of Hiebert's transformational missiology by proposing three propositions for dialogue and discussion in the future.

First, *correspondence with reality as a test of truth is rooted in the divine nature*. Correspondence with the "really real" is not just an abstract principle or a cultural idea; it is a reflection of the very nature of the Creator God "who cannot lie" (Titus 1:2) and of the God of truth for whom it is "impossible to lie" (Heb 6:18).

Second, *noncontradiction as a test of truth is rooted in the divine nature*. Similarly, the idea that A cannot be non-A in the same sense and at the same time is not just an abstract principle or a cultural idea; it is a reflection of the Creator God who is "faithful" and "cannot deny Himself" (2 Tim 2:13).

Third, *convergence of the written Word and the living Word as a test of truth is rooted in the divine nature*. Divine truth or "true truth" can be stated propositionally, but it can never be propositional *only* because Christ the Son of God is truth personified (John 14:6; Rom 3:4). The written Word of God (Scripture) and the living Word of God (Christ) testify to each other, are in accord with the "really real" and "true truth," and together constitute the highest forms of God's revelation to mankind.[26]

The apostle Peter exhorts us to be ready to give a "defense to anyone who asks you for a reason for the hope that is in you"

---

[25] Henry, xi.

[26] See D. J. Hesselgrave, "Reasoning Faith and Global Missions: On Reaching Hindus and Hindu-Like Peoples," *in Reasons for Faith: Making a Case for the Christian Faith*, ed. N. Geisler and C. V. Meister (Wheaton: Crossway, 2007), 392.

(1 Pet 3:15). The operative Greek word here is *apologia*, meaning "verbal defense." Apologetics has an important place in missions. Members of the new International Society of Christian Apologetics should have an important place both in missionary ministries and in missiological dialogues of the future.

RALPH D. WINTER: "THE FUTURE OF EVANGELICALS IN MISSION"

The late Ralph Winter's essay on the future of Evangelical missions has proved to be the most provocative of the three grand essays in this book. That was all but inevitable. Down through many years, Winter's proposals have often been provocative. But if Winter had written on this topic before the turn of the century and therefore before he came forward with his new "kingdom mission," the responses would have been different. As things now stand, all of his respondents express appreciation for his erudition, creativity, and outstanding contributions to the world mission of the church. At the same time Chris Little has serious misgivings because Winter has shifted his focus away from gospel proclamation and church development and in the direction of social transformation and kingdom-building. Mike Barnett takes issue both with some of Winter's interpretations of history and with his view that the future rests more on sodalities than modalities. Mark Terry and Scott Moreau have serious reservations, but both elect to emphasize trends and ideas they believe to be vital to any projections of the future. Ed Stetzer closes his analysis with two paragraphs that, in my view, constitute a fitting conclusion to his evaluation of Winter's essay and also constitute a most fitting conclusion to this book.

The Essence of Ralph Winter's Kingdom Mission

By way of introduction, it might be helpful to point out that, in proposing his "radically new interpretation of the Lord's Prayer and Great Commission," my friend Ralph Winter not only thought "outside the box"; he employed keys of his own making to open a missiological "Pandora's Box" that has already challenged the credulity of many of us. To revert back to a previous metaphor, he added still another enclosure—better, more enclosures—to the missiological maze through which missiologists of the future will be required to find their way.

In hope of bringing a larger measure of understanding at this point, I suggest that it would be helpful to view Winter's kingdom mission as one comprehensive and integrated apologetic for the biblical gospel. In Winter's view this apologetic is necessitated because the increasingly educated peoples of the globalized world of the future *simply will not believe a simple gospel.* He does not doubt the power of the gospel to save. But he doubts that educated people will believe it or even listen to it unless Christians lend credibility and believability to gospel words by doing kingdom deeds. In essence, then, what Winter proposes is a Christian apologetic comprised not so much of faithful words (though biblical truth should be shown to conform with the best of modern science) but of good deeds of all kinds—deeds that combat evil and are sufficiently arresting to demonstrate the validity and desirability of embracing Christ and His kingdom. That having been said, I will attempt an abbreviated analysis and evaluation by use of the three "keys."

Unlocking Winter's New Kingdom Mission

1. Differentiating Between Missiology as Science and Task. It should be noted that Winter's kingdom mission features a whole array of components masterly woven together so as to make a kind of "metanarrative" ("metascientific narrative") of the world as it was, is now, and will become. At ground zero this metanarrative has to do with the struggle between good and evil, with the battle between God and Satan, with taking evil really seriously, as C. S. Lewis did when led to the truth of Christianity. Building on that struggle as a foundation, Winter constructs his new understanding of missions/missiology out of theological/biblical components, yes, but also out of materials that emanate from both social and physical sciences. What citizens of our postmodern globalized world will discover here—and perhaps find compelling—is a blending of components emanating from the sciences as well as Scripture—from astronomy, paleontology, anthropology, sociology, psychology, linguistics, history, and still other sciences. Winter says that his kingdom mission is based on "contemporary scientific consensus" on such matters as those having to do with "Big Bang" theory, certain "extinction events" triggered by the collisions of asteroids, the emergence of noncarnivorous animal life and mankind, and so on. But it also has to do with his reading of these events and of human history from the meanderings of early man right up to the misdirections of "Second-Inheritance Evangelicalism" and his prognostications of successes that would attend the recovery of the social emphases of "First-Inheritance Evangelicalism." This having been said, his interpretation and evaluation of the missionary contribution of the Bible institute movement, for example, will be troubling to many.

Winter's reconstructions and interpretations of prehistory and historical events and movements may or may not be totally reliable, but they are impressive. Skeptics would do well to read H. Ross's book on creation.[27] Much of this material is beyond my poor power to evaluate properly. They are best left for others to ponder and decide. What I would stress here is that, by virtue of his ability to address these matters in words and ways that few missiologists are prepared to do, Winter's approach does evidence a kind of credibility that commends itself to informed unbelievers of whatever geographical and religious background. It may also prove convincing to an emerging generation of Evangelicals already inclined to think of mission in terms of social transformation rather than gospel penetration.

2. Recognizing Scripture as the Standard of Measurement. Given the way Winter sometimes treats the biblical text, I have often wondered (and on one occasion inquired) as to his view on the inspiration and authority of the biblical text.

Having been personally assured by Winter that he believed in inerrancy and the full and final authority of Scripture, I will hazard some thoughts as to the consistency of his hermeneutic in the light of this commitment. Of course, this particular discussion must of necessity be confined to just a few examples taken from a proposal that is exceedingly comprehensive.

The moorings of Winter's kingdom mission are to be found in his appeal to selective texts in the Old and New Testaments that he

---

[27] H. Ross, *The Creator and the Cosmos: How the Greatest Scientific Discoveries of the Century Reveal God* (Colorado Springs: Navpress, 1993),

employs as a biblical basis for the struggle between God and Satan as mentioned above. Genesis 1 is the story of the original creation and then of a new beginning in which the dust settles, light returns, and noncarnivorous animal life and nonviolent human life are created. However, humans are seduced by an extraordinarily powerful Satan, violence returns, and the relatively short history of the Bible ensues. Genesis 12:1–3 and its elaborations indicate that Yahweh called on Israel to take an active, not a passive, role in sharing the promised blessing with surrounding nations. The operative word here is "active."

Coming to the New Testament, Christ's mission was both redemptive and restorative; it yielded both the gospel of salvation and the gospel of the kingdom. Christ came to give His life a ransom for sin (Mark 10:45) but also to war against evil, to set captives free (Luke 4:18–19), and to destroy the works of the Devil (1 John 3:8). The petition "Your kingdom come, your will be done, on earth as it is in heaven" (Matt 6:10 ESV) focuses on *life on earth,* not *life in heaven.* Ultimately, it means that the church should do more than *pray* for the coming of the kingdom; it must also take an active role in advancing the kingdom. Winter's interpretation of Matt 28:18–20 highlights the phrase "observe everything that I have commanded," from which he infers that Christian mission includes all that the Great Commandment, for example, requires. In obeying it, Christians not only demonstrate kingdom principles and values; they also bring them to earth by, for example, eradicating disease-bearing microbes, overcoming poverty, greening the environment, and establishing peace. Winter does make clear, however, that in his view we do not establish the kingdom. The final establishment of the kingdom awaits the coming of Christ.

Certain presuppositions underlie Winter's reading of Scripture and mightily affect his interpretations. First, words without deeds have no meaning. That is what makes Christ's admonition in Matt 5:16 all important. As long as the gospel is merely information and words, it will be insufficient, unconvincing, and even meaningless. Deeds that war against evil *clarify* God's glory even though they do not *complete* it. In a profound sense, therefore, the glory of God manifest in His creative work and the good works of His people are in themselves the *means* of mission. Second,

God is the Author of good only; Satan is the author of evil. Winter commends Gregory Boyd's thesis that essentially says that when bad things happen to good people, God is in no way responsible. In fact, He is as surprised by it as we are. This is, of course, open theism. It attempts to exonerate God in the eyes of the world, but in order to "save" an "all-good God," it sacrifices an "all-knowing God."

The validity or invalidity of Winter's interpretations and applications of the various biblical texts needs to be taken up *ad seriatum*. But the two presuppositions above would seem to be out of keeping with verbal inspiration and biblical inerrancy— and therefore possibly deleterious to biblical mission. The notion that words without deeds are meaningless ultimately implies that human words cannot bear the full weight of truth whether in divine revelation or in human proclamation. If that be so, the proclamation of the gospel is neither sufficient nor central to Christian mission. And, along with undercutting the omniscience of God, Winter's open theism would seem to undermine the full authority of Scripture and emasculate the biblical gospel. Having said this, I recognize that Winter might well counter that, while the Evangelical Theological Society denounced open theism, it nevertheless allowed open theists to retain membership. And to that there seems to be no answer other than that which has already been indicated by others, namely, that to be consistent it is now incumbent upon the ETS to redefine inerrancy. But that seems akin to inquiring as to what the meaning of *is* is!

3. Harnessing the Potential of Discussion and Dialogue. In October 2006, along with almost 30 specialists in education, medicine, and the sciences, as well as theology and missions, I was invited by Winter and his associates to Techny, Illinois, for the express purpose of giving consideration to his "radically new interpretation of the Lord's Prayer and the Great Commission." The consultation was held under the auspices of the Roberta Winter Institute founded for "the purpose of awakening the Evangelical movement to a crucially deeper understanding of God's will in this world." For the better part of two days, participants listened to a major presentation by Winter; examined distributed materials including his essay, "Planetary Events and the Mission of the Church";[28] and participated in discussions featuring both the strengths and weaknesses of the new proposal as viewed by participants.

Before leaving Techny, Winter invited us to reflect on his proposal and continue in dialogue with him. Accordingly, I gathered 18 Rockford colleagues representing various professions, shared the Techny materials with them, recorded their responses, and then forwarded the results to Winter. That was in early 2007, and it began a dialogue between us that extended over a year and a half and numbered almost 50 exchanges of e-mail letters. To me, the fact that Winter continued to correspond despite his serious illness and exhausting schedule was indeed remarkable. However much we may have agreed to disagree, the fact that he gave that much time and energy to dialogue with just one of his missiological colleagues—and a lesser one at that—speaks volumes about the man and his commitment to Christ and Christian truth as he came to understand it.

In that connection I should note that some of what I have written here grows more out of our larger and longer discussions, not just those relating to Winter's grand essay per se. I have deemed this necessary to a better understanding of his changed view of mission. Also, I should mention that during our more recent discussion concerning his kingdom mission, Winter did yield to his critics on one major point: namely, he dropped the notion that we have now entered what he had early on termed a "Fourth Era" in the history of modern missions. This is important because, had he persisted in his Fourth Era thinking, it would have reinforced the idea that the Third Era—with its emphasis on completing the task of evangelizing the peoples of the whole world in our time—has been superseded by kingdom mission and its emphasis on social transformation. As it turned out, his abandonment of the Fourth Era idea means that—at least as far as Winter's new proposal is concerned—we are still in the Third Era. World evangelization is still the goal of Evangelical missions, and world evangelization is a finishable task.

---

[28] See R. D. Winter, "Planetary Events and the Mission of the Church" (D. McClure Lectureship, Pittsburgh Theological Seminary, October 3–4, 2005). See also "The Unfinished Epic: In Five Acts" dated September 2006 distributed at Techny, IL. October 23, 2006.

That brings us full circle. How, after all, *is* mission to be defined and described? Winter seems to have made social action at least necessary to evangelism and church growth. McGavran clearly saw social action as parallel to, but qualitatively different from, evangelism and church growth. "Revisionist holists" (my term) such as B. Myers, J. Engel, and W. Dyrness see them as "full and equal partners" and refuse to separate them. "Restrained holists" (my term) such as J. R. W. Stott and the framers of the Lausanne Covenant see social action and evangelism as partners but give priority to evangelism. "Traditional prioritists" (my term) include all in mission but uniformly think of social action as supportive of, and secondary to, evangelism and church growth.[29]

Clearly at odds with Ralph Winter's kingdom mission is C. F. H. Henry's view that "the closest approximation of the Kingdom of God today is the church, the body of regenerate believers that owns the crucified and risen Redeemer as its Head."[30] As Henry says, the church's *mission* is to evangelize the world by preaching the gospel, converting men and women to Christ, instructing them in the faith, and forming them into responsible churches. The church's *problem* is that many of its own members are unregenerate and remain outside the kingdom, and most others are not taking the Great Commission seriously enough to evangelize the earth![31]

All of the foregoing, and all of the contributors to this volume, are—or at least lay claim to being—Evangelical. But they often differ, and differ widely, as to what their mission actually consists of. So we must ask, "Is there a future of Evangelicals in the future mission of the church?" The answer must be a resounding "Yes" coupled with a provisional "If." As long as Evangelicals courteously and candidly continue to talk and listen to one another, yes, they have a future in mission. If, that is, their coming together and their conversations continue to be based on the full and complete authority of God's revelation in Christ and Scripture.

---

[29] See Hesselgrave (*Paradigms in Conflict*, 120–22) for a discussion of these various positions.

[30] C. F. H. Henry, *The God Who Shows Himself* (Waco: Word, 1965), 88.

[31] Ibid., 102.

CONCLUSION

After all of this, what remains to be said? My long-suffering wife, Gertrude, is of the opinion that not too much more *could* be said. But, of course, that is not so. It is imperative that discussions such as this one continue. Being incapable of improving upon the words of my colleague and coeditor, Ed Stetzer, I now repeat them lest they be forgotten. In answer to the questions, "What will the postmodern church look like? Will we recognize it?" he writes, and I echo, the following words.

> Yes—because our Scripture is the same as that of old. Yes—as long as they maintain absolute adherence to those Scriptures, we've done our best, in our turn, to preserve the faith once delivered. If I've seen any overarching theme through all of these essays, it is this: we must draw a line of communication from the revealed, inspired, infallible, inerrant Scriptures of the Old and New Testaments to a world that has never heard them.

> All of the rest of our issues relate to that task, which we can only do in partnership with, and under the guidance of, the Holy Spirit. We will not arrive at an agreed-upon definition of missions, but this is a good description of what missionaries have always done—or tried to do. We may not agree completely regarding theology, on interpretations of that living Word. Given the history of the church, I can say that I'm pretty sure we won't. We may trace our way into the future with trepidation born of the uncertainty of coming events. We can only suppose what's coming and try to prepare for anything. But we must never let go of that line that stretches from the inspired writers of the Bible to us—nor should we fail to pass it along to others, along with the joy it brings. In this, may we all be faithful—to the glory of God!

BIBLIOGRAPHY

Bavinck, J. H. *An Introduction to the Science of Missions.* Translated by D. H. Freeman. Grand Rapids: Baker, 1969.

Eitel, K. E. "Evangelical Agnosticism: Crafting a Different Gospel." *Southwestern Journal of Theology* 49.2 (Spring 2007): 150–67.

Escobar, S. "Evangelical Theology in Latin America:
    The Development of a Missiological Christology."
    Missiology: An International Review, XIX.3 (July 1991):
    315–29.

Ferm, V., ed. *Classics of Protestantism.* New York:
    Philosophical Library, 1959.

Frizen, E. L., Jr. *75 Years of IFMA: 1917–1992.* Pasadena:
    William Carey Library, 1992.

Henry, C. F. H. *The God Who Shows Himself.* Waco: Word,
    1965.

———. *Toward a Recovery of Christian Belief: The Rutherford
    Lectures.* Wheaton: Crossway, 1990.

Hesselgrave, D. J. *Communicating Christ Cross-Culturally:
    An Introduction to Missionary Communication,* 2nd ed.
    Grand Rapids: Zondervan, 1991.

———. *Paradigms in Conflict: 10 Key Questions in Missions
    Today.* Grand Rapids: Kregel, 2005.

———. "Reasoning Faith and Global Missions: On Reaching
    Hindus and Hindu-Like Peoples." Pages 381–400 in
    *Reasons for Faith: Making a Case for the Christian
    Faith.* Edited by N. Geisler and C. V. Meister. Wheaton:
    Crossway, 2007.

———. "Revelation and Reason in Cross-Cultural Apologetics
    and Missiology." *Journal of the International Society of
    Christian Apologetics* 2.1 (Winter 2009): 5–22.

———. "Will We Correct the Edinburgh Error? Future Mission
    in Historical Perspective." *Southwestern Journal of
    Theology* 49.2 (Spring 2007): 121–49.

Hubbard, D. A. *What We Evangelicals Believe.* Pasadena:
    Fuller Theological Seminary, 1979.

Köstenberger, A. J., and P. T. O'Brien. *Salvation to the Ends
    of the Earth: A Biblical Theology of Mission.* Downers
    Grove: InterVarsity, 2001.

McGavran, D. A. *The Bridges of God: A Study in the Strategy
    of Missions.* New York: Friendship, 1955.

———. *The Clash Between Christianity and Culture.*
    Washington, DC: Canon, 1974.

———. "Missions Face a Lion." Manuscript in the possession of D. J. Hesselgrave (1988). A version of this manuscript was published as "Missions Face a Lion" (*Missiology: An International Review* 17.3 [July 1, 1989]: 335–56).

———. Personal letter to D. J. Hesselgrave (April 7, 1988).

McLaren, B. D. *A Generous Orthodoxy.* Grand Rapids: Zondervan, 2004.

Neely, A. "Missiology." Pages 633–35 in *Evangelical Dictionary of World Missions.* General editor S. Moreau. Grand Rapids: Baker, 2000.

Netland, H. A. *Dissonant Voices: Religious Pluralism and the Question of Truth.* Grand Rapids: Eerdmans, 1991.

Newbigin, L. *The Open Secret.* Grand Rapids: Eerdmans, 1979.

Parsons, M. "Karl Barth." Pages 64–65 in *New 20th Century Encyclopedia of Religious Knowledge.* General editor J. D. Douglas. Grand Rapids: Baker, 1991.

Perry, E. *The Gospel in Dispute.* Garden City: Doubleday, 1958.

Petersen, W. J., and R. Petersen. *100 Christian Books That Changed the Century.* Grand Rapids: Baker (Fleming Revell), 2000.

Ross, H. *The Creator and the Cosmos: How the Greatest Scientific Discoveries of the Century Reveal God.* Colorado Springs: Navpress, 1993.

Winter, R. D. "The Meaning of 'Mission': Understanding This Term Is Crucial to Completion of the Missionary Task." *Mission Frontiers Bulletin* 20.33–34 (March–April 1998).

———. "Planetary Events and the Mission of the Church." (D. McClure Lectureship, Pittsburgh Theological Seminary, October 3–4, 2005).

———. "The Unfinished Epic: In Five Acts." Dated September 2006 and distributed at Techny, IL (October 23, 2006).

List of Contributors

Mike Barnett holds the Elmer V. Thompson Chair of Missionary Church Planting at Columbia Biblical Seminary. He earned the Ph.D. degree at Southwestern Baptist Theological Seminary and served 12 years in the 10–40 Window with the International Mission Board. He has published extensively in the areas of creative access and business and missions.

Keith Eitel is dean of the Fish School of Evangelism and Missions at Southwestern Baptist Theological Seminary. He served as a missionary in Cameroon in West Africa. He earned the doctor of missiology degree at Trinity Evangelical Divinity School and the Ph.D. degree at the University of South Africa. He formerly taught at Criswell College and Southeastern Baptist Theological Seminary.

Norman L. Geisler is professor of apologetics at Veritas Evangelical Seminary in California. He earned his Ph.D. at Loyola University in Chicago and served on the faculties at Dallas Theological Seminary and Trinity Evangelical Divinity School. He cofounded the Southern Evangelical Seminary in Charlotte, North Carolina. A noted writer, he has authored or coauthored 70 books.

Darrell Guder is academic dean and professor of missional and ecumenical theology at Princeton Theological Seminary. He received his Ph.D. from the University of Hamburg. He formerly served as professor at Louisville Presbyterian Seminary and Columbia Theological Seminary. He is a leader in the missional church movement.

David J. Hesselgrave is professor emeritus of missions at Trinity Evangelical Divinity School. He is also a former Evangelical Free Church missionary to Japan, where he served for 12 years. He holds a Ph.D. from the University of Minnesota. He served as executive director of the Evangelical Missions Society, and he authored *Communicating Christ Cross-Culturally* and *Planting Churches Cross-Culturally.*

Paul Hiebert, deceased, was professor of mission and anthropology at Trinity Evangelical Divinity School and earlier at Fuller Theological Seminary. He served as a missionary in India. He received his Ph.D. in anthropology from the University of Minnesota. He authored many books and articles on anthropology and missions.

Andreas Köstenberger is professor of New Testament and biblical theology and director of Ph.D. Studies at Southeastern Baptist Theological Seminary. He earned a Ph.D. in New Testament at Trinity Evangelical Divinity School. He has published widely on the biblical basis for Christian missions.

Christopher Little is professor of intercultural studies at Columbia International University. He served as a missionary in Jordan, Kenya, and Mozambique. He received his Ph.D. degree in missiology from Fuller Theological Seminary.

Scott Moreau is professor of missions at Wheaton College. He served as a missionary in East Africa. He edited *The Evangelical Dictionary of World Mission,* and he currently serves as editor of the *Evangelical Missions Quarterly.* He received his doctor of missiology degree from Trinity Evangelical Divinity School.

Michael Pocock is professor of missions and chairman of the Department of Missions and Intercultural Studies at Dallas Theological Seminary, where he has served for 22 years. He served for 16 years with the Evangelical Alliance Mission in Venezuela. He holds the doctor of missiology degree from Trinity Evangelical Divinity School.

Ed Stetzer is president of Lifeway Research and missiologist in residence at Lifeway Christian Resources in Nashville, Tennessee. He has served as a church planter in North America and on the staff of the North American Mission Board. He served on the faculty of the Southern Baptist Theological Seminary, where he received his Ph.D. in missions. He has lectured on church planting at seminaries in North America and around the world. He serves as a contributing editor for *Christianity Today.*

Mark Terry is professor of missions at a seminary in Asia. He also serves as visiting professor of missions at the Southern Baptist Theological Seminary, where he was formerly the associate dean of the Billy Graham School of Missions and Evangelism. He served as a missionary for 14 years in the Philippines and holds a Ph.D. in missions from Southwestern Baptist Theological Seminary.

Charles Van Engen is the Arthur F. Glasser Professor of Biblical Theology of Mission in the School of Intercultural Studies at Fuller Theological Seminary. He earned his Ph.D. at the Free University of Amsterdam and served as a missionary in Mexico. He is a former president of the General Synod of the Reformed Church in America and currently president of Latin American Christian Ministries.

Enoch Wan is research professor of Intercultural Studies and director of the Doctor of Missiology program at Western Seminary. He currently serves as president of Evangelical Missiological Society and editor of the e-journal www. globalmissiology.org.

Darrell L. Whiteman is vice president and resident missiologist at the Mission Society in Atlanta, Georgia. He has cross-cultural mission and research experience in Melanesia and central Africa, and served as professor of cultural anthropology and later dean of the E. Stanley Jones School of World Mission and Evangelism at Asbury Theological Seminary (1984–2005). He is the past president of the Association of Professors of Mission, the International Association for Mission Studies, and the American Society of Missiology, and served as editor of *Missiology* from 1989 to 2002.

Avery Willis is a retired missionary to Indonesia and a former vice president for Overseas Operations at the International Mission Board of the Southern Baptist Convention. He holds a Ph.D. in missions from Southwestern Baptist Theological Seminary. During his years as an administrator at the IMB he was a leader in the Orality Movement in modern missions.

Ralph Winter, deceased, was the founder and longtime director of the U.S. Center for World Mission. He earned his B.D. at Princeton Seminary and a Ph.D. in linguistics at Cornell University. He served as a missionary in Guatemala, where he collaborated in the development of Theological Education by Extension (TEE). In 1966 he joined the faculty of the School of World Mission at Fuller Theological Seminary. During his time at Fuller, he established the William Carey Library to publish books on missions. He gave the famous address, "Cross-Cultural Missions, the Highest Priority," at the Lausanne Congress in 1974 that called on Evangelicals to identify and evangelize the unreached people groups of the world. He also published and edited the journal *Mission Frontiers,* as well as editing the widely used textbook *Perspectives on the World Christian Movement.*

Name Index

Subject Index

A

absolute truth   *3, 105–6, 135, 148, 152, 156, 159*
affective   *96*
anthropology   *147*
anticolonial   *117*
anticolonialism   *116–17*

B

Bible institutes   *177–78*
biblical theology   *63, 66, 76, 279*

C

China   *239, 254*
Christendom   *34, 52, 54, 57, 60, 273*
Christocentric   *43, 45–46, 66, 79*
Chronological Bible Story Telling   *239*
church growth movement   *16*
cities   *252*
cognitive   *96*
communication   *104, 111, 150, 156, 158*
communication and contextualization   *154*
Constantinian   *13, 32*
contextual   *24*
contextualization   *3, 35, 52, 72, 94, 96, 100, 104–5,* *109–11, 115–18, 120–21, 123, 132, 139, 141, 144–45, 147–48, 150, 152, 156–59, 251*
contextualized   *142*
contextualized hermeneutics   *101*
contextualizing   *31*
critical contextualization   *3–4, 100, 108–10, 117, 123, 145, 156, 158, 280, 283*
critical realism   *108, 136, 162*
critical realist   *93*
critical realist epistemology   *133, 280–81*

D

dynamic equivalence   *107*

E

Edinburgh   *15, 22, 176, 271, 277–78*
emergent   *34, 36–37, 73, 195*
emergent churches   *2*
Emergent Missional Church   *38*
emerging church   *17, 36*
emerging church movement   *35*
epistemology   *91, 115–16*
Evangelical   *21, 22, 106, 164–65, 179, 187, 237, 286*
Evangelicalism   *205*

Scripture Index